EVERYBODY'S BOOK OF BICYCLE RIDING

EVERYBODY'S BOOK OF BICYCLE RIDING

by Thom Lieb

Rodale Press, Emmaus, Pennsylvania

Book design by Kim E. Morrow

Illustrations by John Knaus and Brian Swisher

Copy edited by Susan Weiner

Printed in the United States of America on recycled paper, containing a high percentage of de-inked fiber.

Library of Congress Cataloging in Publication Data

Lieb, Thom.
    Everybody's book of bicycle riding.

    Bibliography: p.
    Includes index.
    1. Cycling.   1. Title.
GV1041.L53   796.6   80-24042
ISBN 0-87857-322-4 hardcover
ISBN 0-87857-323-2 paperback

2 4 6 8 10 9 7 5 3 1 hardcover
2 4 6 8 10 9 7 5 3 1 paperback

To the earth beneath my wheels.

CONTENTS

ACKNOWLEDGMENTS

This book would not have been possible without the help of John Keats, who planted the seed; Sharon Karger, who nurtured it; Eric Rummel, who helped me through the early days; Chuck McCullagh and Kevin Shafer, who provided a forum for my ideas along the way and gave me access to material from *Bicycling®* and *Bike World* magazines; and Heidi Adelman and Dave Washington, who helped me wrap things up; as well as Leigh Phoenix, Jerry Simpson, Holland Peterson, John Marino, John Howard, physical therapist Randy Ice, Ed Burke, John Forester, Charlie Pace, Harlan Meyer, Alan Abrahamson, John Camp, M.D., Creig Hoyt, M.D., David Smith, M.D., and dozens of other cyclists who have shared their knowledge and the joy of cycling with me through the years.

INTRODUCTION

Since the early 1970s, millions of Americans bought bicycles. For many, the purchase was their first, or the first within decades.

The bicycle was advertised as a romantic, effortless answer to pollution, midriff bulge, tension and a dozen other problems, including the gasoline crisis.

But while salesmen were quick to sell millions of bicycles and tons of useless accessories, they neglected, often out of sheer ignorance, to give the buyers what they needed most: education. After all, most assumed, the bicycle was only a toy.

Consequently, millions of new bike owners found themselves helpless when a tire went flat a mile from home, scared half to death when a car drove by, and bruised and sore from riding just a few slow miles. Soon their bikes were left to rust under porches or gather dust in garages.

But a growing group of bike owners realized there was an easy way, a safe way, a comfortable way to ride their bikes, even for more than 100 miles in a day. And they found that whether they used their bikes to save gas, explore themselves or the world around them, or increase their fitness, cycling was the most exhilarating activity they'd ever tried.

Unfortunately, the tens of millions who had tossed aside their bikes never had the chance to tap this enjoyment, the pure exhilaration. Even as the bookstore shelves filled with titles on cycling, there was no book that offered the novice cyclist a guide to enjoying all facets of the sport.

This book is my attempt to correct this situation. I've tried to cover everything of interest to the novice cyclist, with special emphasis on making cycling easier, safer, more comfortable and, ultimately, more enjoyable. Because much of this information has been ignored by the technically obsessed writers who have covered cycling in the past, even cyclists who have been riding for years will find much to improve their enjoyment and health.

Unlike its competitors, this book is not about bicycles: it is about cycling. It will show you the correct way, the safe way, the comfortable and easy way to enjoy the sport of cycling, and will unlock the door to parts of the sport that you may not have known existed. There's a good chance that once you venture beyond that door, you'll never turn back.

PART I
WARMING
UP

CHAPTER ONE
JUST
CYCLING

The sun was slowly sinking behind a bank of dark clouds. I had dodged potholes and angry drivers, had trudged up and swooped down hills at 40 miles an hour (mph) on my way out of the city. Now, after a day at the office, I was far out into the country, safe from the curses and blasting horns of harried people rushing home that Friday evening. It was the perfect time for a ride. The cool air swept over me, but the warmth of the lingering sun kept me from chilling.

As I rode, my mind wandered far from the road to the pages of a half-written article scattered across my desk back home. Suddenly, ideas flashed through my head, and I realized how to rewrite a section that had troubled me for weeks.

I glanced at my speedometer and noticed that I was riding two miles an hour faster than I normally do—and normally, I work as hard as I can. My legs were spinning effortlessly, my pulse was low and the road flowed under my wheels.

It was one of those moments when mind, body, machine and road merged, and nothing I could have consciously done could have made me move faster or more efficiently. And I couldn't have felt more at peace with myself or the world.

I was just cycling.

You cannot jump on a bicycle for the first time and expect to reach that state of clarity and euphoria. It comes only by mastering the basics of cycling and savoring every turn of the pedals. But doing so takes little effort, and can bring countless rewards.

Euphoria is what cycling is all about. Men and women of all ages cycle for a multitude of reasons: to stay in shape, save gas and money, or explore the world. But no matter why they say they cycle, they wouldn't be doing it if it were not fun.

Holland Peterson, a Canadian touring cyclist, paid homage to the euphoria of cycling in his "Cyclist's Manifesto":

> The purpose of cycling is to yield euphoria: to exalt in the mystic allure of the open road; to exalt in salutary exercise in the open air; to savor the sensuous pleasures of a constantly changing scene; to submerge your being into the beauties of nature so that you lose your identity

into something infinitely more vast. This is euphoria. If you have experienced it, you are a cyclist.

The smooth rhythmic act of pedaling can act like a meditator's mantra by freeing your mind from mundane distractions. With little effort, the skilled cyclist's body continues to cycle, but far more efficiently than he could consciously direct it to. Writer and philosopher Michael Novak described the process in *Joy of Sports:*

> This is one of the great inner secrets of sports. There is a certain point of unity within the self, and between the self and the world, a certain complicity and magnetic mating, a certain harmony, that conscious mind and will cannot direct. Perhaps analysis and the separate mastery of each element are required before the instincts are ready to take command, but only at first. Command by instinct is swifter, subtler, deeper, more accurate, more in touch with reality than command by conscious choice. The discovery takes one's breath away.

Cycling is not only a good way to lose yourself, but to find yourself too. Alan Abrahamson, a young writer, recalled the 4,250-mile transAmerica cycle trip he rode at age 17.

"I grew up in a hurry," he said. "It was me against the world, and I'm happy to say I at least kept the world at a stalemate.

"I learned to be friends with myself. I think I developed this capacity when it was just me, the sun and 30 miles of road, and I had to step back and see what I was thinking. How was I feeling? Was I emotionally up or down? Did I think the upcoming ride would make me happy or sad? Why? I think I learned some of the things that make me tick, and accepted myself as myself—not as some idealized version of myself."

Cycling is, admittedly, not the only activity that lets you rise above yourself, transcend your limits and gives you a more positive outlook. But cycling has several advantages over the competition, advantages that make it the best sport around.

For starters, cycling is only as competitive as you want it

to be. You may be satisfied to ride a few miles to work, school or the store, or take a short ride around the park after dinner. Or you may want to better John Marino's 12-day trans-America crossing record. Clubs sponsor 5-mile tours and 750-mile races; there's always something that's just right for you—and something to move on to.

You don't have to track down a partner to enjoy cycling, or wait your turn to use a special facility. After you buy your bike, there's no charge to ride, and you're not confined to a track, pool or short road circuit. In fact, cycling forces you to go out and explore the world around you. Five-time American road-racing champion John Howard recalled his introduction to cycling: "Just getting out of the goldfish bowl of swimming and the ¼-mile track was thrilling, feeling the wind in my hair, the sun on my cheeks, seeing the blue sky above."

Film producer and cycle commuter Greg Kirchin said cycling to work "gives me a chance to explore the back roads around where I live." Greg rides his bicycle at least 12 miles a day on his way to work and back nearly every workday of the year. "You get to see new scenery, people wave to you as you ride by; it's a really nice way to start the day."

Unlike other forms of transportation, cycling does not isolate you from the ground you're covering. Zooming over flat, featureless interstate highways at 60 mph in a chrome-and-glass chariot with the air conditioner and the stereo blasting is no way to experience the richness and variety of the world around you.

And although cycling is slow enough to let you take in the sights, sounds, smells and feel of the planet, it is still fast enough to let you quickly cover a lot of ground. In the time it takes a typical runner to cover 6 miles, a cyclist can cover 20; and while a backpacker might set his sights on a 20-mile day, even a six-year-old cyclist can cover 100 miles or more. Not only is cycling faster than these and other forms of locomotion, but cycling is also easier, so you can ride longer without stopping.

Cycling is a year-round sport too. One of the most pleasant rides I ever took was on a winter day, long after most cyclists hide their bikes for the year. I hesitated for hours before going outside: the mercury hovered at 25°F., a temperature several degrees colder than I'd ever ridden in before. Yet something drew me out to the road, and made me want to explore.

The air was eerily still and pure. After I rode 3 miles, I was warm inside and out, and opened my windbreaker to let the crisp air wash over me. As I cut through the air at 20 mph, my face and body tingled. I felt utterly alive, and sucked in the purest air I'd ever tasted.

About 12 miles from home, near the midpoint of my ride, soft clumps of snow began drifting through the sky. They brushed against my face, softly caressing my red cheeks. Had I not had to show up at the office that afternoon, I probably would have ridden all day.

Cycling is also one of the most democratic sports, one that anyone can learn and master. It is one of the few activities that families and friends of all ages and sizes can undertake together. Size and sex are not handicaps, even in the grueling racing circuit: some of the top male, European professional road racers stand under 5' 2", and weigh less than 140 pounds; female American racers have regularly brought home medals from international competition, where American men have made little headway.

Perhaps nowhere is this democracy more evident than at the annual Tour of the Sciota River Valley (TOSRV), a two-day, 210-mile ride that draws close to 4,000 people to Columbus, Ohio. TOSRV is the Boston Marathon of cycling, but with one important difference: it is not a race. People ride solely for the enjoyment of cycling, and to spend time with families and friends. There are six-year-old boys and girls pedaling high-rise-handlebar and motocross bikes; women and men in their sixties and seventies spin past cyclists two generations younger.

Racers in red, green, yellow and blue jerseys sprint through the rolling course at better than 25 mph; mothers and fathers plod along on their tandems, their children sleeping snugly in trailers behind them.

Cyclists cluster with people they'd like to meet, or with those they've met at other rides, bringing one another up to date on what they've been doing, and offering cycling hints and snacks. Riders stop and share lunch and hugs along the banks of the Sciota River, and stretch out in the spring sun.

The line of cyclists snakes along for miles down the road, a blur of colors. Families who have not seen one another for months—or maybe not since the last TOSRV—exchange stories, recall memories and vow to meet at the next TOSRV.

Cyclists from South Africa and France ask their new-found American friends about riding in the United States, then tell them of the pleasures or horrors of cycling back home.

As the cyclists sprint over the finish line, they toss their helmets in the air or throw their arms skyward, each one basking in the accomplishment and sheer joy of the ride and the company of their warm, enthusiastic partners.

In *Cycling: The Healthy Alternative,* British physician David Kerr says of this phenomenon:

> The strengthening of family or group loyalties and the recognition of interdependence are recognizable advantages, but the wide age range which group cycling can embrace reinforces the former benefits in a way no other sporting group activity can claim so plausibly. The opportunities offered for shared learning, mutual support and communal responsibility on the road could contribute to an improvement in our fragmented society and should be seized on and applied by cyclists of all ages.

Since cycling is a sport for all ages, it's one you can enjoy throughout your life. It's not just a fad, but something you can return to year after year.

And there's a good chance you'll keep cycling because, unlike any other sport, it can be a useful part of your life, rather than a drain on your time. Bike activist Ellen Fletcher, a member of the Palo Alto, California, city council, summed up the advantage in *Bike World* magazine: "It amazes me that so many people get up so early to jog. They spend all that energy running around, and they don't get anywhere. They have to go home and get in their cars to go to work. I would like people to become aware that they can get this kind of exhilaration in a useful way by getting where they need to go"—by bike, of course.

The chances are that once you try cycling, you won't be able to get along without it. And that's because when you take everything into consideration, one conclusion is inescapable: no other activity can offer you such a rich range of experience and personal fulfillment.

Just cycling.

CHAPTER TWO
HEALTH ON WHEELS

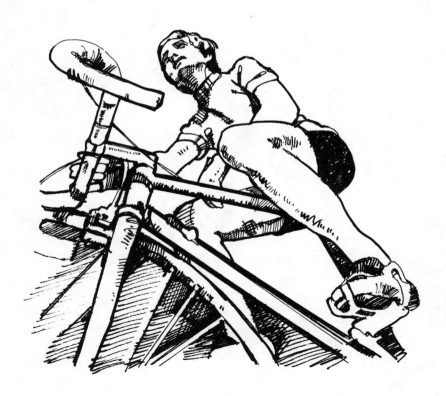

Not only is cycling so much fun, it is good for you too. Many newcomers find it hard to believe that cycling, which is rarely painful and always enjoyable, makes them healthier, too. As John Howard, who dominated American cycle racing in the early 1970s, said: "There's an attitude in America that you have to suffer to exercise. You go out and flog yourself for a few hours. People take up running and say, 'This really hurts—it must be good exercise.'"

Howard is not alone in his observation. Every day more people are becoming interested in improving their fitness, in being able to do everything they want to do, safely and with energy and enthusiasm. Yet many of those people find that exercise, the key to such fitness, is often boring and painful. Instead of helping them enjoy life, exercise seems to many to be punishment.

Cardiologist and syndicated columnist Peter Steincrohn, M.D., writes in his book, *How to Cure Your Joggermania!:* "My guess is that for every person who loves to jog there are five who hate it. Pleasant or not, most people exercise for 'the good it does them'—for the fitness and good health it promises."

While Dr. Steincrohn doesn't care for any type of exercise, there are many people convinced that exercise is good for them, so convinced that they'll put up with an activity they hate for the promise of fitness. Ask a runner why he runs, and he'll probably say, "for my health."

Running vs. Cycling

And there's the big difference between running and cycling: I've never met a cyclist who didn't ride first for the fun of it. For most cyclists, improved fitness is simply a fringe benefit of riding.

But it's an important one: despite rumors to the contrary, the general level of fitness in America is declining. At the same time, each year younger people fall victim to heart disease, which causes every other death in this country. Meanwhile, evidence continues to mount up indicating that exercise protects against heart disease, and in turn, extends life expectancy and slows the aging process.

In 1973, the President's Council on Physical Fitness and Sports reported that nearly half of all Americans over 50 are nonexercisers whose only physical activity on an average day consists of walking to their cars, to lunch, to the kitchen, and to turn on and off the television.

Other studies have found that the average level of fitness in America is far below the norms of Scandinavian countries, and many Americans have fitness levels below those set by the American Heart Association. Women received lower marks than men, with those in their teens and twenties scoring lowest.

Our children are in no better shape. Watching television and eating high-calorie, low-nutrition snacks has produced a generation of coronary-prone children. A University of Michigan study of American children found increased evidence of high cholesterol, high blood pressure, obesity and other conditions implicated in heart disease.

The director of that study, Thomas Gilliam, Ph.D., found that exercise reduced blood fats, one of the implicated factors, and recommended that youngsters should be motivated "as early as possible to engage in strenuous activity for their health's sake and continue throughout their lifetime." What better way than by "riding bikes," which even children prefer to running and other activities.

Another study, by the U.S. Department of Health, Education and Welfare, found that youngsters between the ages of 10 and 17 showed no improvement in physical fitness between the years 1965 and 1975. And a ten-state study found 39 percent of boys between ages 11 and 18 and 33 percent of girls the same age were overweight.

Just look around, and you'll quickly see that most adults, too, are overweight. And even if you meet your insurance company's standards, don't pat yourself on the back: unless you weigh what you did in your early twenties, you're probably overweight.

So when it comes to decreasing the risk factors of heart disease, the Fitness Boom has been a bust.

Unfortunately, heart disease is the number one killer in the United States. In 1978, an estimated 900,000 Americans died of heart disease or stroke, more than twice as many as died of cancer. By age 60, 1 in every 5 men and 1 in every 17 women in the United States have coronary disease.

While there is no indisputable evidence that regular exercise helps prevent heart disease, there is strong support for that conclusion. A 20-year cancer prevention study, "the largest human biological study ever undertaken of life and death," found that, "Among men reporting exercise habits, death rates from coronary heart disease and stroke were far higher among those checking 'none' than for 'slight' or 'moderate' or 'heavy' exercise. Death rates tended to decrease somewhat with increasing amounts of exercise."

Other studies have shown that inactive people run a risk two to three times greater than active people of dying from cardiovascular diseases (those that affect the heart or blood vessels). Those who have been active have a two-to-three times better chance of surviving a first heart attack than those who have been sedentary. And those who undertake an exercise program after a heart attack can expect to live significantly longer than those who don't.

One of the key findings in research on the effects of exercise is that physical training builds collateral circulation. Your heart pumps blood that carries oxygen and nutrients to all the other parts of your body. But your heart does not take oxygen and nutrients from the blood it is pumping out. It can get them only from blood flowing into it through two coronary arteries. If these arteries are blocked, an inadequate blood supply to the heart may cause part of the heart muscle to die: a heart attack.

But exercise opens additional blood vessels in the coronary arteries and in peripheral arteries. If a vessel becomes clogged, the result will not be as severe, since other vessels can take over the transportation of blood with its necessary oxygen and nutrients to tissue near the damaged vessel.

Just as important, regular exercise that requires increased oxygen uptake—the aerobic exercises such as cycling, running, long-distance swimming, skating, aerobic dancing and cross-country skiing—also increases the muscle mass, blood volume and power of the heart. A trained heart is much more efficient at rest and during exercise and returns to its resting rate quickly after exercise. And training also lowers blood pressure during rest.

Still, Dr. Steincrohn, a militant nonexerciser, writes in his book, *Joggermania:* ". . . I do not believe that it has been scientifically proved that exercise prevents coronary heart disease. There are too many other contributory factors, like obesity, high blood pressure, heredity, tension, heavy smoking and drinking—and the simple fact of being a male."

James F. Fixx, M.D., author of *The Complete Book of Running,* adds another 11 factors to the list: activity, fasting, blood sugar, triglycerides, fibrinolysins, diet, electrocardiogram (EKG) readings, uric acid, pulmonary function, glucose tolerance and cholesterol. But, he writes, "Of the [factors], exercise may improve all except heredity. Although smoking and dietary habits, for example, are not directly altered by running [or other exercise], anyone who becomes a regular runner will probably stop smoking, eat less and eat a greater proportion of wholesome food."

Assuming that exercise does help prevent heart disease, it's important to keep in mind that only the aerobic sports offer these benefits to the cardiovascular system. Other sports, including bowling, golf, softball and tennis, do not call for your heart and lungs to work as hard for extended periods. Only extended, vigorous aerobic exercise practiced regularly will give these results.

Short-duration events are not nearly as good, and may in fact be harmful. Ernst van Aaken, M.D., who has coached world-record-holding runners, writes in *Van Aaken Method* (Mountain View, California: World Publications, 1976): "All sports and types of work which require pure skeletal-muscle strength, and increase the heart's work by increasing blood pressure within the heart itself and in the arteries, are detrimental to the durability of the organism and to the work of this most important motor, the heart."

Admittedly, such exercise can help muscle tone and strength. But no one ever died of weak legs or arms.

The Best Aerobic Sport?

In contrast, aerobic sports such as cycling increase the capability of the oxygen supply system. Since all of the body's vital systems depend on oxygen, these sports keep those systems working at their peak and reduce the chance of disease.

Cycling may well be the best aerobic sport. Studies have consistently found champion cyclists to have the largest heart volume of all athletes, as well as the highest ability to deliver oxygen to the muscles, called maximum oxygen volume (VO_2max). Cross-country skiers and marathon runners place second and third.

The earlier you begin cycling, the better the results. In an interview with *Runner's World* magazine, Kenneth Cooper, M.D., the Father of Aerobics, said: "It's a whole lot more cheaper and a whole lot more effective to maintain good health than it is to try to regain health once it's lost."

But it's never too late to improve your health through cycling. In fact, cycling has been successfully used to rehabilitate people who have had heart attacks.

John Camp, M.D., and physical therapist Randy Ice are involved in a program called Specialized Coronary Outpatient Rehabilitation (SCOR) at Rancho Los Amigos Hospital in Downey, California. In the program, coronary patients follow a "prescription" of exercise, diet and other risk reduction factors.

After a period of careful supervision, SCOR patients are given a choice of walk–jogging, running or cycling. The SCOR Cardiac Cyclists Club began in 1974 and within six years had 50 members ranging from 39 to 74 years old. In addition to their weekday exercise prescriptions, the cyclists meet on Saturdays to ride 30 to 40 miles or more as a group.

The odds of staying alive after a heart attack are not good, even after expensive bypass surgery (costing up to $25,000) that temporarily reroutes blood past the blocked arteries. In fact, in a group of 50 coronary patients such as those in the Cardiac Cyclists Club, it's expected that at least 12 would die of heart attacks during a six-year period.

The Cardiac Cyclists don't like those odds. That's why some of them sought out the SCOR program on their own, despite their physicians' advice to rest and take it easy. Amazingly, they've beaten the odds: instead of 12 deaths by heart attack, only one Cardiac Cyclist has died, the only one who refused to stop smoking. He died not on his bike, but while shopping.

The most amazing and inspiring part of the Cardiac Cyclists' tale is that they are not just surviving but have more physical capacity than people decades younger. All are capable of cycling 50 miles in a day, and two-thirds have ridden 100 miles or more. Two of the Cardiac Cyclists have cycled 200-mile rides in less than 15 hours, and one, in his fifties, has ridden 300 miles in a day.

"These men have gone from the condition that is the sickest you can get to one of extreme health," Dr. Camp said. "If everybody in this country did what the Cardiac Cyclists did every day, I'd be out of business."

Despite the impressive results, Dr. Camp has not seen such programs embraced by the medical community.

"I send all of my patients to the program," he said, "but the majority of cardiologists don't. When doctors admit the program is good, they also have to admit that they, too, are killing themselves: more than half of all doctors die of cardiovascular disease.

"People in this country are obsessed with sickness. They want a magic pill. But sedentary people cannot keep saying, 'Cure me! Cure me!'

"People have to realize that doctors will never be able to bring them health. Only you can do it."

Cycling and Aging

Since degenerative diseases, including cardiovascular disease, go hand in hand with aging, arresting or reversing them through cycling effectively reverses the aging process. A study by the University of San Diego's exercise physiology laboratory checked heart rate, oxygen-processing capacity, the pumping power of the heart, and peripheral vascular resistance,* all commonly accepted indicators of aging, in 43 middle-aged men engaged in exercise programs over a ten-year period. At the end of the study, Fred W. Kasch, M.D., director of the laboratory, found that none of the four indicators showed signs of increased age and two—oxygen-processing capacity and the amount of blood pumped in a single heartbeat—suggested a reversal of a commonly accepted aging trend, which shows a lower oxygen capacity and smaller stroke volume with age.

One of the most convincing pieces of evidence that cycling reverses the aging process comes in the form of a cyclist nicknamed Foxy Grandpa. Ed Delano began cycling at the age of 58. In 1975, to celebrate his seventieth birthday, he cycled 3,400 miles from Vacaville, California, to Quebec, Canada, in 34 days.

The most astounding thing about Delano is that the older he becomes, the better he becomes. At age 69, he recorded times of 26.51 for 10 miles and 1:11.59 for 25 miles. At the age of 72, he had cut those times to 26.26 and 1:08.25. Not only have his time-trial times progressively decreased over the years, but his times in his seventies equal those projected for racers three decades younger.

Delano's body-fat level is as low as that of trained young athletes and his maximum voluntary ventilation volume† is about 130 percent of the predicted norm for his age.

The most impressive finding, though, is that Delano's maximum oxygen uptake is better than the "very good" category for men aged 20 to 29 years old and about 30 percent greater than the aerobic capacity of distance runners his age.

Irvin Faria, director of the human performance labora-

---

*Peripheral vascular resistance refers to the resistance of blood flow through the body's small arteries (known as arterioles) and reflects the flexibility or pliability of those small arteries, i.e., the lower the peripheral vascular resistance, the "younger" the vasculature.

†If you breathe in and out as rapidly and deeply as possible, the measured volume of air represents your maximum voluntary ventilation. Typically, this is between 100 and 200 liters a minute.

tory at California State University, Sacramento, summed up
his study of Delano in *Bike World* magazine:

> Even though serious cycling was not begun until he
> was 58, physiological youth has been regained or main-
> tained. It is difficult to identify the causative factors
> for the extraordinary physiological characteristics dis-
> played. The extent to which heredity, residual effects of
> training during early youth and recent training have
> contributed to the present physical status cannot be
> quantified.
>
> It does appear, however, that a combination of fac-
> tors, including cycling, has resulted in delaying physio-
> logical aging. In this instance, there has been a very
> favorable effect of vigorous physical activity continued
> thoughout life. Perhaps for some the fountain of youth
> may be no farther away than their bicycle.

Delano's performance speaks well of the fact that
cycling is a life sport: he not only continues to ride well into
his seventies, but beats cycle racers decades younger.

Many people Delano's age would have been forced to
give up most sports because of physical problems. But
cycling does not tear your body down as it builds up your
cardiovascular system. In fact, the gentle rhythm of cycling
makes it ideal for those who could not otherwise exercise. Dr.
Camp found that many of his older Cardiac Cyclists couldn't
run because of arthritis of the knees and hips. "One of the
cyclists has arthritis of the hips so bad that he cannot walk
without a severe limp," Dr. Camp said. "He can't run, and
there's no way he could perform aerobic exercise except with
a non-weight-bearing method like cycling.

"We also have some very obese individuals. Simply
because of their weight they cannot handle the jarring of
jogging, so they cycle. Cycling lets their leg muscles work,
but they don't have to put their weight on their legs.

"We also have people with foot problems who have taken
up cycling. That's the greatest reason for choosing cycling
over running."

Randy Ice took the topic further: "Go to any sports orthopedist's office and you'll find 15 runners and no cyclists.

They're making a fortune on running injuries. I've never had any of my cyclists *ever* have to limit their cycling because of an injury other than a traumatic one, such as falling off their bikes. And these Cardiac Cyclists are riding as much as 500 to 600 miles a month."

An Injury-Free Activity

Cycling is an amazingly injury-free activity, especially when compared with running. Dr. Steincrohn lists some of the hazards of running in his *Joggermania* book: stress fractures, back pain, hip pain, knee and ankle injuries, shinsplints, hamstring tears and pulls, achilles tendinitis, heel spurs, blisters, inflamed bones on the soles of the feet—and a half dozen others. But cyclists who ride thousands of miles a year rarely develop more serious problems than mild knee pains and saddle sores, both of which are usually caused by improper positioning on the bike, and rapidly clear up if treated promptly.

Researchers who studied 89 Bikecentennial cyclists who rode 4,500 miles across the United States in 80 days concurred that cycling has few ill effects. Daniel N. Kulund, M.D., and Clifford E. Brubaker, M.D., found that most of the participants suffered only minor knee pain, back pain and saddle soreness. "On the basis of the Bikecentennial experience," they wrote, "it seems a reasonable conclusion that bicycle touring is safe and desirable."

Robert H. Michael, M.D., chief of orthopedic surgery at Union Memorial Hospital in Baltimore is convinced that cycling is less likely to cause injuries than other sports, particularly running. In fact, some orthopedists recommend cycling as rehabilitation for certain problems. Among those are back problems: cycling on a "racing" bicycle allows the cushions between the disks in your spine to relax, keeping them from degenerating, which can cause pinching, tiredness, pain and, eventually, ossification of the cushions.

Not everyone agrees that cycling is the best exercise from an orthopedic viewpoint, though. Steven Skinner, M.D., an orthopedist at Hershey Medical Center in Pennsylvania,

feels that from an orthopedic viewpoint there is little difference among the aerobic sports. But Dr. Skinner does find
one major difference between running and cycling: "Cycling
is fun," he says, "running is boring."

Most of the handful of articles on cycling injuries in the
medical literature deal with the one truly unpleasant aspect
of cycling: accidents. But, as you'll see later, most cycling
accidents can be easily prevented, and few involve motor
vehicles. And keep in mind that cycling is not the only sport
in which accidents happen: every sport has its risks. Dr. van
Aaken lost his legs after he was hit by a car while running.

Most of the consequences of cycling are far more
pleasant, though, and there are many more than those already listed. One is that cycling uses every major muscle
group in the body. Harry J. Johnson, M.D., chairman of the
New York Life Extension Institute, a preventive-medicine
organization, wrote in the *Physician and Sportsmedicine*
magazine: "Any exercise that involves the whole body and
does not demand too much at any one time makes an ideal
form of exercise. And an added advantage of bicycling is the
pleasure of it."

Not only does cycling keep most of your muscles in tone
and working at their best, but it also makes you look better,
too. As you train, you will lose body fat and store what fat you
do have in your muscles, where it is not visible. Nonathletes
store fat under their skin, where it creates unsightly bulges
around the waist, buttocks, thighs, hips and breasts.

Cycling will give your muscles better definition and will
make you more compact and attractive. In *The Sportsmedicine Book,* Gabe Mirkin, M.D., writes: "It amazes me
that so many women are worried that exercise will build large,
ugly muscles. It doesn't happen. Ice skater Dorothy Hamill
and gymnast Olga Korbut have sleek, well-formed muscles.
To develop large, bulky muscles, you have to do resistance
exercises such as weight lifting. Rhythmic exercises, such as
aerobic dancing, swimming and bicycling, form long muscles
and a firm, attractive figure."

You'll lose inches before you lose pounds, but the excess
pounds will drop, too. Not only does exercise burn off excess
calories, but it also typically reduces appetite. Medical

authorities agree that the best way to take off weight and keep it off is through a combination of diet and exercise.

Greg Kirchin lost 50 pounds in six months of commuting, riding only a 12-mile round trip to work each day, supplemented with detours and trips to the store.

"I don't think I lost all those pounds through burning off calories in exercise," Greg says. "Instead, I lost because cycling changed my attitude toward eating. I'm not as hungry. The more I exercise, the less need I feel to eat. Eating for me is something I do out of frustration, nervousness and not having something better to do. But cycling takes care of that tension.

"And as I started to lose weight, I began to feel good about the way I looked and felt."

The Mind–Body Connection

As your body improves, your mind should, too. When 60 middle-aged Purdue University faculty and staff members were put on a four-month exercise program, their personalities changed for the better. As they became fit, they also became more emotionally stable, more self-sufficient, more imaginative and confident.

Nancy Rosenberger, now an enthusiastic club cyclist, found this out after a divorce. She used her newfound time to ride her bicycle at every opportunity, and found that cycling benefitted her.

"A divorce really cuts into your self-confidence tremendously," she recalled. "But cycling helped me regain confidence and find myself again."

"I went out riding a lot after work to relax, and I'd do a lot of thinking. While I was enjoying the scenery and listening to the birds, I thought about my life, and got to know myself again. I don't think I could have found the time otherwise.

"I met new people virtually every time I went out for a ride. It's fantastic to absorb everyone elses' experiences and share yours with them.

"I heard a lot of talk about 100-mile rides and I said, 'Why can't I do that?' So I thought I'd try one. I did, and I was

ecstatic. Meeting that goal really helped my self-confidence.
I changed a lot that summer."

Most of the Cardiac Cyclists have changed since they've
begun riding, too. "They can see the differences it's making," Dr. Camp said, "and they say, 'I'm taking over control
of my body and aging. I'm taking control of my disease.'

"Life is worth living again. They don't have to worry
about dying the next day. The wife of one of the cyclists said
to me, 'You don't know how nice it is to be able to plan trips
and know we can make them. Before, we were afraid to plan
anything!'"

It's no wonder, then, that exercise is proving effective
in treating depression, a serious problem for hundreds of
thousands of Americans. After studying about 700 de-
pressed patients, Robert S. Brown, M.D., recommended in
the *Physician and Sportsmedicine* magazine "that any
rational, safe and effective treatment regimen for depression should include a prescription for vigorous exercise. . . .Although the mechanisms of mind/body exchanges
must be further explored, we urge consideration of the pal-
liative impact on depression of appropriately supervised and
continued programs of physical activity." A key finding of his
study was that, "Although physical exertion on the job may
be physically beneficial, recreational or voluntary programs
yield more psychologically useful exercise."

John Griest, M.D., found a jogging program more beneficial than psychotherapy in treating moderate depression.
People who regularly exercise, Greist concluded, "get a
sense of success and mastery from it. When people find
they're able to do something they didn't know they could do,
they begin to realize they can also make other changes in
their life for the better."

Another reason that cycling helps control depression is
that it is a good way to release stress. In *Van Aaken Method,*
Dr. van Aaken writes, "It's much too little-known that human
beings. . .can work off the most serious consequences of
stress by increasing their oxygen uptake in physical
activity—running a few slow miles for recovery after a hard
day's work, for instance, however paradoxical that may
sound to the uninitiated."

Nancy Rosenberger is in agreement. "People think cycling is hard work—they just don't believe how relaxing it can be." And U.S. national 24-hour time-trial record holder Leigh Phoenix concurs: "There's nothing like a good ride to burn off day-to-day frustrations."

As you become fitter in both mind and body, cycling will also sharpen your senses. Among other benefits, this awareness, coupled with your well-conditioned heart and lungs, will make sex more pleasurable. In *The Sportsmedicine Book,* Dr. Mirkin writes: ". . .individuals who are fit don't tire easily during lovemaking and can participate in sexual relations more intensely and for a longer period of time. They find this satisfying and rewarding." And Mirkin quotes sex researcher William Masters, M.D.: "A person who has good physical fitness invariably functions more effectively sexually than a person in poor shape. Sexual function is a physiologic process and every physiologic process works better in a good state of health than in a poor one."

Cycling is also good for improving your balance and digestion and helps you sleep. In fact, when seven experts evaluated 14 popular forms of exercise, cycling ranked second, just a few points behind jogging, and far ahead of activities such as golfing, softball and walking for promoting physical fitness. And the small difference in the ratings between running and cycling seems to be due to the experts' unfamiliarity with the benefits of cycling. For instance, while cycle racers typically hold speeds of 25 mph for four hours or longer, marathoners race for just a little more than two hours. Yet the experts gave cycling only 19 points out of a possible 21, while running got a perfect score.

Even if there were a wider gap in the ratings, though, cycling would still be the sure winner for many because of the infrequency of injuries and, most of all, the sheer joy of cycling.

But no matter how much fun it is and how good it is for you, cycling cannot appeal to everyone. Other sports admittedly have their benefits, and for many, these outweigh those gained from cycling. Some prefer the simplicity of running or the refreshing coolness of swimming; others simply do not like to mingle with traffic.

Still, many people quickly become hooked when they give cycling a fair trial. Unfortunately, there is a naive group that will never give it a fair trial; those who are afraid of injury while exercising.

Ironically, you have a far better chance of dying from remaining sedentary than from exercising, unless you overdo it in the beginning. The sudden shock to the system, akin to shoveling snow or being placed under emotional stress, can indeed level an underexercised, overweight person.

But the myth persists that moderate exercise is a threat. In no small part, this is reinforced by the media. "What people don't realize," Dr. Camp explained, "is that no one puts anything in the headlines about the millions of people who die sitting at their desks. On the other hand, for every million Joe Blows dying at their desks, there's a marathoner or cyclist who dies. That's what gets the headlines."

Peter Wood, M.D., deputy director of Stanford University's Heart Disease Prevention Program, offered these additional comments in *Runner's World* magazine: "Some authorities. . .have predicted a vast epidemic of running deaths as coronary-prone Americans put on their running shoes. It hasn't happened, and no amount of references to a few well-known cases. . .proves that it has." On the contrary, as Dr. Wood points out, many life insurance companies are offering lower premiums to regular exercisers—something they would hardly do if those people had the profit-eating habit of dropping dead early. Occidental Life Insurance Company led the way in 1978 by offering policies with savings of up to 20 percent for cyclists who rode at least three times a week for a year.

It's not hard to find other disclaimers for the exercise-death myth. Even the prestigious *Journal of the American Medical Association,* analyzing a survey of 2,606 sudden deaths, reported that, "Sudden deaths in connection with sporting activities or regular daily routine were rare."

The authors of the survey collected data on more than a million performances of skiers over a 16-year period. In those trips, they found only eight deaths related to the ski hikes, and all victims had had definite and known cardiac conditions.

While the author of the editorial found "a considerable risk of sudden death in connection with strenuous physical exercise in subjects with manifest or latent heart disease," he concluded that, "Sudden death seems to be preventable. . .and the best method of prevention is progressive training and gradual adjustment to physical stress."

So, all things considered, hopping on a bike should do much more to lengthen your life than shorten it. While there's no guarantee as yet that cycling will put more years in your life, it is guaranteed to put more life in your years.

CHAPTER THREE
THE SAVING MACHINE

Not only can cycling save your life and make it more worth saving, too, but it can also help you save other things—such as money.

I'm sure you don't need to be reminded how gasoline prices have soared since the beginning of the 1970s, jumping more than 60 percent in 1979 alone; as supplies continue to dwindle, prices can only soar higher. And the real cost of gasoline is much higher than the pump price: hours wasted searching for open stations and waiting in line; dependence on terroristic oil-producing nations who are hardly looking out for our best interests.

In his January 1980 state of the union address, President Jimmy Carter put the situation succinctly when he said: "Our excessive dependence on foreign oil is a clear and present danger to our national security." Yet far too many of our leaders seem ready to begin World War III rather than enforce legislation to cut that dependence.

The Hertz Corporation found that on the average, American motorists pay 31.9¢ a mile to drive and maintain their cars. In big cities, such as New York and Los Angeles, those costs rise to 44.2¢ a mile. Even at the average cost, driving 15,000 miles a year costs about $5,000, enough to buy and maintain a different mid-quality bicycle for every month of the year.

Maybe you can afford the costs and, in fact, have nothing better to do with your money. But that's still no reason to waste energy unnecessarily. Every time you drive, you take a bite out of the remaining world oil supplies, which some experts predict will be exhausted in 30 years. The biggest accumulations of world oil supplies have probably already been found, and global oil production during coming years is expected to increase less than 1 percent a year, compared with an annual growth of 7 percent in the 1960s and early 1970s. If this proves to be true, *Business Week* magazine noted, "there will be nowhere near enough oil to meet the current 3 percent annual increase in world demand. . . . The resulting scarcity, almost inevitably, will be apportioned by further relentless price boosts, accompanied by stepped-down conservation . . . and economic slowdown in the consuming nations."

With only 6 percent of the world's population, the United States uses 30 percent of the world's energy. To meet this gluttonous demand, the United States has to import half the oil it uses—a staggering 8 million barrels of oil a day.

Stanley Hart, chairman of the transportation committee of the Sierra Club in Southern California, attacked this practice in an article in the *Los Angeles Times:*

"America's per capita gasoline consumption is 4½ times that of France and more than 7 times more than that of Japan—clearly an immoral use of an essential but diminishing commodity. Fifty percent of our consumption is devoted to transportation, mostly by private cars and freight. The inefficiency of American vehicles is well known; it would not be entirely inaccurate to say that the power of OPEC and Iran oil power were made in Detroit."

In refreshing counterpoint to our inefficient autos, the bicycle is the most efficient form of locomotion known. A cyclist can travel 1,000 miles on the energy equivalent of one gallon of gasoline.

But the key is that cycling uses no oil, and so offers a way to conserve our energy supplies, the only way to prolong them. Without conservation, we might live to see the day when we cannot even take the bus to work if we cannot find gas for the car: there simply won't be any oil left, at least not for sale in America.

And don't expect to be bailed out by synthetic fuels and other alternative sources of energy. In *Running on Empty,* three members of the Worldwatch Institute contend that it is conceivable that petroleum substitutes could be developed in time to protect the automobile from the impending downturn in world oil production—"but it is unlikely. The leading candidates . . . all face serious economic, environmental or social problems that are likely to present major barriers to their development.

"An alternative approach—the development of vehicles that do not require liquid fuels at all—is also unlikely to provide salvation from oil shortages."

Even while oil supplies last, we'll continue to pay dearly for them. Only by lowering our oil consumption and need for foreign oil can we hope to fend off the inflation that has racked the country for the past decade. Stanley Hart writes: "Many would argue jobs and prosperity depend on high levels of oil consumption. The contrary is true; the excessive use of oil helps create the foreign trade deficits that are a significant cause of U.S. inflation. The resulting waste and inefficiency handicap American industry in both domestic and overseas marketing of American goods."

Using bicycles instead of cars wherever possible will not only help conserve energy resources and curb inflation, but will help save other resources, too. The material used to make just one car can produce 150 bicycles. And bicycles take up less space, with the added benefit of being able to use narrower roads and smaller parking lots. Since car production requires large amounts of energy, and asphalt is oil based, the savings will multiply.

And, Hart added, "Parking, roads and other auto-related uses take up 40 percent of all space in urban areas (60 percent in central business districts); space that provides neither a return on investment nor taxes to support the community. It also increases urban sprawl, thus increasing travel and real estate costs, as well as gobbling up prime agricultural land. These costs are borne by all of society, not by motorists alone, who benefit from the misuse of this land. In addition, motorists' subsidies, costs that are hidden in grocery and tax bills, are matched by the demand and cost of dealing with automotive air pollution."

The less oil we burn, the cleaner our air and planet will become. Spent energy resources continually foul our air and water, and become garbage, and are becoming increasingly difficult and expensive to dispose of. In cities, the internal-combustion engine contributes up to 85 percent of all air pollution. The effluents from vehicle exhausts mix with other substances to form deadlier poisons, and cause phenomena such as acid rain, which is ruining cropland and sterilizing lakes and streams throughout the world.

A related problem is that the level of carbon dioxide in the earth's atmosphere, called the greenhouse effect, is steadily increasing. While its full effects are not yet understood, it is believed that the increasing levels of carbon dioxide will be unfavorable to all but plant life.

Of course, public transportation is plagued with all the problems of private transportation. To make matters worse, transit systems require so much energy to produce that it may take 30 years or more of continuous use just to recoup the energy used to build a system.

It's obvious that there is a growing need for a type of transportation that will not foul the air we breathe and the water we drink or strip the planet of its nonrenewable resources. Cycling is the perfect answer.

PART II
GETTING INTO GEAR

CHAPTER FOUR
CHOOSING A BIKE

Choosing to use a bicycle instead of an auto wherever possible should be easy for most people: American homes contain one bike for every two people. Even if you don't own a bike, there's a good chance someone else in your family does. Of course, talking him out of his bike may not be the easiest thing to do, so you may end up having to buy a bike of your own.

Despite what many books and salesclerks say, picking a bicycle is nowhere near as complicated as building a nuclear reactor. The bicycle is, in fact, an elegantly simple machine, one referred to in the Broadway play *Spokesong* as "the last thing man invented that he understood."

The most important step in choosing a bicycle is evaluating your needs and budget. If you plan to ride less than five miles at a time over level terrain, a single-speed ("no speed") or 3-speed bike should be sufficient. These "velocipedic burros," as touring cyclist Holland Peterson calls single-speeds, are also good for cruising on the beach or delivering newspapers.

In fact, Peterson, who rides even during the harsh Canadian winters, has sworn by single-speed bikes during his 45 years of cycle touring.

"I think one has to be philosophical to enjoy a single-gear bike," he explained. "After all, the only advantage ten gears have to offer is speed, and speed isn't one of my values. I can appreciate scenery much better at my average of 12 mph in the saddle than I can at a 10-speed average of 16 mph. I unashamedly walk up most hills and stop on the slightest provocation."

Undoubtedly, part of Peterson's enthusiasm stems from the fact that his single-speed bike is custom-built, weighing only 25 pounds. Unfortunately, the bikes you'll find in the stores more typically weigh as much as 50 pounds, making it much harder to cover a given distance, or to lug your bike up to a second-floor apartment.

Many cyclists who commute by bike have found a reasonable answer to these problems: single- and 3-speed bikes that fold in half. These bikes can be folded up in seconds, tossed into small carrying bags, and carried aboard planes and buses or into the office or store. Traditionally, folding bikes have been as heavy as the heaviest conventional bikes, and bulky when folded. But the Bickerton bicycle introduced in the late 1970s weighs less than 20 pounds, folds to the

Comparison of 3-speed and 10-speed bicycle designs. Note the thick saddle, the upright handlebars and the wide tires on the 3-speed on the top. The 10-speed on the bottom has drop or racing handlebars, and narrower saddle and tires.

size of a small suitcase in less than a minute, and comes in single- and 3-speed models. It's not perfect, though: its small wheels can make for a shaky ride, its gearing is poor for hilly areas, there is typically a long wait for delivery, and the price of the 3-speed is about $400.

Advantages of a Ten-Speed

For those reasons and several others, most cyclists are better off with a 10-speed bike, especially if they live in hilly areas. A 10-speed will make even your five-mile jaunts easier, and allows you to travel much farther, comfortably. More importantly, you can use a 10-speed to do anything you can do with a single- or 3-speed, and much more. I've used the same 10-speed to tour, race, commute to school and work, shop for groceries, visit friends, take long recreational rides and even ride in the woods.*

A 10-speed is not ten times as expensive as a single-speed; in fact, it's hard to find a good single- or 3-speed bike for less than $100, while comparable 10-speeds start at just $50 more. For the beginner, 10-speeds in the $150–$250 range are the best buys: they're light, yet sturdy and reliable. The $250 models use lighter but stronger and more attractive components than the $150 bikes, and typically weigh about four pounds less.

The number of gears is not the sole difference between single-, 3- and 10-speed bikes, but it is an important one. A single-speed bike has one gear, suitable for riding on the flats. A well-designed 3-speed also has a gear for riding into head winds or climbing hills, and another for coming downhill or riding with the wind at your back. A 10-speed gives you a much wider range, allowing you to pedal up and down the steepest hills, and into and out of the stiffest winds. But if you don't mind walking hills, a single- or 3-speed may be OK.

---

* There are still several 5-speeds available, but they do not merit serious consideration. They offer the disadvantages of both the 3- and 10-speeds with none of the advantages, yet sell for nearly as much as 10-speeds.

The single- and 3-speeds' gearing is not the only factor that limits their range. Another important one is their design. Single- and 3-speeds are equipped with upright handlebars and wide saddles with springs. This setup is fine for short rides through busy streets, because the upright position lets you keep an eye on traffic.

But try riding more than ten miles in that position and you'll find it far from ideal. Your arms will tire from staying in the same position, and your backside and back will grow sore as every bump and pothole send their full impact straight up your spine. And the wide saddle will chafe your legs.

You don't have these problems with a 10-speed. The dropped handlebars allow you to ride in a variety of positions to relieve fatigue. Leaning forward places some of your weight on your arms, giving your back a rest. As an added bonus, riding in this position lowers your wind resistance, thus allowing you to ride faster without working harder.

The single- and 3-speeds' wide, low-pressure tires help absorb road shocks, but only at the cost of efficiency. These tires give a soft ride because they are wide enough to swallow bumps and stones. But their large area of contact with the road also increases rolling resistance and swallows your effort. It may take half again as much effort to move a single- or 3-speed at a given speed as a 10-speed.

The single- or 3-speed's weight adds to your work. A mid-priced 10-speed weighs 25 to 30 pounds, but a top-of-the-line single- or 3-speed may weigh closer to 50 pounds. Those extra pounds don't make the bike sturdier, but they do make it harder to push up hills.

Another feature of single- and 3-speed bikes that appears to be an advantage to the novice is just as disappointing. Single- and 3-speed enthusiasts make much ado about the gearing and braking systems being tucked safely inside the rear hub. Granted, it's less likely that they will be damaged there, but when they do go out of adjustment, it means you're going to be stuck an expensive repair bill. Even a child can adjust the exposed gear changers and brakes on a 10-speed with a screwdriver in a few minutes.

If you're beginning to suspect that I favor 10-speed bikes, you're right. But only for good reason: 10-speeds are easier to ride and repair and are more comfortable than single- and 3-speed bikes. And a bike with those qualities is going to inspire you to ride farther and more often.

Whichever type of bicycle you decide is best for you, take the time to look in all the bike shops and manufacturers' catalogs you can find. A bike is a major investment that should last ten years or longer.

Where to Shop

Avoid discount houses, department stores and auto supply houses. Prices at such stores may look appealing, but the bikes don't. Bicycles do not have large markups—maybe $40 on a $250 model—so you're not going to find a $65 10-speed that comes even close in quality to one costing $150 or more.

Most discount houses, department stores and the like sell bikes for only one reason: profit. So they look for bikes with high markups or bikes that can be sold at bargain-basement prices. The quality of either type is questionable at best. I know from experience: I worked on the cheap bikes in a discount store's sporting goods department. There was a host of problems with these bikes: brakes that didn't hit the rims (So who needs to stop?), gear changers that were as temperamental as British sports cars (just find your favorite gear and stay there), metal shavings in the ball bearings. The store sold one model because of its incredibly low price. Unfortunately, it also had an especially troubling quirk: the front forks tended to break off while riding downhill.

The other salesmen could not have cared less. They weren't cyclists and, in fact, usually didn't even work in the bike department. Most of them knew more about toaster ovens than about bikes. Instead of hiring a competent mechanic to run its service department, the store left its customers to fumble around with incomplete parts and instructions printed in Japanese.

A bike shop cannot make up its losses on defective bikes that are returned by selling toaster ovens. Consequently, the people at a bike shop will help you pick a bike that's right for your size, needs and budget. The shop will set up the bike properly, and will be there later to tackle repairs—they're not going to drop their bike line, as some discount houses have done. And you don't have to worry about getting a bottom-of-the-line clunker; bike shops don't have the time or money to repair them.

Frame Size

A bicycle is made up of several components, the most important of which is the frame. If the frame doesn't fit you, you'll waste energy while pedaling and never be comfortable.

A bicycle frame is essentially two triangles that you hang parts on. The most important part of the two triangles is the tube they share, the *seat tube*.

The seat tube runs from the center of the *bottom bracket* (the cylinder in which the crank axle rotates; the pedals are attached to the *crankarms,* which attach to the axle) to the *top tube* (the one running parallel to the ground). Most 10-speeds with 27-inch wheels are offered with a choice of 19-, 21-, 23- or 25-inch seat tubes. The selection is limited on 26-inch-wheeled bikes (single- and 3-speeds, as well as inexpensive 10-speeds), which may be offered only in 21- or 23-inch frame sizes.

Unless you are extremely short, you should buy a diamond frame (men's) bike. This design is stiffer and sturdier than the dropped (women's) model, and has a higher resale value. Short men and women may not be able to find a diamond frame small enough; if possible, they should buy a mixte frame instead of a dropped frame. On a mixte, the top tube is dropped as it is on a traditional women's frame. But instead of joining to the seat tube, the top tube on a mixte runs back to the rear wheel axle, making a much sturdier frame.

There are several ways to determine frame size, but only two work well. The simplest method is to measure your inseam (from your crotch to the floor) in your bare feet, then subtract ten inches.

To get the most precise fit, though, it's best to measure

(continued on page 42)

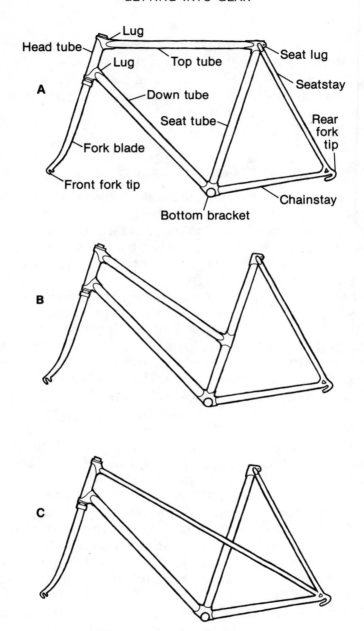

Diamond, or men's, bicycle frame (A). On dropped, or women's, model (B), there is no top tube. Instead, a tube runs from the head tube to the seat tube. On a mixte frame (C), a tube or pair of tubes runs from the head tube all the way to the rear axle dropouts.

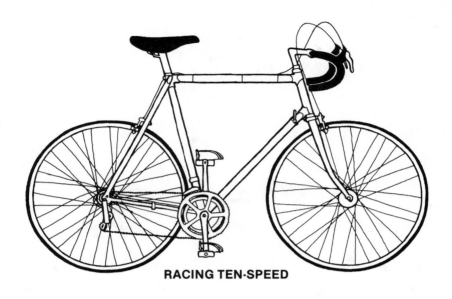

RACING TEN-SPEED

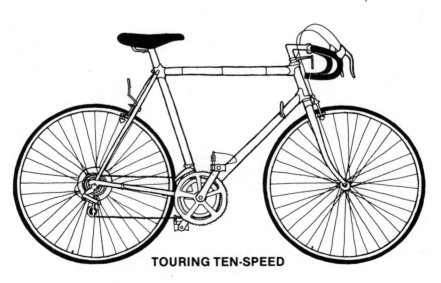

TOURING TEN-SPEED

Comparison of racing and touring 10-speeds. As a general rule, the racing model has a shorter, more upright design and a smaller rear sprocket while the traditional touring frame is longer, has shallower angles and a larger rear sprocket. But many so-called touring bikes have measurements and angles closer to those of a racing bike.

As a rule of thumb, you can determine your proper frame size by straddling the bike in your bare feet. There should be just about an inch of clearance between your crotch and the top frame tube. For a more precise fit, measure the distance from the top of your thighbone to the floor and subtract 13¾ inches.

the distance from the top of the thighbone to the floor, again in bare feet. Then subtract 13¾ inches from that measurement to determine the correct frame size.

When considering a bike, ask the salesperson if it's available in your frame size. Not every manufacturer offers the same frame sizes: some make 22- and 24-inch models instead of 21-, 23- and 25-inch frames. If your dream bike isn't offered in the exact size you need, take the next smaller size.

Don't accept a frame that is far too large or too small because it's the only one in stock. I made this mistake with my first good bike. The store had stocked only 21- and 23-inch models. Although I needed a 25-inch frame, I assumed that a 23-inch frame was the largest made. When I got home and tried to raise the seat high enough so I could extend my legs fully, the seatpost pulled right out of the seat tube. I finally tracked down an extralong seatpost, but it was too flexible, and part of my pedaling effort was wasted in side-to-side motion.

A frame that's too big can be even worse. Children are often unwitting victims here: parents will buy a bike as they would a pair of pants so that the child can "grow into" it. But a bike that's too big is impossible to control.

In addition to different sizes, you'll also find different designs. Single- and 3-speeds come in one style only, designed for short rides on level ground. But you'll find two styles of 10-speeds: "touring" and "racing" designs. The touring bikes are designed for comfortable, leisurely recreational riding, and have been used for commuting to work and crossing the country. The racing design is primarily for hard, fast day trips.

On $150-$250 racing bikes, the *wheelbase* (the distance between the front and rear axles) is shorter than on tourers, typically 39 to 40 inches as opposed to 41 to 42 inches for touring bikes. The racing bike's frame angles are steeper, making the tubes more upright. Typical racing frames have seat tube and head tube angles of 72 to 74 degrees, while the tourers have angles of 70 to 72 degrees. The *fork rake* (the distance the front forks are offset from the line of the steering axis) is also straighter on the racer than on the tourer.

These differences don't overwhelmingly change the character of the ride, but each has an opposing purpose. The short, steep racing bike is designed to deliver all of your power to the ground as efficiently as possible. The longer, more comfortable touring frame trades off efficiency for better shock absorption. Unless you're seriously considering racing or are just an out-and-out masochist, a touring model is probably the better choice.

Gearing

Another important difference between racing and touring bikes is in the gearing design. Gearing isn't difficult to understand. A 10-speed bike gets its 10 speeds by using a freewheel cluster of five gears on the rear wheel), teamed with two *chainrings* (front gears). Front and rear *derailleurs* (gear changers) move the chain from one gear to another.

The lowest gear (the one that's easiest to pedal) uses the smaller front chainring and the largest rear sprocket. With this combination, it's easy to turn the pedals, but you don't move as far forward with each pedal revolution. You use low gears to climb hills or when riding into stiff winds.

The highest gear uses the large front chainring and the smallest rear sprocket. This combination is much harder to pedal, but moves you farther down the road with every revolution.

Most racing bikes have front chainrings with 52 and 42 teeth, and rear cogs with 13 or 14 to 24 or 28 teeth. A typical rear setup would be 13–15–17–20–24. The highest gear would use the 52 and 13 combination (written as 52 × 13 and correctly pronounced as "fifty-two–thirteen") and the lowest would use the 42 and 24 combination (42 × 24).

Using the 52 × 13 combination, each time you turn the front sprocket (which happens every time you turn the pedals), the rear wheel will turn four times. The distance covered will be four times the circumference of the wheel. The circumference of a wheel is equal to its diameter multiplied by pi (3.14).

A 27-inch wheel has a diameter of 0.6858 meter. Multiply that by pi and by the four revolutions this gear combination gives, and you'll find that you move down the road a total of 8.6 meters (about 28 feet) for each pedal revolution. This gearing combination (52 × 13) is said to have a development of 8.6 meters.

Aside from showing the distance covered with every turn of the pedals in a given gear combination, development also lets you compare combinations. A 56 × 14 or a 48 × 12, for instance, gives the same development as the 52 × 13 combination. To find the development of any combination, use this formula:

$$\text{development (in meters)} = \frac{\text{teeth front sprocket}}{\text{teeth rear sprocket}} \times 3.14 \times 0.6858^* \text{(in meters)}$$

The touring bike gets its wider gearing range by using a wider spread between sprocket teeth. Typical combinations are 52 to 40 on front, 14 to 28 or 34 on rear. The high gear is 52 × 14; low gear is 40 × 34. It is easier to turn the touring bike's low gear than the racing bike's higher low gear, but of course you won't move as far for each pedal revolution.

Don't worry about the highest gear combination on the bike you're considering. Most bikes come with gears high enough to win the fastest bike races. Do worry about the low-gear combinations. If you live in flat or mildly rolling country, a 42 × 24 setup should be sufficient. For hilly terrain, you need at least a 42 × 28 combination. For extremely hilly or mountainous terrain, or for carrying baggage over even mildly rolling terrain, look for a 42 × 32 or lower gear. You may even find a bike with a 36 × 28 or 34 × 32 setup, but these aren't commonly available.

A good dealer will replace the stock freewheel that comes with your bike with one better suited to your needs. This takes only a few minutes. To correctly adjust this setup, he should also lengthen the chain if he's installing a freewheel with larger sprockets. Making this change on certain racing bikes may require changing derailleurs, as well.

Some 12-speed setups offer wider gear ranges than 10-speeds, but factory combinations are usually poorly selected. A 12-speed also requires more careful shifting tech-

(continued on page 48)

* Many American cyclists still use an archaic variation of this system. By multiplying the gear ratio (front sprocket divided by rear) by 27, you arrive at a figure (in inches) that is useful only for comparisons. You cannot compute how far you've traveled unless you further multiply your results by 3.14 and divide by 12.

Gear Development in Meters for 27-inch Wheel
(0.6858 meter)

Number of Teeth on Rear Sprocket

On Chainring	12	13	14	15	16	17	18	19	20	21	22	23	24	25	26	27	28	29	30	31	32	33	34	
26	4.66	4.30	3.99	3.73	3.49	3.29	3.10	2.94	2.79	2.66	2.54	2.43	2.33	2.23	2.15	2.07	1.99	1.93	1.86	1.80	1.74	1.69	1.64	26
27	4.84	4.47	4.15	3.87	3.63	3.41	3.22	3.05	2.90	2.76	2.64	2.52	2.42	2.32	2.23	2.15	2.07	2.00	1.93	1.87	1.81	1.76	1.70	27
28	5.02	4.63	4.30	4.01	3.76	3.54	3.34	3.17	3.01	2.87	2.74	2.62	2.51	2.41	2.31	2.23	2.15	2.07	2.00	1.94	1.88	1.82	1.77	28
29	5.20	4.80	4.45	4.16	3.90	3.67	3.46	3.28	3.12	2.97	2.83	2.71	2.60	2.49	2.40	2.31	2.22	2.15	2.08	2.01	1.95	1.89	1.83	29
30	5.38	4.96	4.61	4.30	4.03	3.79	3.58	3.39	3.22	3.07	2.93	2.80	2.69	2.58	2.48	2.39	2.30	2.22	2.15	2.08	2.01	1.95	1.89	30
31	5.56	5.13	4.76	4.44	4.17	3.92	3.70	3.51	3.33	3.17	3.03	2.90	2.78	2.66	2.56	2.47	2.38	2.30	2.22	2.15	2.08	2.02	1.96	31
32	5.74	5.29	4.92	4.59	4.30	4.05	3.82	3.62	3.44	3.28	3.13	2.99	2.87	2.75	2.64	2.55	2.46	2.37	2.29	2.22	2.15	2.08	2.02	32
33	5.92	5.46	5.07	4.73	4.44	4.17	3.94	3.73	3.55	3.38	3.22	3.08	2.96	2.84	2.73	2.63	2.53	2.44	2.36	2.29	2.22	2.15	2.08	33
34	6.10	5.63	5.22	4.88	4.57	4.30	4.06	3.85	3.66	3.48	3.32	3.18	3.05	2.92	2.81	2.71	2.61	2.52	2.44	2.36	2.28	2.21	2.15	34
35	6.27	5.79	5.38	5.02	4.70	4.43	4.18	3.96	3.76	3.58	3.42	3.27	3.13	3.01	2.89	2.79	2.69	2.59	2.51	2.43	2.35	2.28	2.21	35
36	6.45	5.96	5.53	5.16	4.84	4.55	4.30	4.07	3.87	3.69	3.52	3.36	3.22	3.10	2.98	2.87	2.76	2.67	2.58	2.50	2.42	2.34	2.27	36
37	6.63	6.12	5.69	5.31	4.97	4.68	4.42	4.19	3.98	3.79	3.62	3.46	3.31	3.18	3.06	2.95	2.84	2.74	2.65	2.56	2.48	2.41	2.34	37
38	6.81	6.29	5.84	5.45	5.11	4.81	4.54	4.30	4.09	3.89	3.71	3.55	3.40	3.27	3.14	3.03	2.92	2.82	2.72	2.63	2.55	2.47	2.40	38
39	6.99	6.45	5.99	5.59	5.24	4.93	4.66	4.41	4.19	3.99	3.81	3.65	3.49	3.35	3.22	3.10	2.99	2.89	2.79	2.70	2.62	2.54	2.46	39

Number of Teeth

	12	13	14	15	16	17	18	19	20	21	22	23	24	25	26	27	28	29	30	31	32	33	34
40	7.17	6.62	6.15	5.74	5.38	5.06	4.78	4.53	4.30	4.10	3.91	3.74	3.58	3.44	3.31	3.18	3.07	2.96	2.87	2.77	2.69	2.60	2.53
41	7.35	6.79	6.30	5.88	5.51	5.19	4.90	4.64	4.41	4.20	4.01	3.83	3.67	3.53	3.39	3.26	3.15	3.04	2.94	2.84	2.75	2.67	2.59
42	7.53	6.95	6.45	6.02	5.65	5.31	5.02	4.75	4.52	4.30	4.11	3.93	3.76	3.61	3.47	3.34	3.22	3.11	3.01	2.91	2.82	2.74	2.65
43	7.71	7.12	6.61	6.17	5.78	5.44	5.14	4.87	4.62	4.40	4.20	4.02	3.85	3.70	3.56	3.42	3.30	3.19	3.08	2.98	2.89	2.80	2.72
44	7.89	7.28	6.76	6.31	5.92	5.57	5.26	4.98	4.73	4.51	4.30	4.11	3.94	3.78	3.64	3.50	3.38	3.26	3.15	3.05	2.96	2.87	2.78
45	8.07	7.45	6.92	6.45	6.05	5.69	5.38	5.09	4.84	4.61	4.40	4.21	4.03	3.87	3.72	3.58	3.46	3.34	3.22	3.12	3.02	2.93	2.84
46	8.25	7.61	7.07	6.60	6.18	5.82	5.50	5.21	4.95	4.71	4.50	4.30	4.12	3.96	3.80	3.66	3.53	3.41	3.30	3.19	3.09	3.00	2.91
47	8.43	7.78	7.22	6.74	6.32	5.95	5.62	5.32	5.05	4.81	4.59	4.39	4.21	4.04	3.89	3.74	3.61	3.48	3.37	3.26	3.16	3.06	2.97
48	8.61	7.94	7.38	6.88	6.45	6.07	5.74	5.43	5.16	4.92	4.69	4.49	4.30	4.13	3.97	3.82	3.69	3.56	3.44	3.33	3.22	3.13	3.03
49	8.79	8.11	7.53	7.03	6.59	6.20	5.86	5.55	5.27	5.02	4.79	4.58	4.39	4.21	4.05	3.90	3.76	3.63	3.51	3.40	3.29	3.19	3.10
50	8.97	8.28	7.68	7.17	6.72	6.33	5.98	5.66	5.38	5.12	4.89	4.68	4.48	4.30	4.14	3.98	3.84	3.71	3.58	3.47	3.36	3.26	3.16
51	9.15	8.44	7.84	7.32	6.86	6.45	6.10	5.77	5.49	5.22	4.99	4.77	4.57	4.39	4.22	4.06	3.92	3.78	3.66	3.54	3.43	3.32	3.22
52	9.32	8.61	7.99	7.46	6.99	6.58	6.21	5.89	5.59	5.33	5.08	4.86	4.66	4.47	4.30	4.14	3.99	3.86	3.73	3.61	3.49	3.39	3.29
53	9.50	8.77	8.15	7.60	7.13	6.71	6.33	6.00	5.70	5.43	5.18	4.96	4.75	4.56	4.38	4.22	4.07	3.93	3.80	3.68	3.56	3.45	3.35
54	9.68	8.94	8.30	7.75	7.26	6.83	6.45	6.11	5.81	5.53	5.28	5.05	4.84	4.65	4.47	4.30	4.15	4.00	3.87	3.75	3.63	3.52	3.41
55	9.86	9.10	8.45	7.89	7.40	6.96	6.57	6.23	5.92	5.63	5.38	5.14	4.93	4.73	4.55	4.38	4.22	4.08	3.94	3.81	3.70	3.58	3.48
56	10.04	9.27	8.61	8.03	7.53	7.09	6.69	6.34	6.02	5.74	5.48	5.24	5.02	4.82	4.63	4.46	4.30	4.15	4.01	3.88	3.76	3.65	3.54

nique than a 10-speed. Fifteen-speed setups have the same problems.

A 3-speed offers you neither the gear range of a 10-speed nor a choice of gear ratios. It also gives you only one choice of shift lever position: on the handlebars. On a 10-speed, you can opt for shift levers that mount on the handlebar stem, on the *down tube* (tube running diagonally from the head tube to the bottom bracket) or in the ends of the handlebars. I prefer the handlebar-end position. It lets you shift without taking your hands off the handlebars or your eyes off the road. In an accident, stem-mounted shifters could possibly injure you. And at times, shifting either stem-mounted or down tube shifters can affect your steering control.

Wheels

After you've looked at a bike's frame and gearing, check the wheels. Kicking the tires won't do much good, but looking them over and asking a few questions will add to your knowledge and allow you to make better choices.

Look for alloy rims and high-pressure tires. These are best for three reasons:

1. The wheels of a bike act as flywheels. The heavier they are, the harder it is to bring them up to a given speed, slow them or turn them. This means heavier wheels make you work harder and are not as safe or responsive as lighter ones.

2. High-pressure tires, rated at 75 pounds per square inch (psi) or more, roll more easily than low-pressure models, giving you an even higher return on your power output.

3. Alloy rims provide better braking power than steel rims when wet. Even if you do not plan to ride in the rain, this could prove to be a lifesaving advantage. A solitary puddle or sudden summer shower can quickly cut your braking power to dangerously low levels. I learned how ineffective steel rims were one night as I was cycling home from a coin laundry. It had begun to drizzle while I was doing my laundry, and the roads were slick as I was rolling quickly homeward. Unfortunately, a

traffic light turned red as I was approaching it. I hit the brakes—but kept gliding almost as fast as I had been traveling. Luckily, I was wearing thick-soled shoes.

Contrary to popular myths, a cyclist who rides sensibly can ride on alloy rims and high-pressure tires without turning the rims into pretzels and the tires into patchwork quilts. After riding thousands of miles in Pittsburgh, Pennsylvania, the Pothole Capitol of the Nation, I've come to the conclusion that proper cycling technique and tire inflation will keep even the lightest wheels rolling for years. Not long ago, as I was flying down a hill at 40 mph, I ran into an unavoidable 15-foot stretch of 6- to 10-inch-deep potholes. Although the impact punctured my tubes in five places, with careful maneuvering my ultralightweight rims and tires survived unscathed.

The wheels are the only parts of your bike where lightness reduction is critical to cycling performance. Granted, any part that revolves—pedals, chainrings, chain, even your shoes—should be as lightweight as possible to make acceleration and hill climbing easier. But rims and tires are the most critical parts because they revolve faster than any other part of the bike. A $150 bike with lightweight wheels is more pleasurable to ride than a $1,000 bike with heavy wheels.

Saddles

A good saddle is also important for cycling enjoyment. No matter how well your frame fits, how low your gears reach or how light your wheels are, cycling will be sheer misery if your saddle is uncomfortable.

Single- and 3-speed bikes have wide, padded saddles with springs, which look comfortable at first but will chafe you and bounce away your energy on longer, faster rides. Most 10-speeds in the $150-$250 range have narrow, padded vinyl saddles that are more comfortable in the long run. I rode on one for my first 100-mile ride with no discomfort. Watch out for padded saddles with metal bases, though; when you compress the padding, you wind up sitting directly on top of the metal.

Even padded saddles with nylon bases rub some people the wrong way. Women particularly have problems, because the female pelvis is wider than the narrower male pelvis most saddles are designed for. If, after 100 to 200 miles of cycling, you find your saddle uncomfortable, consider switching. Avocet manufactures anatomically designed, padded saddles for both men and women, and Brooks and Ideale produce fine leather ones. Good saddles aren't cheap: expect to pay $20-$40. And leather saddles can take years to conform to your contours. But a good saddle could make the difference between you riding your bike or throwing it into a corner of the garage.

While there are dozens of brands of bikes on the market, there are only a handful of component manufacturers in the world. This has two advantages for you as a buyer. First, since a few companies produce hundreds of thousands of parts, costs are lower and replacement parts easier to get than if each company made every part it needed. Second, this standardization makes it hard to buy a bad mid- to high-priced bike. Most of the popular component brands are uniformly good.

Still, there are several other things to check if you want to make sure you're getting the most for your money. Checking to see if the bike has—or in some cases, does not have—these features can greatly increase your cycling safety and pleasure.

Brakes

For starters, take a look at the brakes. There are two types: coaster and caliper brakes. Coaster brakes are virtually worthless, unless you are buying the bike for a child with weak hands. A coaster brake stops the bike by the friction of skidding. You can easily lose control, and just as easily blow out your rear tire by sliding on it. With luck, a coaster brake will stop you in the nick of time.

And while coaster brakes are tucked away in the rear hub out of harm's way, this is not necessarily an advantage. While a good coaster brake may go years without needing adjustment, when one does go bad, it requires dismantling, and often replacing, the rear hub. A coaster brake is acceptable only on single-speeds that are ridden around the block or on the beach.

There are two types of caliper brakes. On sidepull brakes, the brake cable enters the brake arms (calipers) from one side. On centerpulls, the cable pulls the arms from a central, transverse cable.

Ironically, the best and worst brakes made are sidepulls. On $150-$250 bikes, you'll find some of the worst. These brakes constantly pull to one side, dragging on the rims and slowing you down. Go with centerpull brakes if possible. If you're buying a 3-speed, you may have no choice but side-pulls.

With either type, make sure the brake pads contact the rims squarely. Some bikes come with brakes that do not fit, and the pads hit the tires instead of the rims. This is danger-ous and will cause excessive brake pad wear.

You'll also find different types of brake levers. Three-speeds and some 10-speeds have "touring" levers designed to be used only from the upright position. Most 10-speeds have "racing" levers designed to be used from several riding positions.

Many 10-speeds also come with extra "safety" levers. These run parallel to the top of the handlebars and sup-posedly make cycling safer by making it easier for you to brake while sitting upright. Novices often assume that with-out safety levers, they can actuate the brakes only from the crouched-over position. That's not true; cyclists usually ride in a modified crouch with their hands resting on the rubber brake-lever housings, and apply the brakes by squeezing the levers with their fingers.

Not only are safety levers unnecessary, but they are also unsafe. They limit the amount of travel of the main brake lever. On a long downhill run or with wet or out-of-round rims, the brake levers may run out of travel before effectively stopping the bike. They reduce steering control by allowing you to apply the brakes while sitting upright, instead of crouched over, the best position for emergency stopping. If the bike you choose has safety levers, ask the dealer to re-move them before he adjusts the brakes. Once the safety levers are removed, the brake levers should be lowered to just above the middle of the bend in the handlebars.

If you have small hands, make sure you can comfortably

grip the brake levers. If not, your dealer might be able to substitute smaller levers.

Other Components

If you have limited storage space or plan to carry your bike inside your car, you should also check to see if the bike has quick-release hubs. These allow you to remove a wheel with just a flick of the lever, and are also valuable for fixing flats on the road.

Take a look at the pedals. They should be metal rattraps, and have adjustable ball bearings. The dealer will know if they do. They should not be counterweighted (made with long side plates that hang down to keep the pedals upright) because this type of pedal sometimes scrapes the ground in turns and cracks easily.

On 10-speeds, make sure that the pedals come with, or

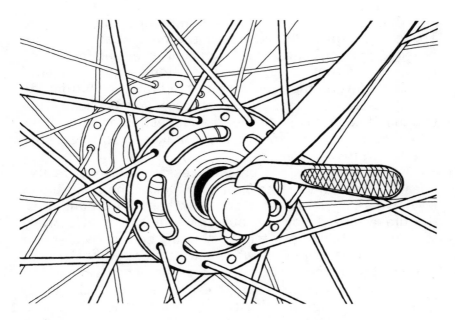

Quick-release hub mechanism, which is a boon to cyclists who want to remove wheels for storage or transportation. Pull quick-release lever down to release the wheel.

will accept, toe clips and straps to hold your feet securely in place. You don't have to use them at first, but later they can make your riding much easier. Clips and straps allow you to pedal throughout all of the circular pedaling cycle rather than just pushing on the downstroke, greatly increasing your efficiency.

Check to see if the frame tubes have reinforcing lugs at the joints. These metal sleeves are used to distribute stress at the joints, and are used on nearly all medium- to top-quality frames. On some Schwinn models, the lugs are inside the tubes.

Next, look at the crankarms. The least expensive bikes have one-piece Ashtabula cranksets; these are heavy and limit your choice of chainrings. Good 10-speeds have cotter-less cranksets. All cotterless cranksets allow you to remove and replace the inner chainring; the best also let you replace the outer chainring. Check to see if both can be replaced on the bikes you look at. If not, you must replace the entire crankset when the teeth wear out.

Avoid cranksets that have crankarms held in place by cotter pins. These pins often freeze in place, making it impossible to clean and lubricate the axle bearings.

Finally, check the rear dropouts where the rear wheel axle is held in the frame. If you plan to use your bike for touring or even shopping, you'll want dropouts that have eyelets for the attachment of carrier racks.

The next thing to check is not a part of the bike, but could be more important than any of them: the warranty. Most manufacturers offer warranties of about 90 days on all parts except the frame and forks; those are usually warrantied for life. Some dealers offer free adjustments after your first month of riding; others can be talked into it. Whatever promises your dealer makes, make sure you have them in writing.

A Secondhand Bike

If you're not positive you're going to like cycling, or just cannot afford a new bike, start with a used bike.

It takes time to find a used bike that meets your needs and budget. But that time might save you money. Then again, it might not: if you buy a used bike that needs repairs and new parts, you may end up spending more than if you had purchased a new one. And inflation has driven bike prices so high that a bike that sold new for $200 five years ago may bring $300 used.

Check the want ads in your local newspaper, and those in the "pennysavers." If you don't see what you want after a few weeks, place an ad yourself. Seeing your ad may make a reader remember that the bike he bought for exercise three years ago has been sitting in the attic for two years and 11 months.

Take a trip to the student unions at local colleges and universities. If you don't see what you want advertised on the bulletin boards, post your own ad. Check the campus papers, too, particularly at the end of the spring semester, when many students sell their bikes for vacation money.

Check in the local bike shops, too. While most shops don't handle used bikes, they may be able to put you in touch with a customer who wants to sell a bike.

Local cycling clubs usually run ads from their members in their newsletters. It may be worth joining a club to check the ads and place one of your own. Even if you don't belong to a club, you may be able to place an ad in its newsletter for a dollar or two.

The rules for buying a new bike also apply to used machines. Find out your frame size, and decide what gearing setup and design are best for your needs.

When you find a bike that seems to fill the bill, try to get a knowledgeable cyclist to look it over with you. Look for a basic, simple machine, without exotic—and hard to replace—parts such as hydraulic brakes or unusual gearing systems.

Ask the owner about the bike: how much it's been ridden; how long he's had it; what's been replaced. If it's been used for racing, the bike is probably not a good buy: racers can beat a bike mercilessly, and ruin it in no time.

Check the bike to see if it's been wrecked. Look at the front forks: if they are bent backward, that's one sure sign. Thank the seller and be on your way.

Look for dents and bends in the tubing. Wrinkles in the paint are also a sign that the frame has smashed into something. Minor nicks and scratches are acceptable; in fact, a flawless, new paint job may indicate that the owner is trying to cover up dangerous weaknesses in the frame.

See if the rims spin smoothly between the brake pads and that there are no dents or bumps in the rims. Replacing a rim can cost $20 or more.

Shift the gears, making sure everything works smoothly. Grab a crankarm in each hand, and try to wobble them up and down. If there are problems with the gears or cranks, you could be in for a whopping repair bill.

Try the brakes, too, and check the brake pads, brake and derailleur cables, and chain. If any of these are worn, you'll have to replace them.

Check the tires. If they are cut or the tread is bald, figure on adding another $10-$30 to the tab.

If repairing the bike will bring the cost up to the price of a new one, forget it. But if, even after repairs, the price is reasonable, ask the owner for a test ride. If the bike rides well, haggle over the price, even if you're willing to pay what he's asking.

If you decide to buy, ask for the original bill of sale. If the seller cannot produce one, the bike may be stolen, and you could be charged with receiving stolen goods if you buy it.

Useful Accessories

After you buy a used bike, you'll undoubtedly have to take a trip to the local bike shop to pick up replacement items. You'll also find accessories here that every cyclist should carry.

One necessity is a pump that can be carried on your bike. This allows you to keep your tires at the proper pressure no matter where you are, and to repair flats on the road. Some pumps are so hard to use that inflating your tires by mouth almost seems easier. Others explode when you try to pump more than 70 psi into your tires. The best pump I've found is the Zefal hp. It sells for less than $15, and includes adapters so that it can be used with American Schrader valves or the

European Presta valves that are used on many lightweight tires.

You'll also need a patch kit. Forget about those thick hunks of rubber your dad used to burn onto your tubes; there are far better ways of repairing a flat. The best repair kit available is the Rema Tip-Top, selling for a dollar or two. Second best is the Velox kit, about the same price.

You'll also need tire irons. These are levers used for prying the tire out of the rim to fix a flat or change a tube. Two or three will do the job, at less than a dollar each.

The only other accessory most cyclists will need is a water bottle and cage. A bottle of water can be a lifesaver on long rides, or even short treks on extremely hot days.

If you plan to take along your children who have not yet reached cycling age, you'll also need a carrier. The youngest can be carried in a backpack, but those a little older or heavier will need a seat of their own. The best seats mount behind the saddle and have enclosed sides to keep the little one's feet out of the spokes. Make sure that the seat mounts securely to your frame. Some models have a quick-release feature, but most carriers are light enough to leave in place when you're riding without your passenger.

Most child seats are good for children only up to 30 or 40 pounds; you may well want to take the children along on rides when they're bigger than that. A popular solution is the bike trailer. These can carry loads up to 80 pounds or more without undue stress on you (of course, you'll have to pedal harder), and many can be fitted with a two-child seat insert. The biggest drawback is the price: from $80-$250.

If your bike doesn't have a kickstand, don't bother buying one. In fact, if it does have one, take it off; a kickstand is not necessary. Bikes balanced on kickstands inevitably fall over and might be damaged. It's better to get into the habit of leaning your bike against a building, tree or signpost that will keep it from falling.

If you're buying a new bike, you may have a long time to choose your accessories: bike shortages are common, and you may have to wait up to six months for the bike you want. More than 10 million Americans a year have been buying bikes during the last several years. The bicycle industry is having problems keeping up with demand. Choosing a bike as soon as possible makes sense not only from this standpoint, but from another as well: bike prices have risen a steady 15 to 20 percent a year throughout the last decade, and inflation and shortages will keep the prices spiraling upward. A bike that sold for $250 in 1972 now costs nearly $1,000.

Even if you have to wait or pay an inflated price, though, you'll find that a bike that fits you and your needs is a bargain at any price.

CHAPTER FIVE
SETTING IT UP

Even the most expensive and refined bike is of little use if it is not set up properly. Before you start riding your new bike, or even the old one that's been lying in the basement, you should take the time to set it up to fit you. Only by doing so can you find out how enjoyable cycling can be.

"You have to adjust your bike so it feels just like a part of you," racer Tom Chew told me, "so it becomes merely a part of yourself. I change my bike around for every race so it feels most comfortable.

"Your bike has to fit *you*. I remember once I lent my bike to another racer, Mac Martin, who's about the same size as me. He went out for a ride and came back and said, 'Your bike's set up all wrong'—because it didn't fit him." Although Tom and Mac are about the same size and weight, their arms, legs and torsos measure differently. What was comfort for one was pain for the other.

Because cyclists are built differently, there are no hard and fast rules on setting up your bike to fit you. There are, however, starting points that will help you find the most comfortable and efficient position quickly.

The first, and most crucial, adjustment is saddle height. The correct saddle height lets the muscles in your legs work to their maximum potential; an incorrect position strains muscles and cuts your efficiency.

To find your proper saddle height, take off your shoes. If your bike has toe clips, remove them. Using the bolts underneath the saddle, adjust the top of the saddle so that it is level. Loosen the bolt at the top of the seat tube (you may need an allen wrench for this), and raise the saddle until your heel just reaches the pedal when it is in the lowest position of the pedal stroke. Make sure there is still at least two inches of the seatpost in the seat tube.

Have someone hold the bike upright, while you put your heels on the pedals and pedal backward. Your hips will probably sway. Lower the saddle about ¼ inch at a time until you can backpedal without swaying. With the saddle at this height, your knees should be just barely bent.

Turn the crankarms until they are parallel to the floor, with the right pedal forward. Have your helper drop a plumb line from the center of your right knee. Move the saddle

To determine proper saddle height, place your heels on the tops of the pedals. At the bottom of the pedal stroke, there should be a slight bend in your knee. If your pedals come with toe clips, remove them before checking this measurement.

forward or back (using the bolts underneath to loosen it) until the center of your knee is in line with the center of the pedal. The first adjustment compensates for differences in leg length; the latter compensates for different thigh lengths.

To compensate for torso and arm length, sit with your hands on the drops of the handlebars, looking straight ahead. Have your helper drop the plumb line from the tip of your nose. If the handlebar stem and top tube are the correct lengths, the line will drop about an inch behind the handlebars.

If the line falls much more or less than an inch behind the bars, you will need a new handlebar stem. These come in lengths of 45 to 140 mm, and cost as little as five dollars. They do, however, require you to dismantle one brake lever and, possibly, your shift levers, to replace them. And there are three different diameters available; none compatible with the others. It's best to have your dealer make these changes before you take delivery. On bikes with upright bars, you'll have to feel your way to the proper fit.

All that remains now are a few minor adjustments.

The forward/aft position of the saddle is correct when, with the balls of the feet on the pedals, a plumb line intersects the middle of the knee and when the foot is in the forward position with the crankarm parallel to the ground.

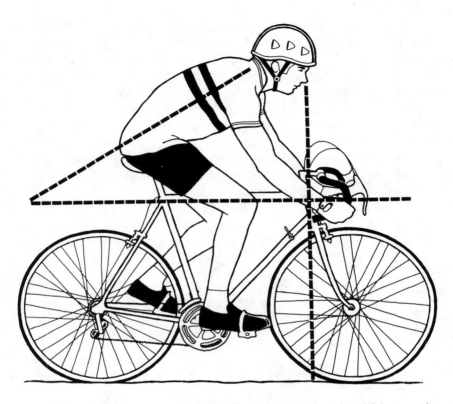

To determine proper stem extension, your arms should be on the drops and your back at an angle less than 45 degrees. If your stem is the right length, your nose should be slightly behind the handlebars. You can check this measurement with the help of a friend and a plumb line.

Loosen the expander and binder bolts on the top and front of the handlebar stem. Adjust the top of the handlebars so that it is parallel to the ground, and about an inch below the top of the saddle. Make sure at least two inches of the stem remain hidden inside the head tube. Most stems are marked with a line to indicate the minimum insertion level. If you ignore this marking and position the stem too high, the stem or the head tube could crack.

    If you want to use toe clips, make sure they are the proper size. Small fits men's shoe sizes 5 to 7, Medium, 8 to 10, and Large, 11 to 13.

Remember, these are just starting points. Allow a few weeks' trial before you make any changes, then make gradual adjustments by raising the saddle a ¼ inch or changing its tilt a degree or two. European road racers adjust their saddles in millimeters.

While these are just starting points, don't neglect them. Like most riders, I began riding with my saddle positioned so low that my legs could never fully extend. After a mile or two, my knees felt as though I'd just come off a torture rack. When I finally raised the saddle to proper height, I left the bars down in the same position and ended up with terrible pains in my neck and back. A stem that is positioned either too low or too high will also cause neck and back pains.

If you're short, unfortunately, you may have to endure a certain amount of discomfort. The bicycle industry is apparently still run by long-limbed height chauvinists who have little concern with designing bikes to fit shorter people. I've seen 20-inch frames with top tubes as long as those found on 23-inch bikes. This makes no sense, and can cause problems; extrashort stems are rare. One of my 5' 4" friends spent months hunting for a stem that would put the bars close enough to her so that she would not have to stretch to reach them and she has extremely long arms. If your arms and torso

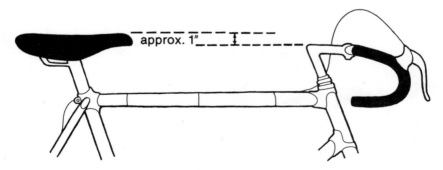

Your handlebar stem is properly adjusted when the top of the bars is parallel to the ground and about an inch below the top of the saddle. At least two inches of the stem must remain inside the head tube.

are short, be prepared to stretch, at least until you can afford $600 or more for a custom-built bike.

Another problem for short and tall people alike is that the stem and handlebars may not raise high enough to allow an upright riding position, yet still keep two inches of the stem hidden. There are longer stems available that will solve this problem, but these are as rare as the extrashort ones, and so may require months of searching.

Once you've adjusted your bike to fit you, though, it's done (unless, of course, you're still growing). Spending less than an hour to make adjustments in the beginning will help make your rides comfortable and enjoyable.

CHAPTER SIX
RIDING TECHNIQUES

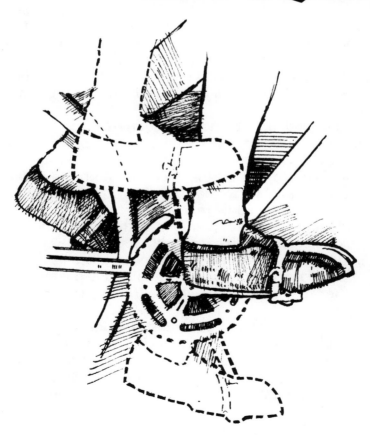

Now that your bike is ready, it's time to concentrate on your riding. There's much more to efficient cycling than just hopping on your bike and pedaling—but it needn't take you long to master the basics.

Riding a bike is much like driving a car. When Mario Andretti enters an auto race, he wants to wring every ounce of potential from his machine. He does this by shifting at just the right moments and using his brakes as little as possible. And Andretti knows exactly what engine speed is most efficient. Just as he doesn't want to waste power, neither does he want to burn out an engine.

Before you ever get on your bike, though, make sure you are ready to ride. If you've been physically active, the worst you can expect from starting to ride is a few aches and pains in muscles that you haven't used for a while. But if you've been sedentary, a smoker, are overweight, or have a personal or family history of heart problems, cycling could hurt or even kill you. If you fit into this group, you should have a physical examination before getting on your bike. What kind of exam and how extensive depends on your age and background. In Chapter Ten, the various tests are defined and explained in detail.

It's a good idea to find a quiet street or parking lot with a mild grade for your first lessons on the basics of cycling. If you have a 3-speed bike, shift into second or "N" gear. If you have a 10-speed, get off the bike, turn it upside down, spin the pedals and shift so that the chain is on the small front sprocket and the middle rear sprocket.

Straddle your bike. Spin one of the pedals into the two o'clock position. You'll have to lift your back wheel off the ground if you have a single- or 3-speed bike.

Push down on the forward pedal, while pushing off with the other foot and raising yourself onto the saddle at the same time.

If your bike has toe clips and straps, ignore them at first. After you can easily mount, loosen the straps so that you can easily slide your feet in and out. Instead of stroking the pedal as you start, slip your foot into the clip first. Reach down and tug the strap tight, but not so tight that you cannot remove your foot.

To properly kick off, stand astride the bike with one foot in the toe clip and the other on the ground.

After you kick off and get rolling, turn the cranks so that the free pedal is at the 12 o'clock position. Tap the rear edge with your free foot to turn it upright, then quickly slip that foot into the clip. This is a difficult maneuver to master, but it quickly becomes almost second nature.

After you slip your second foot into the clip, you can leave the strap loose for emergency stops or reach down and tug it snug, too. If you tighten both straps, make sure that you loosen one before you attempt a stop. This may seem obvious, but I once saw another cyclist who forgot to do so and tumbled over sideways, "Laugh-In" style, as he stopped.

If you don't have time to loosen a strap before you have

to stop, you can still free a foot in time. Turn the cranks so that they are parallel to the ground. Push down on the left crank without moving it. At the same time, pull your right foot up against the strap securing it. The strap will loosen enough for you to slide your foot out.

Turning and Stopping

Once you get moving in a straight line, you must be able to turn, as well. Some cyclists who have been riding for years still haven't mastered this.

To turn, lean in the direction you want to go. Turn your handlebars slightly. Hit the rear brake before you start to turn if you are riding too fast. As you turn, raise your inside pedal so that it doesn't scrape the ground and cause you to crash. Point your inside knee toward the inside of the turn to help maintain your balance.

Pick a line through the turn and stay with it. Many times, a cyclist will start through a turn, then decide halfway through that he is going to come too close to the edge of the road. He swings the handlebars to change his course and crashes to the ground. In most cases, staying with the original line would have been perfectly safe; it's hard to estimate how close to the edge of the road you are, especially when you're just starting to ride. Unless you see that your course is going to take you off the edge of a cliff or into a deep pothole, stick with it. Surveying a turn before you enter it will help you pick the best course through it.

When you have to stop, look for a curb. You can rest one foot on the curb while you stop, staying in the saddle so that you do not have to remount. If there is no curb or if you're ending your ride, slide forward off the saddle just as you come to a complete stop.

Choose one foot to remove from the pedal, and stick with it. I use my right foot, since there is usually a curb on my right side.

If you stay in the saddle at stoplights and stop signs, you might find that you cannot get as good a kickoff as you could if you were standing. A good way to start quickly is by standing on the pedals. As you start, get up out of the saddle and throw your weight on the one foot you've kept on the pedal. This will get you going fast, but may cause you to weave back and forth the first few times you try it.

Even more important than starting, of course, is being able to stop. There's more to proper braking than just frantically squeezing the brake levers; knowing how to stop correctly could save your life.

There's a common cycling superstition that if you touch your front brake lever, your bike, like a crazed bronco, will throw you over the handlebars headfirst. There is a grain of truth to this, but it is a distortion of the whole truth.

As you try to stop your bike, your weight shifts forward over the front wheel. It's true that grabbing only the front

To stop in an emergency, you should move down and back on your bike. This gives you a lower center of gravity and puts more weight on your back wheel, preventing you from skidding or flipping forward under hard braking.

brake lever with all your power will lock the front wheel and send you flying over the handlebars. But it's also true—and far more important—that properly applying only the front brake will stop you twice as fast as using only the rear brake. And using the two in tandem gives even better results.

If you're stopping from a cruising pace or want to reduce your speed, you can use the rear brake alone. But if you have to stop fast, or from a high speed, such as at the end of a long descent, you have to use both brakes.

To stop as fast as you can, first drop down and slide back on your bike. This lowers your center of gravity and the chance that you will be pitched over the bars. Squeeze both the front and rear brake levers hard, but not hard enough to lock either wheel.

On long downhills or on rainy days, don't grab the brakes, but pump them as you would in your car on an icy road. Otherwise, they may heat up and fade, leaving you brakeless, or lock one or both wheels, causing you to skid.

Skidding is caused by braking too fast on normal road surfaces or merely applying normal pressure to the brakes on wet or bumpy roads. In the first case, you lock one or both wheels; in the second, you lower the already reduced traction of your tires to the point where you have almost no contact with the road.

If you skid, remember that old rule of winter driving: steer into the skid. Pump your brakes. Accelerate if you can, and if it helps. Stay loose and don't fight the skid and you'll quickly regain control.

Pedal Cadence

Just about anyone who has ever ridden a bike can start, stop and turn competently. These are skills that are never forgotten once learned. But there's a big difference between being a barely competent cyclist and getting the most out of what efforts you put into your riding.

A key difference is spinning. Many cyclists, even skilled ones who have raced or toured for years, have never learned this simple but vital technique. Cycling without spinning not

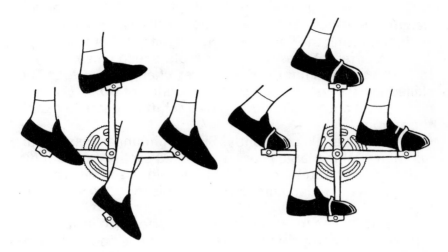

Spinning vs. pushing pedaling motion. The figure on the left shows the pedal action of a cyclist who pushes and jabs at the pedals, usually in a high gear. The figure on the right shows the leverage of the spinner's foot on the crank. The cyclist who spins transfers a smooth, circular flow of power rather than choppy jabs.

only wastes your energy, but can cause injuries and equipment problems.

Spinning is the technique of pedaling rapidly in low gears. This reduces the forces your muscles and joints must transmit and results in less wear and fatigue. Spinning places the demands of cycling on your heart and lungs, where you want them.

The rate at which you pedal is called your cadence. A typical rider probably pedals less than 40 revolutions per minute (rpm). A skilled cyclist turns the pedals 60 to 120 times each minute. He may not travel farther or faster, since he uses low gears, but he will not tire as quickly.

Spinning doesn't reduce the amount of work you have to do, but spreads it out over a larger number of pedal strokes, making each one easier. Think of it this way: you can lift a

100-pound weight over your head once, or lift a 20-pound weight five times. Either way, you do the same amount of work, but lifting the lighter weight will not tire you as quickly.

The different gear ratios on a multi-speed bike allow you to hold your optimum cadence over changing terrain. The skilled cyclist maintains a steady cadence of 60 to 120 rpm on the level and up and down hills by shifting gears to match the terrain.

And he pedals constantly. Since spinning is less fatiguing than pushing large gears, the skilled cyclist can hold his cadence indefinitely. This lets him hold a smooth rhythm that doesn't tax his joints, and keeps his muscles warm and loose.

Spinning can make a tremendous difference in your performance. After my first 50-mile ride, and five hours of pushing my biggest gears, I felt horrible. My thighs, calves and knees felt as if someone had been smashing them with a sledgehammer all afternoon.

After the ride, I signed up at headquarters for the weekend cycling club outing and stumbled to my room. The door barely slammed closed behind me before I collapsed on the bed. Within minutes, I was sound asleep—but not before grimly realizing that there was another 50-mile ride ahead of me the next day.

That evening, a cyclist named Paul, who at 20 years old had already ridden dozens of 100-mile rides, asked me how I liked the ride. I told him how hard I'd found it, and how I wasn't looking forward to riding the next day.

"You're probably pedaling too slow," Paul said, "most novices do."

"Paul," I said, "I couldn't have pedaled any faster today if my life had depended on it."

"But you were probably using the wrong gears," Paul said. "You'll do a lot better if you use low gears and pedal faster. Don't even use your large front sprocket until you learn to spin."

The next morning I started out using my small chainring, rather than the large chainring I had used the first day. My legs spun easily as I knocked off mile after mile. In an hour and a half, I had completed 27 miles. Within three hours, I had finished the ride—and was ready for another 50.

For your own sake, give spinning a try. There is nothing gained by "grunting" around in your highest gears. You are just wasting your energy and taking a chance of seriously injuring your knees or pulling muscles. As John Forester writes in *Effective Cycling*, the expert cyclist isn't the one who rides in his highest gear at all times, but the one who rides in the correct gear at all times.

Learning to spin takes time, especially if you're already a pusher. A quote by photographer Ansel Adams describing a photographic process comes to mind: "It takes a novice an hour to learn, but someone with experience will need longer."

Unless you can afford a digital tachometer, which is a great training aid but may cost as much as your bike, your initiation into spinning will be crude. A good rule is: if your legs burn, the gear is too high; if your lungs burn, it's too low. Work toward keeping your legs spinning as fast as comfortably possible for as long as you can. At first, you won't be able to pedal fast for long: you'll use all your energy just turning the pedals. But every time you go out for a ride, try to hold a fast spin for a little longer than you did the time before.

Stick with your middle to low gears. A good starting gear on a 10-speed would be 42 × 16 to 42 × 19. If you're riding through an area with rolling hills, use a lower gear in the 42 × 20 range.

Don't be embarrassed to use such low gears. I use extremely low gears, but can beat most pushers up any hill. As they grunt along in pain, I twiddle my way up.

Gear Shifting

After a few weeks of practice, you'll find a cadence that feels right to you. On a single-speed bike, when the wind or terrain makes it too easy or hard to hold that cadence, you'll have to change from your ideal rhythm. On a 3- or 10-speed, though, you shift into another gear that lets you maintain your cadence.

To shift a 3-speed bike, you must ease or stop pedaling. Put your weight on the raised pedal as you shift, to keep the strain off the shift mechanism.

To shift a 10-speed, ease up slightly on the pedals, but

never stop pedaling. And don't try to shift while you're back-pedaling, either: doing so will jam your chain, ruin your sprockets, and cause you to crash.

If you have handlebar-end shifters, you can shift without taking your hands from the bars. I hold my hands near the ends, where the levers are, and shift with my little fingers.

To shift levers on the down tube, though, you have to take one hand from the bars. Move your right hand so that it's over the center of the handlebars, with the stem under your palm, then take your left hand from the bars. If the bike wobbles drastically, put your left hand back on the bars until you regain control. It won't take long until you are able to control the bike with just one hand.

Don't take your eyes off the road for more than an instant to look for the shift levers. Search for them by feel. It's better to miss the levers than to take your eyes from the road and miss seeing a pothole or a car running a stop sign.

Learning to shift a derailleur bike may take a full summer or longer. Go easy at first, pulling your levers back, or pushing them forward, a little at a time. Gear levers are not marked "P–R–N–D–L" like those of a car, so you have to learn the gears by feel. At first you will overshift and undershift and will have to jiggle the levers each time to put the chain exactly where you want it. But after a while you will know exactly how much you have to move the levers to shift up or down one gear.

If you hear a rattling sound after you shift, the chain has not set properly on the sprockets. Move the shift lever gently back and forth until the noise stops. Scraping noises call for the same treatment: the chain has set properly, but a derailleur cage is not in the right position, causing the chain to rub against it. If you allow the chain to continue rubbing, it may break the derailleur cage.

On derailleur bikes, the left lever controls the front gears, the right controls the rear (same as for brakes). In the beginning, you may find it easier to work first on mastering the rear gears. To do this, shift into the smallest front sprocket—and forget about the front gears. After you get the feel and hang of shifting the rear gears, then you can work on the front ones.

When you shift the rear gears, you move into a lower, easier-to-pedal gear by pulling the shift lever toward you. When you push the lever toward the bike, the chain drops onto a higher, harder-to-pedal gear.

Most front derailleurs work just the opposite way. When you pull the shift lever toward you, the derailleur moves the chain onto the large front sprocket, which is a higher gear. While some front derailleurs work the other way, the general rule is: pull only the rear shifter all the way back for your lowest gear; pull only the front shift lever back for your highest gear.

With both 3- and 10-speed bikes, you should always downshift before stopping. This puts the bike in a lower gear, and makes it easier to start again. On a 3-speed, it is helpful to backpedal as you downshift; with a little practice, you can downshift a 10-speed by pedaling half a revolution as you brake.

Don't wait until the last minute to shift. Anticipate what gear to shift into for the conditions and terrain ahead, and learn when to shift into it. If you do this, you won't get stuck in the middle of a hill, losing all your momentum as your chain jumps off the sprockets.

When you start using both the front and rear gears on a 10-speed, you'll notice that the gears are not set up in sequence as they are on a 3-speed or a car. You don't just run through all the rear gears on one front sprocket, then shift to the other front sprocket. Instead, you have to shift from one front sprocket to another as you shift across the rear cluster.

To ride efficiently, you must know where the next higher or lower gear is at any time. There is a simple way to do this. Draw a grid like the one below that corresponds to the number of teeth on the front and rear sprockets of your bike (you may have to count the teeth):

	14	17	20	24	28
52					
42					

Now turn to the Gear Development chart in Chapter Four. From that chart, fill in the proper figures in your grid, for example:

	14	17	20	24	28
52	7.99	6.58	5.59	4.66	3.99
42	6.45	5.31	4.52	3.76	3.22

Next, cross out the large–large (52 × 28 in this example) and small–small (42 × 14) combinations. You should never use these, because they make the chain run at severe angles, rapidly wearing down your gear teeth. It's possible to break a chain by shifting into the large–large combination.

Now you're left with eight gears. Most likely, you have at least one set of duplicates. If so, plan your shift sequence around the most convenient one of the two combinations. With this sample gearing setup, the gearing would run:

Gear	Combination	
1 (low)	42 × 28	(easiest to turn)
2	42 × 24	
3	42 × 20	
4	52 × 24	
5	42 × 17	
6	52 × 20	
7	52 × 17	
8 (high)	52 × 14	(hardest to turn)

Racers sometimes tape a copy of their bike's gear sequence onto the top tube with waterproof tape. It's a good way to learn the proper shift sequence.

As you master the gears, you will gradually acquire the quality that separates the expert cyclist from the novice: suppleness. Racers and accomplished tourists pedal fluidly, their legs flowing at the same rate over every type of terrain. There is nothing rough about their pedaling technique—just a smooth, highly efficient flow of power.

Suppleness comes primarily through long hours of cycling, but you can help it along. Try moving your feet in an even, circular motion throughout the pedal cycle instead of pushing choppily. Toe clips and straps will help you do this by letting you apply power all the way through the circle. Becoming supple will take time: even the best cyclists favor different legs each time they ride. But consciously concentrating on pedaling in circles will help you advance more quickly to the point where the smoothness comes unconsciously.

Sometimes it may seem like it will take forever for you to become a smooth, skillful cyclist. But the hours you spend concentrating on just the basics will pay off later when you find yourself merging with your bike and cycling better and easier than you ever dreamed possible. That's when you'll know the joy of just cycling.

CHAPTER SEVEN
HILLS

On your road to becoming a proficient cyclist, you'll find many obstacles. None of them is insurmountable, and knowing how to cope with them will make your hours in the saddle safe and enjoyable.

Undoubtedly, the biggest obstacle in most cyclists' eyes is hills. When I first began cycling, I dreaded facing some of the endless climbs around my southwestern Pennsylvania hills. Only monsters or superhumans could make it up them by bike, I reasoned, not a scrawny guy like me.

After a while, though, I became tired of riding the same few miles of bikepaths and expressways, the only flat areas around. And I began to see pictures of people just as scrawny as me climbing the Rockies and the Alps on their bikes.

Within three years, my fear of hills turned into a passion for them. I came to see every hill as a challenge, a measure of my ability and resolve. Many of my cycling friends think I'm crazy, and think climbing hills is only for masochists.

To some extent, they have a point. Riding up long hills is not always fun. Sometimes it hurts, even after you gradually build your strength.

If you're out for pure fun, there's no reason for you to tackle Mount Everest. You may well be content without ever going near a hill.

But while it does take effort to climb a hill, and it may hurt on the way, there's nothing like the feeling you get when you reach the top. During my second 100-mile ride, my friend Brian Karger and I struggled up a steep, West Virginia hill for what seemed like an hour. Every time we thought we could see the summit, it turned out that the road had just twisted out of sight as it kept climbing. Just when we thought we couldn't ride another minute, we reached the top.

The sight was breathtaking. We were at the highest point for miles, and we could see at least 15 miles away. We sat on the edge of the hill, overlooking the lush green valley far below and the peaks rolling off into the distance. After a long rest we remounted and chased each other down miles of a cool, shady descent.

But the satisfaction and enjoyment of reaching the top of a hill under your own power are not the only reasons to do it. T. S. Eliot once wrote, "If you haven't the strength to impose your own terms on life, you must accept the terms it offers you." If you turn back at every hill, you'll miss a wide variety of experiences, both pleasurable and slightly painful. You then put false limits on yourself, limits that keep you from exploring your full potential. But if you know how to ride up hills, you can go anywhere you like. You are in control.

Easy Does It

The key to getting up any hill is taking it easy. If you accept the hill as part of your journey, and accept the fact that it's going to take longer than other sections, you've already won half the battle.

If a hill is short or shallow, you can bully your way up in the same gear just by giving it a little more oomph at the top. Coming down, you can stay in the same gear by raising your cadence.

There's no way you're going to bully your way up longer or steeper hills, though. But there are ways to make the climb easier.

First, try to get a running start. If you're coming down one hill and into another, push a little on the way down, but not enough to strain or tire you. Your momentum will boost you up the next hill and, if it's not too long, will push you over the top.

By the time you reach the base of the hill, you should have shifted into your lowest gear and be spinning at your normal cadence: there will be no pressure on the pedals at first, but as your momentum drops, you'll be able to maintain your cadence. Don't try to pedal as fast as you can in your lowest gear: you'll run out of breath before you make it part-way up the hill. Take it easy and you'll make it.

If you find pedaling in your bottom gear is too easy, you can shift up to the next gear. Be careful, though. More than once, I've confidently shifted to a higher gear in the middle of a hill, only to run out of breath as the grade grew steeper.

If you shift into your lowest gear and find it is still im-possible to hold your normal cadence, spin the pedals only as fast as you comfortably can. If you try to hold your normal cadence on a hill that's too steep or too long, you'll never make it.

Ideally, you should shift before you begin the climb. But there will be times when you have to shift on the hill, either because you might have underestimated or overestimated the steepness, or the grade changes, or you tire. The most important rule in shifting on a hill is to do it easily and smoothly. Pedal as lightly as possible to take the tension off the chain, and shift into one gear at a time. If you pedal too hard or try to shift too fast, you can easily jam the chain in the sprockets, stalling you and possibly damaging your drive train.

Even in your lowest gear, and at a lowered cadence, you may not be able to climb some hills without stopping. If that happens, stop. You're not racing, and pushing farther could cause serious harm. I've had to stop in the middle of several-mile-long hills, my heart pumping 200 beats a minute and my body burning up. After a two-minute break and a cool drink, though, I've gone on to finish the climbs with little problem.

The only problem with stopping on a hill is starting up again. Many times, I've stopped in the middle of a hill, then found it was too steep to get going again. The best way to avoid this problem is by stopping in a driveway or side street. When you finish resting, check for traffic, then get a running start up the rest of the hill.

Educating Your Body

The more you practice, the better you'll become at climbing in general. To speed up your training, find a long hill that's not terribly steep and ride up it at every opportunity. If you want to become a good climber, spend some of your riding time working only on that hill: ride up, then come back down and cruise around until your heart stops pounding. Ride up again, and repeat until you have only enough strength left to get back home.

After you ride for several weeks, you'll find yourself growing stronger and using ever higher gears to climb hills. Greg

Kirchin recalled his first days of cycle commuting to work and back over a hilly six-mile route:

"Riding home the first day, I thought I'd never make one long hill. But I shifted into my lowest gear and eventually made it. A couple days later, I was using my next higher gear, and a few days after that, my next higher yet. Within a few weeks, climbing that hill was nothing."

At first, your body will object to climbing hills, but you can trick it into going along with your plans. There are two ways to do this. The first is by ignoring the hill. As you ride up, look ahead only occasionally to check the road conditions and traffic. Most of the time, you should keep your eyes on the road beneath you or on your feet. Take a drink of water, sing a song—do anything but worry about getting to the top of the hill.

The alternative is to keep your eyes out front, concentrating on intermediate goals. Don't worry about the summit, but instead try to reach the telephone pole or driveway 50 yards ahead. Once you reach it, pick another goal, and continue to inch your way to the top. Racers use this technique to make it to the end of grueling events.

There's a proverb that says, "When you get to the top of the mountain, keep climbing." It applies equally well to cycling: when you get to the top of a hill, keep pedaling. As you crest a hill, your first inclination will be to stop pedaling and coast down the other side. Don't. As you reach the summit, maintain your cadence. This will keep your legs limber and your power output constant. It also helps you pick up momentum on the way down, momentum that can start you up the next hill. Upshift as you descend, using gears that allow you to hold your normal cadence or overspin a little.

If it's been a long, hard climb, particularly on a hot day, you may be covered with sweat and feel dizzy by the time you reach the crest of the hill. If so, take a short break. You don't want to make an error in judgment as you fly down the other side at 30, 40 or 50 mph.

Even when temperatures are in the 30s or below, you can work up a good sweat while climbing. Unless you cover your chest and torso on the way down, your sweat may freeze, causing discomfort and possibly leading to sickness. On one fall ride I took a few years ago, the temperature hovered near 40°F. for most of the morning. By the time I reached the top of every long, brutal hill, I was soaked. Even after zipping my wool jacket closed over a wool cycling shirt, I couldn't stop the wind from chilling me on the shaded 40-mph descents. A windbreaker would have solved the problem, but I had not brought one along. So I made my own: I stopped in the next town, bought a newspaper and zipped it in under my jacket, just like the European professional road racers do. It worked perfectly. Make sure you always have something along with you to keep you warm on chilly descents.

As you spin down the hill, it's a good idea to drop down on your bike as low as you can, lowering your chest between your elbows. Cyclists call this "tucking it in." This position

To descend a hill properly you should crouch down and back on bike, with arms tucked in and hands on the brake levers.

cuts wind resistance, letting you descend faster (speed skiers do it, too) and, more importantly, increases your stability and handling by lowering your center of gravity. Also, it's easier to use the brakes when you're in this position.

Your position while you're climbing is not as important, but you'll be able to breathe more easily if you sit upright.

It won't take you long to become a better hill climber if you keep at it. But don't overdo it. It's easy to strain your knees while climbing, and a knee injury may keep you off your bike for months, and trouble you for the rest of your life. For that reason, it's best to stay in the saddle and let your thigh muscles do the work.

Climbing Out of the Saddle

But as you grow stronger, you may want to try climbing while out of the saddle to break the monotony or pick up speed. Most racers use this technique, leaping onto the pedals at the slightest hill. But U.S. Olympic Team coach Jack Simes, a multiple U.S. national cycling champion, recommends staying in the saddle as long as possible to help develop your strength.

Still, you might want to try standing while you climb. There are two ways to do it. The first is to use your middle gears at a slower-than-normal cadence. This requires, and will build, great muscular strength.

Racers who specialize in climbing use a different technique: they spin their lowest gears rapidly. These riders are typically lightweight and do not possess exceptional muscular strength. But they have tremendous lung capacity, which is vital to using this technique. If you don't believe it, try this technique sometime and see how quickly you begin to pant.

For most riders, standing on the pedals is too demanding. Still, you can spin the pedals a few times during a long climb to break the boredom and give your legs a brief change of pace.

Even after you get into good shape, there may be some hills that you just cannot climb. That's where you have to use your ultimate low gear: your legs. If you can stay on the bike,

To climb a hill out of the saddle, angle your body over the pedals with your hands gripping the brake-lever hoods.

though, by all means do so. Cycling will help make the climb easier the next time around, and is more efficient than walking. You actually end up working harder if you dismount and push your bike.

Unless you hope to race, how fast you can climb a hill is not important. Indeed, for most of us, it's not important whether we can climb a hill at all. But it's a great feeling to be able to conquer them all, and to go wherever your heart takes you.

PART III
GETTING STARTED

CHAPTER EIGHT
YOUR PLACE ON THE ROAD

Now that you know the basics of safe and efficient cycling, and your bike is set up properly, you'll need a place to ride. You could, of course, spend the rest of your cycling days circling a deserted parking lot or a small bikepath, occasionally sprinting up a local hill for good measure. But that would defeat the purposes of cycling: exploring new ground, moving from one place to another.

Fulfilling these objectives means using the roads and, in most cases, sharing them with larger and faster vehicles.

Unfortunately, most of us have been raised to believe that the roads belong to cars and trucks. We cringe at the thought of sticking our frail bodies out there on slow, light bicycles for the predatory motor vehicles to devour.

Well, while survival of the fittest may be the rule of the jungle, it's not the rule of the road. If this were true, as John Forester points out in *Effective Cycling*, the only vehicles that would be left out there would be cement trucks and Corvettes.

The road is actually a safe place to be, if you use it properly. Most motorists do not want to hit you, and will readily accommodate you if you let them know your intentions. Cyclists have a legal right to ride on the roads, and any motorist who tries to deny them this right faces fines and imprisonment.

In case you're not convinced that riding on the road is for you, consider this: cycle commuters, who ride in the worst weather and lighting conditions during periods of heaviest traffic, have the lowest accident rate of all cyclists. Cyclists using bikeways have nearly three times as many accidents per mile ridden.

I'm not suggesting that the picture is rosy. There are thousands of cycling accidents every year, and about 1,000 U.S. cyclists have their lives cut tragically short. But—and this is the biggest tragedy—most of those accidents involve children under 16 years old. And in more than half of them, the cyclist is at fault or at least has broken a law.

Moreover, an overwhelming majority of cycling accidents don't even involve motor vehicles. Of all cycling accidents, only about 12 percent involve cars, trucks and buses. And of these, many are caused by the cyclist hitting the motor vehicle, not vice versa. Most cycling accidents are in fact caused by falling or running into dogs or other cyclists.

Ironically, the type of accident that cyclists fear most, being hit from behind, while usually severe, is one of the least frequent types of car–bike collisions. Your skill is the most important factor in preventing accidents. The more skill you have, the more the likelihood of an accident decreases.

Protect Your Head

No matter how skillful you are, there is always a chance that you'll be involved in an accident through no fault of your own. Therefore, the first line of defense is to wear a helmet.

Three-quarters of all cyclists who die in accidents die from brain injuries. Countless others survive, but suffer permanent disability. Even a fall from a stopped bicycle can kill you or cause permanently disabling brain damage.

A helmet can prevent these injuries and may well save your life. True, wearing a helmet on a long climb on a 90°F. day is not comfortable—but dying is an even less comfortable thought.

Get a hard-shell helmet made specifically for cycling. They are expensive, costing as much as $40, but, with luck, a helmet is an investment that will last a lifetime. Bell's cycling helmet is generally considered to be the most comfortable and safest. Don't waste your money on the "leather hairnet" helmets that bike racers wear: they merely give you a false sense of security.

Write your name and an emergency phone number inside your helmet. If you crash, send your helmet back to the manufacturer to be checked for hairline cracks that could make it worthless in another crash. If you must, replace it: if it saved your head, it's repaid your investment.

Unfortunately, helmet or not, some cyclists seem to feel that they have the right to be reckless. Your helmet should be simply a backup in a two-part safety plan: stay out of situations that can cause accidents, and know how to escape the unavoidable ones.

Obey the Rules

The first step in avoiding accidents is obeying the rules of the road. Not only is this common sense, but it is also the law. Most state vehicle codes have a section to the effect that:

> Every person riding a bicycle upon a roadway shall be granted all of the rights and shall be subject to all of the duties applicable to the driver of a vehicle by this act.

The rules of the road are the basic driving instructions that hold together the traffic system. They are designed to make that system predictable and safe. Since they govern the entire system, they are equally applicable to every vehicle in it. While this might seem obvious, a survey in Santa Clara, California, showed that almost 90 percent of the population believed that cyclists have to obey traffic laws—but almost the same percentage believed that the laws cyclists had to follow were not the rules of the road.

Violating the rules of the road throws the cyclist into conflict with other vehicles, instead of placing him in harmony with them. In more than half of all car–bike collisions, the cyclist had violated a rule of the road.

If you are involved in an accident where you have violated a rule of the road, you may not be able to recover damages, since the crash is partially your fault.

The most blatant and potentially lethal violation that cyclists make is riding on the wrong side of the road. Any real or imagined benefits of being able to see oncoming traffic are negated by the liabilities of riding into oncoming traffic. Nearly a fifth of all car–bike collisions are caused by wrong-way cycling, and one study has found that the rate is even higher for riders aged 14 and older, who should know better.

The greatest danger in wrong-way cycling comes at intersections. There are no paths for the cyclist to follow, and any path he takes is a possible collision course with a motor vehicle. Drivers always look left, then right as they start to move. If you're coming the wrong way, they won't see you until it's too late.

When a wrong-way cyclist is hit, the results are much worse than if he had been cycling the correct way. If a cyclist riding the wrong way at 15 mph collides with an oncoming car traveling 25 mph, the speed at impact is a combined 40 mph. Had the cyclist been traveling in the correct direction, the net speed would have been only 10 mph. Not only does the greater speed at impact decrease the amount of time available to avoid it, but it also greatly increases the hazards. Since kinetic energy varies with the square of the speed, the wrong-way cyclist's potential impact is 16 times as great as for the cyclist who rides with traffic—the difference between falling from a second story or a thirty-second story building.

Riding on the correct side of the road also allows other vehicles to wait behind you if the road ahead is not clear to pass. A car on a collision course with a wrong-way cyclist does not have this option.

Violating other rules of the road can place you in equally bad situations. I used to run traffic lights that were turning red until the day a motorist coming from my right decided to run his light before it turned green. I barely made it out of that one alive, and have since learned to stop as soon as I see yellow.

Running stop signs, of course, can put you in the same undesirable position. The temptation is there, but if you want to make sure you live to see the next stop sign, come to a full stop and look around. Wait until there is no cross traffic before entering the intersection.

It is also your responsibility to yield at yield signs and intersections where you do not have the right of way. And be careful as you enter the road. Make sure there is no traffic coming before you pull out. Then move onto the road and carefully mount your bike. Mounting on a gravel shoulder or in a parking lot separated from the roadway by speed bumps and sewer gratings can send you tumbling down in front of oncoming traffic.

Remember, you are legally obligated to follow all the rules of the road. One of my friends was ticketed for failing to make a complete stop at a stop sign, and the violation was recorded on his driving record after he presented his driver's license as identification. And recently a 23-year-old cyclist was convicted in a Lubbock, Texas, court of running a stop-light. The prosecutor lost his fight to have the cyclist fined the maximum $200, but the young man did have to pay $95.

Those are not the only violations you can be tagged for. A lawyer with the Securities and Exchange Commission in Washington, D.C., was arrested and fined for cycling 30 mph in a 20-mph zone. John Marino was pulled over in Albuquerque, New Mexico, during his 1978 record transcontinental crossing for riding at 59 mph.

Following the rules of the road will mean little unless you're visible to other motorists. If you make motorists aware that you are also on the road, you'll have a much better chance of gaining their cooperation.

Anytime a motorist hits another vehicle or pedestrian, the response is always the same: "I didn't see him!" This is usually true, and is usually the reason for the accident. Recent research suggests that cyclists are particularly susceptible to not being seen, because motorists are not cued to see them. Motorists look for other large vehicles or pedestrians, but not bicycles. Since they are not looking for cyclists, they literally do not see them in many cases. I've seen an oncoming driver pull directly across a cyclist's path, forcing him off the road and nearly running him over. It was in broad daylight, and the cyclist was only a few feet from the car when the driver made a left turn. The driver's plea: "I didn't see him!"

The strongest argument against using bikepaths centers around this problem. A cyclist on a bikepath is not visible to motorists. At some point, any point-to-point bikepath must merge with traffic, usually at intersections. Since the motorists are not aware that cyclists are riding nearby, they won't look for cyclists when, for instance, making a right turn across the bikepath onto a side street.

To be more visible, then, you have to be out there with the cars. Although the laws in most states require that cyclists ride as far to the right of the road as is practicable, it is unsafe to weave in and out of parked cars or to sweep over to the right side of a right-turn lane, then have to swing back into the straight-ahead lane.

It's also unsafe to ride on the shoulders of the road. Sooner or later, the shoulder will end, or you'll have to move onto the pavement to avoid an obstacle. Motorists will not be watching for you, so making such a move will jeopardize your safety. If you had been riding on the pavement all along, you would not have this problem.

The safest place to ride is about four feet from the right curb or, if there are cars parked on the right, four feet out from the cars. This gives you room to get away from cars that come too close, as well as to avoid potholes, glass and other obstructions. If a car door opens in front of you, you are out far enough to miss being clobbered.

In wider traffic lanes, other vehicles will still have enough room to get by you without crossing into the opposite lane.

In narrower lanes, however, other vehicles will have to swing into the oncoming traffic lane to pass you. If traffic is light or your side of the road is badly chewed up, hold your ground. In fact, if you're riding in light traffic on a four-lane road (or a two-lane, one-way road), feel free to take the entire lane to yourself. I regularly do this on a five-mile, 25-mph stretch that tractor-trailers blast through at about 60 mph. I have never had a close call: motorists simply move into the other lane. Also feel free to stay in the lane anytime you're going as fast as the traffic. If you're going faster, move to the left of the traffic.

On heavily traveled, narrow streets, I hang as close to the right as possible. It's not only illegal to hold up traffic in such a situation, but it's also a good way to make motorists impatient and mad enough to pull stupid and dangerous moves.

Even on such streets, though, you are perfectly within your rights to ride the center of the lane if the side is ripped up or otherwise unsafe. Remember, the law says "practicable." It's not practicable to deliberately ruin your bike and endanger yourself.

Keep in your lane at the crest of hills and through blind

turns, too. Some motorists have unbelievably strong urges to pass cyclists at these spots.* If they want to pass, force them to do so in the other lane. When a car comes roaring along from the opposite direction, you'll have plenty of room to stop or get out of the way.

Always be realistic, though. If a drunken motorist is breathing down your neck, get out of his way. Being right isn't worth much if someone like that turns you into mulch.

If a chewed-up, narrow road is full of speed demons, take another road. If there isn't an alternate road, an increasingly common problem in these days of superhighways, ride as far to the right as you can, traveling slowly and cautiously. If anyone gives you trouble, get his license number.

Make Yourself Visible

Most states have laws that require bicycles ridden at night to have reflectors or lights. John Forester believes that "the older rules requiring a headlamp and a rear reflector meet all known safety and operating conditions, while newer rules that require nine other reflectors but no headlamp are based upon ignorance of collision movements and a desire to publicize the bicycle."

If you are going to ride between dusk and dawn, your bike should have at least a rear reflector. The Society of Automotive Engineers-approved, SAE-A70 (amber) and SAE-A71 (red) auto reflectors are the brightest available. These are about three inches in diameter and have all their reflectivity directed to the rear. The reflectors sold in bike shops typically are smaller and reflect light from the sides as well. Some cyclists feel this is a good idea, but there is no denying that it reduces the amount of reflectivity from the rear. The amber reflectors are the brightest, but are illegal for rear use in some states. The greater brightness of larger and amber

---

* If you crest a hill and there is no traffic directly behind you, it's a good idea to move to the right so that you are out of the way of any unsuspecting motorists approaching from behind.

reflectors is particularly useful in lefthand turns. There, smaller reflectors are only marginally bright enough to attract the attention of an approaching motorist using his low-beam headlamps.

There is wide debate in the cycling community on wheel reflectors and reflective tires. The devices are bright, but I have to agree, along with Forester, that they're probably useless. If a motorist is barreling down on you from the side, by the time he sees those reflectors, you won't have a prayer. If he's going slow enough to see the reflectors in time to avoid a crash, he'll also be able to see you.

There's no argument, however, that a headlight is essential for night riding. A good headlight not only lights the road so that you can avoid potholes and other hazards, but shows motorists that you are there.

You have two choices of headlight design: generator powered and battery powered. Generator lamps are always on your bike when you need them and are fairly inexpensive, but use part of your pedaling effort to operate. Battery-powered lights fall into two categories: those with enclosed batteries and those with separate batteries. The enclosed-batteries type, which includes the arm light, is inexpensive but doesn't put out much light. The separate-battery models light the road like a floodlight, and make you highly visible, but are expensive. With either battery-powered type, there is no guarantee that you'll have it along when you need it or even if you do, that the batteries will work.

While there is agreement on the need for a headlight at night, taillights are more controversial. Some cyclists prefer rear reflectors over taillights, since reflectors are typically brighter. But if a car is approaching without its lights on, or if it passes you on a left curve, where its low beams may be shining to the outside of the curve, a reflector is worthless.

Among those who swear by taillights, there is yet another debate. Some prefer flashing lights, which can attract an oblivious motorist's attention. But others point out that a flashing light does not allow a motorist to judge how fast or which way the bike is traveling, so he cannot react as quickly as needed.

You can increase your nighttime visibility by wearing

bright or reflective clothing, or adding reflective tape to your clothing and helmet. The Bell helmet comes already adorned with highly reflective tape.

Unfortunately, you can pile on reflectors and flashing lights and you still won't be able to avoid the biggest hazard of night cycling: drunken drivers. In a study conducted during the mid-1970s, it was found that half the motorists involved in nighttime collisions with cyclists had been drinking. The only way to decrease your odds of encountering a drunk is by sticking to the main roads you know well, preferably ones that are well lighted.

Night isn't the only time when good visibility is essential. During bad weather, particularly in rain or snow, you should wear light, bright colors and ride with your lights on. Your rain gear and bike bags should be yellow, since it's the most visible color in bad weather.

Even on clear days, you cannot always count on being seen. At certain times of the day, motorists may not be able to see you because glare from the rising or setting sun blocks their vision. Be especially cautious when you're riding into the sun at either of those times of the day, and stay as far to the right as possible. If the only time you can ride is just before sunset, plan your rides so that you'll return home with the sun at your side or back, rather than directly in front of you.

Be Predictable

After being seen, the next most important rule is to be predictable. Following the rules of the road and making sure you are visible will give you a head start. But there's more to it.

When a motorist is going to do something out of the ordinary, he signals with a turn signal or brake lights. You, as a cyclist, must also let others know your intentions, but have to use your hands, eyes and body to do this.

To signal a right turn, you can either extend your right arm or hold your left arm straight up. For left turns, hold your left arm out to the side.

To let motorists behind you know that they have to stop ahead, hold out your left arm with the back of your hand flat and facing them. I also use this signal when I am in the middle of a lane and it is unsafe for others to pass.

Signaling is part of making a safe turn, but there is much more to it. A right turn is usually not a problem. Since you're already on the right side of the lane, you simply signal and make your turn. The only complications arise when there is a separate right-turn lane. Then you must signal (here, the righthand signal definitely works better) from the straight-through lane, check the traffic behind you, and move over to the right side of the right-turn lane.

A left turn is made the same way. Signal and look behind you. When it's clear, move over to the left side of your lane. If there is more than one lane, you'll have to move to the left side of the farthest left lane. The only safe way to do this is by moving one lane at a time, checking for traffic each time before moving to the next. Cutting across three lanes at once is asking to be clobbered.

When I approach an intersection where other vehicles are likely to dart out in front of me from the side streets, I hold a hand up in the air, palm out, facing them like a British bobby, to let motorists know I'm coming through and have the right of way. I find this also works with people waiting to make a left turn across my path.

I need another signal at other intersections. I regularly ride through a busy intersection where most of the traffic turns off to a bridge on my right. I have to watch that the on-coming vehicles don't sweep across my path, and I also have to let those behind me know that I'm going to follow the main route to the left. This is important, because a frequent type of car–bike crash is caused by a motorist misjudging how fast a cyclist is riding, and running into him or cutting too closely in front of him during a right turn. To avoid this, I position myself well out into the lane and point my left arm out. I've never once had a close call in that hectic intersection.

There are time, however, when you cannot use hand signals. Just before the street where I live, there is a sweeping, downhill righthand curve, riddled with potholes. I have to come out of the curve and make a left turn within 50 feet.

Just before my turn, then, I have to: (1) slow down; (2) make a sharp turn; and (3) dodge potholes. If I take my left hand from the handlebars to signal my turn, I lose half my stopping power and much-needed control of the bike through the potholes.

If there is heavy traffic behind me, I just ride along and make a left turn farther down the street. But if there is only a car or two, I'll let them know what I intend to do with body language. Coming into the downhill curve, I move into the center of the lane. As I near my turn at the end of the curve, I slip all the way to the left, slowing almost to a stop. This lets those behind me know I'm going to make that turn, and gives them room to pass me on the right.

Sometimes neither hand nor body signals work. At another pockmarked intersection near my home, I have to make a left turn into a side street where there are always dozens of cars waiting to pull out. Just letting them know I intend to make the turn doesn't gain headway. They're desperate and will try truly idiotic maneuvers to break out of that intersection. Since I need both arms on the bars to wriggle through the potholes, I cannot give them my stop signal. So I try to establish eye contact. Once you're sure they're looking at you, you've won half the battle. But remember that they may look right at you and still not see you. At that intersection I've had people pull out a few feet in front of me after I thought I'd made eye contact with them.

If you cannot attract a motorist's or pedestrian's gaze, let him hear you. You can buy bells, horns and Freon-powered noisemakers, but I've found that simple lung power can be a lifesaver.

I was cycling with my friend Brian Karger one beautiful afternoon. As we cruised along, I noticed a car waiting in the oncoming lane. It did not have a turn signal on, but I figured the motorist was waiting to make a left turn, which would directly cross our path. He seemed to be looking right at me, so I assumed he would wait for us to pass.

Just as we pulled up within ten feet of the car, the driver began to make his turn, and was headed directly for Brian and me. We swerved to the right and simultaneously screamed at the top of our lungs. Instead of the crunching of metal and bones, the next sound I heard was the screeching of the car's tires as the driver slammed on the brakes, missing us by inches. So when all else fails, scream.

Be sure that you leave room for other vehicles, too, when you turn. Proper signals are of little use if you pull over just feet in front of a car that's overtaking you at 60 mph, or make a left turn just feet in front of a fully loaded oncoming tractor-trailer. Always check behind you before you move too. The only way to do this is by looking over or under your shoulder: mirrors give too limited a picture, and can be jarred out of alignment by bumps. Be sure to practice looking behind you so that you don't swerve out into the lane as you look back: swerving into traffic causes one out of every six car–bike collisions.

As you ride more, you should be able to judge how much traffic is behind you and how far back it is just by the sound. In addition, you should be able to anticipate potentially hazardous situations. The Zen archer's credo should also be yours: "Expect nothing. Be ready for everything."

While traffic laws allow you to anticipate what another driver is likely to do, never assume that is what he will do. You have to continually assess traffic, and should consider what you will do if your predictions are wrong.

One spring day, as I was cycling through the countryside of central New York, I crested a hill to find a long stream of traffic rolling toward me in the opposite lane. Then I saw a car flying past the line, in my lane, headed right for me.

Under the rules of the road, I could have assumed that this fellow would move back into his lane as he saw me coming. But I knew better, and just managed to ride off the road before he tore through my lane.

If you stay on top of the whole picture as you cycle, you should be able to ride thousands of miles without a mishap. That's because a good cyclist, an aware one, flows with the traffic rather than hinders it. When you can become part of that flow, there will be many miles of safe, enjoyable cycling ahead for you.

CHAPTER NINE
COPING

Even after you master riding in traffic, there are dozens of other potential hazards awaiting you every time you hit the road. Many of them can be found not only on the roads, but on bikepaths and other routes you may ride.

Again, the key to safe and pleasurable cycling is being alert. Every potential hazard can be avoided, if you're aware of it. Knowing how to avoid these hazards will put you in control and will give you the peace of mind to make every mile you ride more enjoyable.

The types of hazards you'll encounter most frequently vary with where you live and the roads you ride. But a few problems seem to be universal.

Hazard Number One: Potholes

One of these is potholes. I'm a native of Pittsburgh, Pennsylvania, where there are more potholes than roads. Riding in other states has made me aware, though, that Pittsburgh does not have a monopoly on potholes. They're a danger everywhere.

Shallow potholes are no big deal. If you lift your weight from the saddle and place it on the pedals and handlebars, you can ride through them without hurting your bike or losing control. But deeper holes can trap your front wheel and send you headfirst over the handlebars, or at least ruin your wheels and toss you to the ground.

The best way to deal with potholes is to watch for them and avoid them. But you cannot always do that: sometimes a pothole will be hidden by a shadow or another vehicle, and you won't see it until it's too late.

In his book *Effective Cycling,* John Forester recommends a technique for avoiding potholes that he calls rock dodging. He says that just as you're about to hit the hole, rock or other obstruction, you should haul back on one side of the handlebar without first leaning. If you pulled the right side, you'll go to the right, then start to fall to the left. But you can catch yourself as soon as your wheels clear the hazard by steering

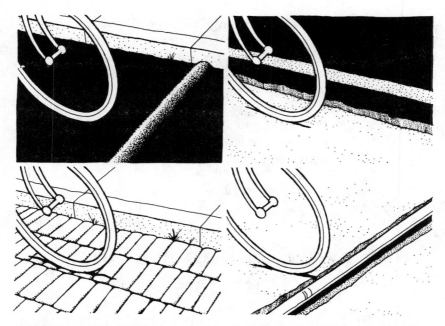

Ridge hazards. Clockwise, a ridge across the roadway. Cyclist has to lift his bike as the pavement rises. At the edge of the roadway. Here the pavement is usually higher than the road, preventing the cyclist from moving from the shoulder onto the roadway. Railroad and streetcar tracks, which can cross the cyclist's path at any angle. Cobblestones and bricks.

more left than normal. Your wheel will snake around the obstruction, but your body and handlebars barely move, so you won't hit a car or a companion in the process.

If you don't have time for rock dodging, though, there's another way to get around obstructions. I was cycling with a group of about 12 other riders one Sunday morning. The roads were deserted, so we were riding 3 abreast across our lane.

Suddenly, we ran into a patch of deep potholes that ran across almost the entire lane. The front riders yelled back to the rest of us to alert us to the holes, then the cyclist on the left veered into the oncoming lane and the one on the right pulled off onto the shoulder.

The rider in the middle, however, had nowhere to go in the seconds before he'd run into the holes. So he lifted his bike from the ground and jumped over the holes.

Jumping your bike isn't the easiest skill to master, but it may save your bike or your life someday when you find yourself between a rock and a car. Belgian professional racing cyclists have developed their jumping abilities to the point where they can jump their bikes sideways over curbs.

If you have no choice but to jump your bike, first accelerate. Just before you reach the obstacle, set your feet in the three and nine o'clock positions. Then jump up out of the saddle, pulling up evenly with your arms and legs.

Never do this if your toe clips aren't tight. My buddy Bob Snyder tried once and smashed his groin on the top tube.

Some places do not have potholes, but deep cracks in the pavement, which range from a hair's breadth to more than an inch across. Once when I was riding with a friend, my front wheel caught in a crack as I was trying to make a left turn. My front tire was torn from the rim, and I tumbled to the ground.

Had I not been watching my friend—who knew every crack and pothole in the road—but watching the road, I would not have crashed. Even though that was the only time I've ever been thrown by a crack or pothole, I have hit bad ones more times than I care to remember. And every time, it's been because I wasn't alert. I'd be talking to a friend, or tailgating a car just starting out from a red light. By the time I saw the holes, I had no choice but to hit them.

As long as you're alert, you have no excuse to run into holes and cracks. Cut around them if you can, or stop and wait for traffic to ease up so that you can cut out farther into the lane. When the road is chewed up for more than a few feet, stay out in the lane where you can avoid the holes.

Sometimes there will be a line of potholes about a foot or two from the right edge of the road. If that last foot or two is not chewed up, I ride there. There's not much room to maneuver, but the line of potholes to your left will act as a barricade between you and other motorists. Drivers don't like to hit potholes any more than cyclists do.

Hazard Number Two: Ridges

A problem similar to potholes is ridges. You can find these where sections of road have been repaved, or a shoulder has been added after the roadway was built. Usually, they are less than an inch high, and are tapered so that you can roll right up and down. But when there is no taper, it's just like riding into an inch-high wall: the impact, especially if you hit the ridge from the side, may knock your front wheel out from under you.

Ridges are most likely to be hazardous when they run parallel to the roadway. I was riding at 35 mph on the shoulder of an expressway once, heading downhill with the wind at my back, when I noticed that the shoulder ended ahead. I knew the roadway was higher than the shoulder, but the difference looked minuscule. I swung my bike to the right, so I could ride over the ridge at close to a 90-degree angle, then swung up onto the roadway.

Well, I tried to swing up onto the roadway. I think my front wheel made it, but the rear wheel caught on the ridge and I was quickly dumped into the middle of the road. Fortunately, I wasn't run over, but I couldn't ride again for a month.

There are other obstacles that are just as dangerous as a pavement ridge if you hit them at the wrong angle. Railroad and streetcar tracks and bricks and cobblestones in the road surface are good examples. When you see any of these, slow down and try to cross them at as close to a right angle as possible.

In the West, watch out for cattle guards. These are series of railroad ties or steel pipes spaced three to six inches apart over a pit. These serve as barriers across the roadways to keep cattle from crossing.

You also have to keep your speed down when you ride on unpaved roads. Although there are not many gravel and dirt roads in most parts of the country, I've had to ride miles of them several times, even on organized rides. Many times, the condition is only temporary as the road is being readied for resurfacing. But temporary or not, an unpaved road may well be the only route to your destination.

Even more dangerous are isolated patches of gravel and dirt, often found in turns, where your traction may already be perilously low. You'll also find bumps, oil, water and ice in turns, so keep your speed down.

You may also come across patches of broken glass, but these are more common on the level. The farther to the right that you ride, the more glass you'll find: traffic sweeps glass over to the right side of the road. If you have to ride over glass or cinders, go slowly, lift your weight off the wheels, and check your tires as soon as you pass through to remove the fragments before they work their way in and cause a puncture.

Hazard Number Three: Wet Spots

Even on the best roads, you have to watch for slippery spots that can make you skid and crash. Wet manhole covers, leaves and lane markers are particularly hazardous. You will also find patches of oil where cars wait for traffic lights.

About the worst conditions occur shortly after the start of a rainstorm, though. During the first half hour, the rain mixes with oil and grime on the road and forms a slippery solution that can cut the friction between your tires and the road to half of what it would be on a dry surface. This loss of friction reduces your steering and braking control, causing you to skid if you brake too vigorously or spill if you take a turn too fast or too sharply. To make matters worse, when caliper brakes become wet, they lose up to 95 percent of their effectiveness.

After the first half hour of a storm, most of the road grime and oil is washed away. Your traction rises to three-quarters of what it would be on a dry surface, but you still need about twice as much distance to stop as you would on a dry road. At even 16 mph, you need about 65 feet to stop; coming down a hill at 50 mph, you need about 500 feet, a full tenth of a mile. The emergency braking technique discussed in Chapter Six will stop you the fastest: keep your weight low and toward the back, and pump the brakes.

One particular problem of riding during or after a rainstorm is puddles. You can never tell when a puddle merely sits on the surface of the road, or fills a foot-deep hole. Try to avoid as many puddles as you can, and creep through those you cannot. Riding through a puddle does the same thing to your brakes as a full-scale rainstorm: it cuts their effectiveness drastically. After you ride through a puddle, pump your brakes several times to squeegee the water from your rims.

Ice is even more hazardous than rain. Ice can collect in turns and shadows even when the temperature is above freezing, and can destroy your traction. Even if you manage to stay upright, you'll have little chance of stopping if you need to. If you're willing to ride extremely slow in your lowest gears, you can safely get through a few inches of snow. But if there's ice on the road, you are simply asking for trouble. Take a bus or go skiing instead.

Even after the roads have been cleared, you may still run into patches of ice. Often you'll find them along the side of the road, where the snow was piled to clear the center lanes. You may also find ice at driveways, where people throw the snow from their yards onto the road, and it is compressed into ice by the passing cars.

Shaded areas can hide all sorts of hazards. If the entire road is shaded, your eyes will quickly adjust and be able to see detail in the shadows. But if there are patches of sun and shade, you won't be able to see details in the dark areas. Those shadows can hide slippery spots, potholes, ridges and a host of other hazards.

Even on well-lighted, smoothly paved roads, there are dangers. One of the biggest is sewer gratings along the edge of the road, running parallel to the road. I'll never forget a cartoon I once saw, in which a highway engineer is holding a piece of crisscross grating. His boss is chewing him out, saying, "What kind of grate is that? It won't trap a bicycle wheel!"

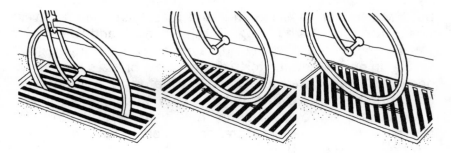

Road gratings may be parallel to the roadway, perpendicular to the roadway, or cross grated. Gratings that are parallel to the roadway represent a hazard to cyclists, as do bridge expansion joints that are wide enough to swallow a cyclist's front wheel.

Fortunately, many communities have replaced the parallel-bar gratings with the safer crisscross or diagonal grates, but sometimes only after a cyclist has been seriously injured. The dangerous grates are not completely gone, though, and occasionally show up in parking lots as well as on the road. If you cannot avoid a parallel grating, get off your bike and walk.

Hazard Number Four: Bridges and Tunnels

You'll find a similar problem on bridges. Larger bridges have expansion joints running across their entire width. The gap in the joints is often large enough to trap a bicycle wheel and send you toppling.

Open-grid metal bridges pose a similar problem: missing grids can also trap your wheels. I've never seen a bridge with missing grids, but I jump out of the saddle for a better view anytime I start over one.

Some bridges are also too narrow. When I lived in Binghamton, New York, the only route to my office included a four-lane, 45-mph bridge. The bridge was barely wide enough for four cars, let alone trucks, and there was no way to safely cycle when traffic was heavy. You could ride on the sidewalk, but the only barrier between it and the Susquehanna River was a three-foot-high railing. One false move and SPLASH!

The only way to safely ride across such a bridge is by taking an entire lane. Unfortunately, some bridges have only one lane in each direction, and many motorists are not keen on sitting behind a cyclist holding 15 mph over a two-mile, 55-mph bridge. You can either hold your ground, find an alternate route or means of transportation, or walk your bike on the sidewalk—if there is one.

Tunnels, too, can really put the squeeze on you. Aside from general claustrophobia, you'll find that most tunnel lanes are just wide enough for a standard-size truck. That doesn't leave much room for a standard-size car and a bike, and none at all for a bike and a truck. To make matters worse, most drivers are petrified upon entering a tunnel. And the road surfaces in most tunnels are slippery. If there are no lights in the tunnel, everyone's vision is reduced. (Don't forget to remove your sunglasses before entering.) Use the same riding tactics as for crossing hazardous bridges.

Even on wide four-lane roads, passing trucks, recreational vehicles (RVs) and buses can cramp you. These vehicles will as often as not cut in front of you without leaving you enough room. The drivers don't realize how much room a cyclist needs, how fast he may be traveling and how long their own vehicles are. Be prepared to bail out if the back end of a vehicle swings into your path. This is a good argument for riding three or four feet from the edge of the road: even if there is no shoulder, you still have a safety zone.

Commercial truck drivers are usually good at judging how much room they and you need, but often commit another error in judgment. When a large vehicle makes a turn, the back end of it moves closer to the inside of the turn than the front end. A television cameraman was killed near my home when the inside rear wheels of a truck jumped onto the sidewalk and ran over him. The driver never knew it happened. Obviously, riding through that turn on a bicycle as the truck was turning would not have been a good idea. Don't let yourself be forced into this situation: if there is a truck, bus or RV hot on your heels as you enter a turn, either get in front and take over the lane or pull over and wait.

Another problem with these vehicles, and with cars pulling trailers, is the use of large side mirrors. People who drive trucks and buses for their livelihood have to know exactly how wide their vehicles are. But when the average person gets behind the wheel of his motor home or adds a set of side mirrors to his car, he cannot be trusted. There is little you can do except to keep looking behind you, and watching your mirror, if you have one.

Large motor vehicles can also harm you in another, less direct way: through air blasts. When a truck, bus or RV passes you, it first pushes along a huge wall of air, then creates a suction in its wake. If there is a crosswind blowing from your left, the vehicle can also block it momentarily.

All of these effects last for just seconds, and therein lies the problem. By the time you correct for the sudden gust or lack of wind, conditions return to normal. Then you are overcompensating and can easily crash.

Many cyclists use this as an argument to avoid riding on main highways and interstates.* I ride with 55-mph truck traffic all the time, and I've never found the gusts to be a major problem. On the other hand, I would not advise taking your first rides on an interstate. But once you're a capable and confident cyclist, you should have little problem coping.

Assorted Hazards

There is an entire group of road hazards unique to riding in cities or business areas. One of the most frequently cited hazards is the opening car door. I've seen this happen: a cyclist was riding close to parked cars when the driver in one opened his door to get out. The cyclist was only feet behind the car when the door swung open, and he plowed into it. The bike stopped there, but the cyclist flew forward and landed on his head.

You'd think that drivers would look before opening their doors, but many don't. And even when they do, there's the

---

* Some states prohibit bicycles on interstate highways.

old problem of not noticing cyclists as they scan for larger vehicles. The solution is obvious: stay a door's length away from parked cars. If you have to ride closer, watch for people in the cars and be ready to brake. Being on the lookout won't always work, though, because the headrests in some cars make it impossible to tell if there is anyone inside.

Watching for people inside parked cars will also keep you on the alert for cars about to pull away from the curb. You can often tell that a driver is planning to pull out by the way he scans his mirrors, or by exhaust smoke coming from the car. Be ready to brake, and keep an eye to the left to check if you'll have room to swing out in case the car pulls out in your path.

Watch for people stepping out from behind parked cars, too. They can be as oblivious to cyclists as drivers are. People just don't realize that being hit by 150 to 200 pounds of bicycle and rider at 20 mph is not a pleasant experience. Many pedestrians don't realize how fast a cyclist may be traveling or how much room he needs to stop. Watch for these folks, especially when it's raining, as they'll sometimes make mad dashes in front of cars, trucks and cyclists to get out of the rain.

And watch out for novice cyclists on bikes. Just because you know how to ride is no reason to assume that anyone else on a bike does. Every few weeks a wrong-way cyclist forces me out into traffic. Jerry Kaplan found in his study of League of American Wheelmen (LAW) members that skilled club cyclists hit other cyclists as frequently as they hit or are hit by cars.

Joggers are a problem, too, especially on bikepaths. I can empathize with joggers in that there are few places to run where you can avoid pedestrians, traffic and intersections. And I don't mind when I see them running single file on a bikepath, even though it's not designed for them and their presence endangers the safety of those it was built for. But when I see a group of joggers strung across the entire width of the bikelane, running straight toward me, I become mad. The main reason why bikepaths have so many accidents per mile is that they are full of inexperienced cyclists. I've seen many on the paths who have trouble just staying upright, let alone maneuvering between hordes of joggers. I don't ride my bike on the course while runners are competing in the Boston Marathon; joggers should stay off bike trails or at least have a modicum of courtesy and common sense.

Not long ago, a movie, *Breaking Away,* was released in which a young cycle racer was shown following a tractor-trailer at 60 mph. A few months after the movie was released, letters began appearing in the cycling magazines complaining about glorifying an unsafe practice, just as parents protested the "Superman" television series that, they were sure, would lead their offspring to try jumping off tall buildings.

I thought the criticism of the movie was silly; after all, I don't know many incompetent cyclists who can hold speeds of 60 mph. But there is an underlying point that is valid: you shouldn't follow any vehicle closely, even at low speeds. My friend Bob Snyder was once tailgating a car as it slithered up a busy hill. Both were probably traveling less than 10 mph. But when the car had to brake suddenly, Bob plowed into its rear and nearly flipped onto the trunk.

As I've already pointed out, riding too closely behind another vehicle can also obstruct your view of potholes and other road hazards. So while it may feel good to keep up with a motor vehicle as it sucks you along in its slipstream, it can also be extremely dangerous.

A motor vehicle too close in front of you can also kick up dirt or blow its exhaust in your eyes as it starts up. And even your own vehicle can cause trouble. Your bike's tires can spit gravel and dirt in your face. In warm weather, bugs will often find their way into your eyes. And if your front tire blows, it could shoot up a piece of rubber.

The only way to protect yourself is by wearing glasses. If you do not wear prescription glasses, buy a good pair of sunglasses. If you have to ride at night or on dreary days, you can get yellow lenses that help your vision.

I've long been a firm believer in wearing sunglasses while cycling, and not long ago witnessed a demonstration of their worth.

I was descending a long, steep two-lane road at about 45

mph. The road was smooth, but there was a patch of dirt and gravel running along the centerline.

For some incomprehensible reason, a man in a pickup truck decided I was not going fast enough and pulled around me to pass. As he did, he sprayed dirt and gravel into my face. If I had not been wearing glasses, I would have been blinded—if not permanently, at least long enough to lose control of my bike and crash.

Sunglasses also shield your eyes and face from the sun. Even on overcast days a few hours' exposure can wash out the pigment in your retinas, making it hard for you to see when night falls. Sunglasses will also keep you from squinting and, consequently, from getting headaches.

Problems with Dogs

One of the biggest headaches for cyclists who ride in suburban or rural areas is dogs. I know cyclists who consider dogs to be their worst enemies, and will eagerly bludgeon a yelping dachschund.

The simple truth is that most dogs are only trying to protect their territory from invaders or feel like chasing something. Most of the time, I simply outrun them. If I can't, I scream and bark at them before they get the chance to bark or lunge. They are usually so stunned that they stop dead in their tracks. This has even worked with Dobermans. If the dog beats me to the first bark, I try talking softly ("Good dog, nice dog") or firmly ("No!") depending on how fierce the animal looks. And I keep one foot free so that I can stop if necessary.

By using these techniques, I've managed to get through all but one encounter with dogs. That one called for special tactics.

Bob Snyder and I were cruising through the countryside near Syracuse, New York, one afternoon when we spotted two shepherd dogs and a mongrel sitting together down the road, eyeing us as though we were to be their dinner. I didn't think we could dismount and reason with them, so we slowed to a crawl while we tried to decide what to do.

Just then, we heard a truck coming up from behind. Bob turned and flagged down the driver. He went over, talked to the man, then came back to me.

"Let's go," he said.

"What about the dogs?" I asked.

"Oh, don't worry. This guy's going to drive interference for us in his truck." And we pedaled down the road beside the truck until we were safely past the dogs.

Had those mutts charged us with froth running down their chins, we would not have had that option. Assuming that you cannot outrun dogs in such a situation, it's probably best to get off your bike and use it as a shield between you and the dogs. Talk firmly, and wield your pump if necessary. Be careful your pump doesn't get caught in the spokes. Just the sight of the pump should scare most dogs.

A survey of the League of American Wheelmen found that collisions with dogs are as likely to cause serious injuries as are collisions with motor vehicles. Recently ex-Mayor John Lindsay of New York suffered a broken collarbone in a collision with a dog. I also know of one racer who killed a collie when he collided with it.

Dogs are not the only animals that can block your path. As I crested the top of a small hill near Columbus, Ohio, one afternoon, a turkey buzzard with about a ten-foot wingspan took off from the road a few feet ahead and soared within inches above my head. On more than one occasion, I've had to dodge snakes that were sunning themselves on the road. One young local rider who didn't dodge got a live copperhead intertwined in his front wheel. I've heard of deer and moose running into cyclists, and a professional racer was killed a few years ago during the Tour de France when he ran into a flock of sheep while roaring down a mountain.

Don't underestimate the smallest creatures, either. As I was flying down a hill one hot summer day, a yellow jacket flew down the open neck of my shirt. By the time I could stop, he had bitten me. If you are allergic to bees and wasps, or have never been bitten, don't leave home without medication to combat beestings.

Problems with People

The most dangerous and vicious animal is the human. The worst offenders, without a doubt, are males between the ages of 16 and 25. For some reason, this age group has little conception of the consequences of their "frivolous" actions. They have grabbed at my bike from car windows, thrust windshield scrapers and umbrellas at my friends, thrown firecrackers in my path and purposely forced me off the road.

I'm not a violent person, but I truly enjoy a story John Forester told me. While a group of cyclists were out on a weekend club ride, a deranged motorist forced one off the road. The racers in the group saw the incident and took off after the motorist. Not far ahead, they caught him, dragged him from his car and beat him to a pulp.

A patrolman happened by and asked the cyclists what was going on. They explained, and he said, "I didn't see a thing. Get back on your bikes and get out of here." Justice prevailed.

That's just one reason why it's a good idea to always ride with others. Another is that you are less likely to be attacked in the first place if you are riding with a companion. And he can ride for help if you are attacked or have an accident.

Whenever anyone threatens your safety, report them to the police. If they're in a motor vehicle, get a description and the license number; if they're on foot, get a good physical description. In either case, try to find a witness. And if the attacker seriously hurts you, prosecute to the maximum.

One sure place to find attackers and other assorted derelicts, hoodlums and junkies is in a large city park after dark. Places such as New York's Central Park are not really safe for cyclists even during the daylight hours.

Despite your riding ability and ability to dodge potholes, dogs and assailants, there's a good chance you're eventually going to crash. Even skilled club cyclists have accidents that cause damage to their bikes or require medical treatment about once every 10,000 miles. Cyclists without that much riding experience have accidents as often as once every 100 miles.

The Right Ways to Fall

Most cycling accidents are simple falls that cause only minor bruises and scrapes. And even collisions with motor vehicles are not necessarily fatal, or particularly harmful, if you know how to crash. The difference between knowing and not knowing may mean the difference between a few bruises and a long stay in a hospital bed.

The most important rule is a simple one, but can be extremely hard to follow: don't panic. If you stay relaxed, you have a much better chance of escaping serious injury. Drunks and babies survive disastrous car crashes because they are relaxed and absorb the shocks, while their tense companions freeze in panic.

The most frequent type of accident is the sliding fall. This is what happened to me when I hit a pavement ridge at 35 mph. I slid on my right hip and shoulder, tearing up my skin and clothing but keeping my bones and bike intact.

The best bet in a sliding fall is just to go with it. William Sanders, author of *The Bicycle Racing Book,* recommends tucking your arms against your chest and using your hands to protect your face. Throwing out your arms, he says, can easily sprain your wrists or break your arms.

A second type of crash is the tumbling fall. This happens when you hit a pothole or car, or lock your front wheel on a descent, flying over the handlebars headfirst. You can reduce the severity of the accident by breaking the inevitable collision that follows into smaller collisions. Sanders recommends tucking your head against your chest, with the arm on the impact side curved around your head for extra protection. You should not be totally relaxed, he says, but should keep enough muscle tension to remain springy.

Direct impact is potentially the most serious type of collision, and you're better off if you try to turn it into a glancing blow. If a car makes a right turn in front of you and you hit your brakes, you'll either plow into it or skid and fall under its wheels. But if you can glance off the car or let it hit you from behind, the impact will be far less severe.

One way of doing this is by making what John Forester calls an "instant turn." Forester describes the process in *Effective Cycling:*

> Suppose a car coming towards you at an intersection turns left on a collision course with you. This is the most common motorist error that causes car–bike collisions. You want to whip into that cross street to get away. Here's how. You turn your front wheel left—the wrong way, towards the car. By doing this, you've forced a right lean, and you'll start to fall right. The moment you've got a good lean started, a tenth of a second or so, turn your front wheel right and you'll find yourself in a tight right turn. Do you understand what you've done? To make a right turn, you must lean right, so to hurry up the leaning process, you made your bike track to the left a few inches. Then you are leaning over properly and you can steer a right turn.
>
> This doesn't ever feel natural, and you must train yourself to do it. It is a jerk in the wrong direction at the start of an instant turn when you deliberately unbalance yourself by steering the whole bike out from under you.

If you are hit from behind, either in an instant turn or at any other time, do not use your brakes. Instead, you should accelerate and pull over to the right. You'll probably be able to get out of the offender's path.

If a direct impact is inevitable, you may be able to let go of your bike at impact and sail over the vehicle or bounce across its roof or hood. This obviously doesn't work well, though, if the vehicle is a huge truck or bus or if it is an oncoming vehicle with a line of traffic behind it.

You may be able to save yourself from serious injuries in a direct collision or in other circumstances, too, by dumping your bike. Former U.S. Olympic Team cycling coach Oliver Martin told *Popular Mechanics* how the technique came in handy for one of his riders.

A group of Oliver's cyclists were training one day. As they were making a sweeping turn on a mountain descent, traveling at about 50 mph, the rear tire blew on one rider's bike.

When a rear tire blows, using the rear brake can cause a skid. Clamping on the front brake usually causes a flight over the handlebars. The best bet is usually to pump both brakes and gradually roll to a stop.

But this rider was heading for the edge of a cliff, and was going too fast to stop in time. So he dumped his bike, and slid along the ground until he came to a stop. Doing so saved his life, but obviously you cannot do this just anywhere: laying your bike down in traffic is the last thing you want to do.

Fortunately, most flat tires don't call for such drastic action. You will usually have enough room to stop, even if you are riding fast. The flat tire will slow you, and pumping your brakes will soon stop you.

A flat front tire can be tricky, though. When your front tire goes flat, you lose your steering control. If you turn the wheel you'll crash. So you have to keep the front wheel straight while you come to a stop. Keep your arms relaxed while you do this, or you may make the front wheel shimmy and lose control.

There's not much more you can do to protect yourself than to remain alert and relaxed and wear a good helmet. If you own an expensive bike or frequently crash, you may want to add a rider to your insurance policy that covers all damages to your bike. Most household policies cover only theft and fire, have high deductibles and don't pay a penny if you wipe out your $2,000 Colnago in an accident. Sure, the other guy's insurance will pay—if there is another guy, if he has insurance and if he's found guilty. These policies usually run about $10 for every $100 your bike is worth, and carry deductibles of $5–$10.

I'm sure some of you will, after finishing this chapter, call the local newspaper to place a Bike for Sale ad. Please don't. The purpose is not to frighten you, but to let you know what dangers lurk on the roads ahead. Despite all of them, cycling is fun. Statistically, there are far more dangers in eating, yet none of us forsake the pleasure of it because of those dangers. Just knowing what to look for will help in avoiding the potential dangers on the road, making you ready for anything.

CHAPTER TEN
YOUR
FIRST
RIDES

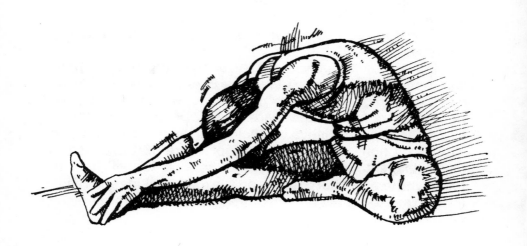

Now that you know what to watch out for, it's time to get down to the joy of cycling.

One of the best things about cycling is that virtually anyone can just hop aboard a bike and ride off into the sunset. There is no pounding or heavy work to worry about; pedaling at a relaxed pace does not strain an underused heart like the rigors of running or racquetball. In fact, doctors often prescribe cycling for coronary patients to help rebuild their weak hearts.

Still, to be on the safe side, it's a good idea to spend a few minutes filling out a risk-factor profile.

A risk-factor profile is a survey of your life-style and habits to determine your relative risk of having heart trouble. Any good internist will be able to draw up a profile for you, including information on your blood pressure, cholesterol, glucose levels and other factors.

If you fall into the low-risk range, it's safe for you to start cycling immediately. If you have a higher risk, though, or want to have more peace of mind, it's a good idea to have an electrocardiogram (EKG) before you begin cycling.

An EKG is a record of how your heart is functioning. A stress test is an EKG taken while you run on a treadmill or ride a stationary bike, to monitor differences in your heart's performance under a workload. Some doctors feel that anyone over age 40 should have a stress test before beginning an exercise program. Others wryly suggest that those who plan to continue their sedentary life-styles are the ones who need a stress test most.

While the medical literature suggests that proper stress testing accurately reveals cardiovascular disease 60 to 90 percent of the time, testing is not always done properly. Kenneth H. Cooper, M.D., who popularized aerobic exercise, wrote in a *Bicycling* magazine article that the stress test most often given—a submaximal test that checks heart performance only up to 85 percent of maximum heart rate—fails to identify coronary problems in up to half of those tested.

Still, Dr. Cooper feels proper stress testing is vital for many who are planning to begin an exercise program. For anyone under age 30, he recommends a complete medical history and physical exam within a year before the exercise program begins. If you're between 30 and 35, Dr. Cooper recommends the same routine, but within six months before you begin exercising, and advises that you also have a resting EKG. Over 35, he recommends an exam, medical history and resting EKG within three months before exercising. A stress test is optional, but recommended. If you're over 40, Dr. Cooper feels that a stress test is mandatory.

Dr. Cooper's suggestions are conservative. Other doctors strongly disagree, and feel no elaborate preparation is necessary as long as you don't overdo it in the beginning. If you have a problem, they reason, it will soon show up: chest pains, shortness of breath and other indicators. Then you'd better see a doctor.

The First Weeks

Whether you have a physical and stress test before starting or just start out cold, it's important to go easy in the beginning. Don't plan to ride 100 miles in your first week; the day will soon come when you'll be able to, and you'll only delay it and injure yourself by pushing too hard in the beginning.

If your only exercise in the last couple of years has been jumping to conclusions, it's a good idea for you to begin your cycling program by walking. Start out by walking around the block a few times and work up to the point where you can walk two or three miles. Even an octogenarian should be able to cover three or four miles in an hour.

If you have a pair of unused running shoes cluttering the closet, pull them out and jog. Again, take it easy, and gradually work your way up to two or three miles before you begin cycling.

Whether you start out on your bike or work your way up through another program, this same moderation is important on your first rides. Use your lowest gears and ride short distances. When you tire, call it quits for the day.

Even if you're active in another sport, you may find yourself tiring quickly. Mike Kane, a systems analyst and tennis player from Washington, D.C., recalled, "I was surprised how tired I got on my first rides. But just as amazing was the difference in endurance after I rode my first few rides."

Before beginning any ride, you should warm up. Warming up gradually raises your body temperature and increases your circulation, preparing your system for the work ahead rather than jarring it into action. A warm-up is also good for your joints, and helps to prevent injuries. For those over age 30, failing to warm up can restrict the blood supply to your heart during the beginning of the exercise session.

By stretching before you ride, you kill two birds at once; not only do you warm up but you also loosen muscles that cycling tightens. When you ride you repeatedly use the same muscles over a limited part of their range. Those muscles, particularly the hamstrings in the backs of your thighs, grow tight. Stretching keeps them flexible.

Toe touches are good for stretching, as are lower leg (calf) stretches. To do a lower leg stretch, stand about three feet from a wall or tree, with your palms touching it and your feet about two inches apart. Slowly shuffle backward, keeping your feet flat on the ground, until you feel strain. Hold the position for about 30 seconds, letting the muscles relax, then repeat another time or two.

To stretch the muscles in my back and neck, I bob from the waist five to ten times. If my neck feels tighter than usual, I lie on the floor on my back, lock my hands behind my head and pull it forward, rotating it to the sides, as well.

With all of these exercises, the key is smoothness. If you stretch in short, sharp motions, your warm-up may do more harm than good.

All together, your stretching should take about 10 minutes. But sometimes you might not have even that much additional time. Whether you do or not, you should continue to warm up once you start cycling. Don't just jump on, shift into high gear and grunt away. During your first 10 to 15 minutes, start out very slowly, using your lowest gears. When you begin to sweat, you're ready to pick up the pace.

Don't push yourself so hard or far that you become so tired that you cannot ride another inch. And don't work so hard that you're constantly out of breath. The best way to train is to break a sweat but still be able to comfortably carry on a conversation.

John Marino suggests checking your pulse every morning to make sure you're not overdoing it. As soon as you wake up, before you get out of bed, take your resting pulse. If it increases more than six beats from one day to the next, Marino writes in *Wheels of Life,* you're overdoing it. In fact, if you're following a sensible routine, you should soon notice your pulse rate dropping as your heart becomes more efficient.

A common mistake made by novices is to ride away from home until they tire, then find themselves facing a long return trip. It's far better to set up a short loop for your early rides, maybe a ½-mile circuit. That way you're never more than a ¼ mile from home, and even the most exhausted cyclist should be able to ride that far.

The Right Cadence

Ride smoothly. Do not push as hard as you can for five minutes, then coast the next five. Ultimately, you want to be able to find a cadence between 60 and 120 rpm that you can hold constantly. At first you'll use all your energy just trying to pedal that fast, but you can help your spin along by keeping your bike in its lowest gears. On a multi-speed bike, you should ride in a gear where you can feel just a slight resistance.

Pedaling constantly is good not only for your cadence, but for your health as well. When you cycle, your heart pumps a larger amount of blood than normal. The blood returns to your heart with the pumping action of your legs. If you suddenly stop, you prevent this return of blood, causing your blood pressure to drop rapidly. This is also why it is so important to cool down after a ride, or even when stopping for a break.

When you feel like stopping—to rest, talk to someone, admire the scenery—by all means do so. But, unless your heart is pounding furiously, keep your breaks short. If you stop for more than 10 to 15 minutes, warm up again before taking off.

Keep your rides short, too. Fifteen to 20 minutes is good for your early rides, but you may not be able to ride even that long in the beginning. Instead of trying to become better by pushing hard once or twice a week, it's much better to go easy five or six times a week. That's the only way to build strength and endurance.

When cardiac victim Harris Neft first jumped onto his bike after recovering from a heart attack, he could barely make it to a mailbox 300 yards away.

"I was huffing and puffing so bad I didn't think I'd make it back," he recalled. "Fortunately, it's downhill from there, so I coasted back."

For months, Harris rode back and forth on the street in front of his house, riding a few yards farther each time. Finally, on a warm Sunday morning, he rode a mile and a half to the park, then turned around and rode home. Within months he was riding up to 50 miles at a time.

As your ride more, watch for signals from your body that you're overtaxing it or doing something wrong. Most likely, your backside will hurt at first, but only until you become used to the saddle. Your neck and back muscles may ache, too, but only because you rarely use them. The muscles will eventually grow strong, and the aches will disappear.

But if your legs, and most importantly your knees, hurt, you're pushing too hard. Use lower gears and pedal easier or you may disable yourself.

And if you get chest pains or severe shortness of breath, stop riding and see your doctor immediately.

When you finish a ride, you should gradually cool down. Dropping from all-out effort to a standstill can trap blood in the muscles you've stopped using, causing dizziness and nausea. Spend five to ten minutes in your lowest gears at the end of each ride to eliminate the chance of this happening. I also stretch afterward, and massage my legs to remove the poisons that accumulate during exercise. After a five-minute massage, my legs no longer feel dead and heavy, but alive and springy.

Overcoming Obstacles

Many people take up cycling, running or any of a multitude of other sports to keep them fit and trim, but soon lose interest. One of the biggest factors is time. The average person believes he does not have time for regular exercise. Cycling has a definite edge: you can use your bike to do errands that have to be done.

Another problem is being self-conscious and feeling silly. A woman in her early forties told me about the time she sneaked her son's 10-speed out for a ride around the neighborhood. She enjoyed the ride, she said, but felt that everyone in the neighborhood was staring at her and saying, "Look at that kook!"

Even if they had been staring, her neighbors would undoubtedly be more understanding today. The energy crisis has made people realize that cycling is a wise and inexpensive alternative to driving a car, and they are now more likely to ask a cyclist for information than to laugh at him. When I began riding, the only comments I ever elicited from motorists were rude ones. Now I get more power salutes and "right on!"'s than threats and curses. When Ray Muia, a chemical engineer and past president of the Western Pennsylvania Wheelmen cycling club, began cycling to work, he expected his co-workers to harass him. Instead, they asked him for information on cycle commuting. "And they became a lot nicer during the gas crunch of '79," he said.

A third problem that keeps people from sticking with their grand exercise plans is boredom. It can happen even to cyclists: riding the same route day after day is bound to become boring sooner or later. As well it should, though: part of the fun of cycling is exploring new routes and places. Scout out different routes and ride them on alternate days. Deviate from your route at the slightest provocation: an interesting side street, heavy traffic, boredom. You can always find your way back. I've moved many times during the 1970s, and this is the way I've always explored my new surroundings. There's no better way to discover the beauty of a new—or old—neighborhood.

Mechanical problems are another deterrent, but are far

less important than most cyclists believe. If you keep your bike clean and lubricated, and your tires inflated, you shouldn't have to worry about anything more than a flat tire every 1,000 miles or your chain falling off occasionally.

If you're riding only around the block, you don't have to worry about getting home if you have a flat or other problem. Even if you break down 50 miles from home it's no big deal if you have change for a phone call and someone willing to pick you up.

But if you don't have a willing partner, or would rather finish your ride by bike than by car, you need only carry a few items with you and take a few precautions.

Before you head out, make sure your tires are inflated to the proper pressure. It should be indicated on the sidewalls of the tires. If you have quick-release hubs or brakes, make sure they're secured.

If your bike is new, check the saddle, handlebars and stem before your first rides. On my fourth or fifth ride on my first 10-speed, I neglected to check those things, and my handlebars came loose halfway down a steep hill.

Squeeze your brake levers to make sure your brakes are working. You should be able to pivot the bike on the braked wheel when you grab one brake lever.

Take your pump, patch kit, tire levers, spare and tube, a small, adjustable wrench to remove your wheels if they are not the quick-release type, and money for a phone call. Identification could come in handy in the event of an accident or if you are stopped for a traffic violation. Don't take your driver's license: cycling offenses can be recorded on your driving record if you present your license for identification.

Don't count on finding a gas station open if your tires need air or have a flat. Even if you are fortunate enough to have all your flat tires near gas stations, there's no guarantee that they'll be open or have working air hoses. If you're not sure how to fix a flat, read Chapter Twenty-One.

If you plan to ride less than a half hour, that's all you'll need. For longer rides, take a bottle of water or electrolyte-replacement fluid, such as E.R.G. or Gatorade. If you plan to ride for more than an hour or to have a picnic en route, take along easily digestible food such as bananas, apples and peanut butter (with or without jelly) sandwiches. I always carry extra money or a credit card in case I have a major breakdown and cannot get home, or find an appealing restaurant or ice cream shop along the way.

Once you're packed, you're ready to roll. You can, of course, ride at any time of day or night except for those times you have to spend at school, work or watching the kids. Still, some cyclists do their riding during lunch breaks, taking a 90-minute break to allow time for a good ride, a snack, and a shower or toweling off. Noon is actually the worst time of day to ride, though. Traffic is heavy, pollution and temperatures are high. In the winter, the higher temperatures are welcome, but not the pollution and traffic.

Before nine o'clock in the morning and after six o'clock in the evening are the best times I've found to ride. It's cooler then, traffic is light and there's less pollution. As an added bonus, most winds kick up during the middle of the day, but are quiet in the morning and evening.

No matter when you ride, try to avoid eating heavy foods for at least two hours beforehand. Digesting these takes a lot of blood and energy, so you won't be able to ride well. If you do, you may become nauseous or develop a side stitch.

If you follow these simple hints, your first rides should be pleasurable ones. And, like Harris Neft, you'll probably soon be ready to move on to longer and more challenging rides, and to make cycling a part of your day-to-day life.

CHAPTER ELEVEN
CYCLE COMMUTING

One wise way to make cycling a part of your day-to-day activities is by riding your bike to work, school, a store or a friend's house. As thousands more acknowledge every year, the bicycle is not just an alternative to the automobile for many of these trips, but is the only sensible vehicle for them.

It has taken the ultimate inducement to get more Americans to turn to cycle commuting: a jab at the wallet. With gasoline prices soaring rapidly to $1.50 a gallon and beyond, cycling has become the logical way to save money while you have fun and become healthier.

But that's only one of the many reasons for cycle commuting. The main one is that it is practical. Eighty percent of all automobile use in the United States takes place within eight miles of home. The U.S. Department of Transportation reports that 43 percent of all urban auto trips are less than four miles in length one way; 67 percent are less than eight miles one way. And other researchers have consistently found that the average commuting speed by car is less than 20 mph.

While any reasonably fit cyclist can hold that speed for a short period of time, most bike commuters average between 12 and 15 mph, about three to four times as fast as walking. Over typical commuting distances, the difference between traveling by car or bike is usually a matter of minutes. And, of course, while the cyclist carries his bike right into the office or locks it outside the store, the motorist often has to search for a parking place and walk to his destination—always facing the possibility of having a breakdown or having to sit in long gas-station lines.

Even with a full tank of gas and an indoor parking space reserved in his office complex, the motorist may save only 20 minutes in a typical commute. For the small, additional amount of time the cyclist spends commuting, he gets a big reward. For that extra 20-minute outlay, John Forester points out in *Effective Cycling* that the cyclist gets 45 minutes of enjoyment and exercise to help him keep fit and live longer. And he also saves money, helps keep pollution down and has the chance to explore new areas. And that's just the beginning.

Frederick Wolfe, a bicycle-transportation-system planner, writes in *The Bicycle: A Commuting Alternative:*

> I believe that this daily beginning (commuting to work by bike) provides an excellent, stress-free way for preparing for one's daily activities. I know that in my profession, I am often caught up in morning meetings, scheduling conflicts and project deadlines. In preparing for these known and unknown events, pressures are created that I feel both physically and mentally. During this morning ride, I can "get my head together" without worrying about that traffic accident up ahead, finding a parking space, getting more gasoline, or wasting precious time idling with morning peak-hour traffic. . . . This ride also affords the chance for regular aerobic exercise and a taste of adventure, exploration and independence—all of which can be real tonics for the body and soul. And the evening ride home is the perfect opportunity to work off the frustrations or satisfactions the day's events have created. Every day begins and ends with a positive feeling.

While you can gain some of the same benefits by using public transportation, obviously there are many that come only through cycling and study after study has shown that cycling is faster than taking trains, buses and subways: you don't have to stop for passengers, and can snake through traffic jams that tie up larger vehicles for an hour or longer. I've even beaten buses to my home four miles away when I walked home from work. And many areas have inadequate public transportation—if any.

If you live more than 10 to 15 miles from your destination, or have to cross water or bad bridges, you may want to combine cycling with public transportation. Cycle part of the distance, then take the bus, trolley, train or ferry, or even drive. Many commuter trains and ferries allow bikes on board, and in San Diego, Seattle and a growing number of other cities, cyclists are allowed to carry their bikes on board buses or else secure them to special outside racks. You can pedal up to a bus stop, lock your bike on the back of the bus, board it as a passenger, then grab your bike when you get off and ride right up to your office, classroom or home.

Choosing a Route

Cycle commuting is simple, but it can be much more enjoyable if you make a few preparations. The first step is picking a route. If you plan only to ride around the corner to pick up a loaf of bread or visit a friend, this is not much of a problem. But if you'll be riding miles to the office, school, a store or a friend's house, picking a good route is more important.

The prime consideration in picking a route is directness. The cycle commuter wants the shortest route that he can cover with the least effort. This route will typically cover the main roads; the reason they are so well traveled is because motorists have the same requirements.

But there are times when such a route is not practical. As a cyclist, you may be prohibited from riding on sections of the best route, or you may opt for a flatter, but longer route where the main traffic takes a shortcut over a hill.

You may also find that part of the most direct route is too hazardous or nerve-racking. I avoid the most direct route from my home to my office for those reasons. The last two miles of the four-mile route runs on a narrow, heavily traveled four-lane road. Although the speed limit is 35 mph, motor vehicles hold 45 to 60 mph. Traffic is always heavy.

Just before I enter the city, the route crosses a four-lane, 55-mph bridge. In less than 1,000 feet, vehicles must cross as many as three lanes so they can take the correct exit. There is at least one accident on that bridge every week. Back roads may take longer, but they're far more tranquil.

Another factor in choosing a route is pollution. On routes where traffic is regularly backed up or routes that run through tunnels, pollution can make you physically ill, and may have long-term effects. Again, you may want to trade off the most direct route for one that will let you breathe a little easier.

Pollution is no reason to stay off your bike, though, unless the Pollution Standards Index is so high that there is a warning issued, or unless you have a respiratory problem. Surprisingly, a preliminary study by the U.S. Department of Transportation found that cyclists had less carbon monoxide in their blood than motorists after the same amount of time on the road. This may be because air intakes for auto cooling vents and air conditioners are located close to the ground, where vehicles are spewing their emissions. By the time the emissions reach the cyclist, they've already dissipated.

But the study also found that cyclists were more susceptible to sore eyes and throats, as well as laryngeal irritation. When you can avoid heavy pollution, by all means do so. And when the Pollution Standards Index tops 100, leave your bike at home.

If you don't know your area well and don't care to explore it, the best way to choose a bike commuting route is with a map. City street maps provide virtually all the information you'll need for short metropolitan rides, but they don't extend far beyond the city boundaries. If you live farther out, topographical maps will be more helpful. These show changes in elevations along the routes, and include even the smallest roads. Topo maps in 1:24,000 (7½ minute) scale cover areas of about six by eight miles; other series cover larger areas.

Topo maps use concentric rings to show altitude. The amount of height each ring represents is constant on a given map, but varies depending on overall elevation. On a typical map, each ring might represent 200 feet of altitude. An area surrounded with four rings, then, is 800 feet higher than the surrounding area. If you want a quick, flat route, you'll look for another one. One hint: routes along railroad tracks and rivers are the flattest.

A free index of topo maps for your area is available from Branch of Distribution, U.S. Geological Survey, 1200 South Eads Street, Arlington, VA 22202 (if you live east of the Mississippi River) or Box 25286, Federal Center, Denver, CO 80225 (west of the Mississippi). Outdoor supply shops often carry topo maps, too.

After you plot your proposed route, give it a test ride. Driving it by car on the way to work will give you an idea of trouble spots and traffic density; riding by bike on your day off will let you leisurely observe road conditions and get an idea of how much time you'll need to cover the distance.

No matter what route you decide to use, it's a good idea to ride it as often as possible. Even though you'll miss exploring by doing so, motorists along the route will come to expect you, making your journey safer and easier.

Look for other cyclists, too. They may make good riding companions, and can be helpful when you have a problem.

Even if you find an ideal route, you may need an alternate at times. For example, there's a one-mile descent on my regular route to work. When the hill is covered with rain or snow, it is treacherous, and I take another route.

Make sure you are physically and mentally ready for the trip before you try cycle commuting. If you have confidence in your ability to commute by bike and are not intimidated by traffic, you have licked the mental part. If you have been regularly riding equal distances, the physical part will be no problem. The first few rides will take a lot out of you if you are not in good shape, but you'll quickly become stronger.

Allow plenty of time for your first commutes. You may need time to rest or to repair a flat tire, or you may have to take a detour to avoid an accident. It also takes longer at first to park your bike and freshen up than it will after you become a regular commuter. Riding under an unnecessary time strain can take all the joy from cycle commuting.

If your bike needs servicing, do it the night before. Don't plan to change a tire or adjust your brakes and gears in the morning, unless you have another way to get to work. Keep Murphy's Law in mind: If anything can go wrong, it will, at the worst possible time.

Lay out your clothing and supplies the night before for the same reasons. Cycle commuting should be fun, and it's no fun to have to rush to get to work.

Don't skip breakfast. You might be able to get away without eating if you ride to work by bus or car, but it's not as easy when you have to propel yourself. Anyway, nutritionists regard breakfast as the most important meal of the day, and studies have shown that the healthiest and longest-living people are those who eat breakfast.

Avoid milk and cheese. They take too long to digest, and will just lie in your stomach and bog you down. Grain products, such as bread, cereal, pancakes, English muffins and granola bars, are digested quickly and give instant energy. Some can be eaten en route. Fruit and juices are good, too. The important thing is that you eat something to give you the energy you need to reach your destination. Coffee, even with gobs of sugar, is not enough.

Carrying Gear

There are two schools of thought regarding what to wear for cycle commuting if you have to dress formally at your destination. One group of cycle commuters chooses to wear what they work in. If your route isn't grueling or dirty, this makes sense. You can even wear a suit while cycling as long as the weather is cool enough. If it's warmer, you can wear just your shirt, and carry your coat and vest. Always wear trouser clips so that your right pant leg won't get tangled up with the chain.

But if the route is strenuous or dirty, the weather bad or if you are riding to the store or classroom, it's more practical to ride in cycling or casual clothes or a warm-up suit.

If you decide against riding in your work clothes, you're faced with the problem of getting your clothes to the office. Ray Muia drives his car to work once a week with his work clothes. He stores his clothes at his desk and changes into them after he cycles to work each morning.

The alternative is to carry fresh clothes with you every day. This requires planning on a day-to-day basis, and is not practical for suits and other expensive clothing. But if there is no other place to stow your clothes at work, this may be your only solution.

If your office doesn't have a place for you to store your clothes or clean up, you may want to check with the local YMCA or YWCA or college gym. A good shower can work wonders after a long or hard ride, and gives you a chance to untangle matted hair and clean off road grit.

If you don't have to cycle far, or like to ride leisurely, a shower won't be necessary. You can still cover ground quickly by traveling right below the sweating point, and that point moves higher as the temperature drops.

George A. Sheehan, M.D., "the runner's doctor," writes in *Dr. Sheehan on Running* that the athlete's sweat—

> . . .needs no deodorant. Honest sweat has no odor. The sweat that comes with effort and exertion, with running hills and bases and slants off-tackle is a dilute salt solution of mint purity. . . .There is, therefore, no reason to worry about honest sweat covering your body or saturating your clothes. . . .
>
> Showers are time-consuming and can lead to a chill and all the complications thereof. Showers are also unnecessary to rinse a dilute, odorless salt solution off your body.

Dr. Sheehan goes on to point out that there is another type of sweat which comes from an entirely different set of glands and is triggered by crisis. This is the sweat that has an odor. Dr. Sheehan says that one way to contend with this sweat "is to get rid of the trigger mechanisms of fear and anxiety and apprehension. And one of the better ways to do this is to work up an honest sweat. The ensuing relaxation and feeling of being in touch with yourself can bring you safely through confrontations that would ordinarily set the aprocrine glands into action."

Even if you do work up a sweat while cycling, then, the only real problem will be drying off. You can easily carry or store a towel, or even use paper towels in the office or school washroom.

Being wet becomes more of a problem if it is the result of being caught in an unexpected storm. If you're caught on the way home or the storm starts before you leave for home, you can grin and bear it (assuming you're not wearing a $350 wool suit) or find another way home. But being caught on the way to work is another matter. If there's a chance of rain, it's best to carry your good clothes in a waterproof bag and wear your rain gear. If worse comes to worse, stop somewhere and call a cab.

Even if you don't intend to carry clothes or a towel with you on your bike, there will still be things you'll occasionally need to carry: briefcase, reports, newspaper, items you've picked up in town, even your bike tools.

The simplest way to carry these things is in a saddlebag. Saddlebags come in a wide range of sizes: from small enough for a spare tube and tire tools to large enough to live out of for a week. They attach to clips under your saddle or, if there are no clips, to the two rails of the saddle.

Saddlebags are readily available and inexpensive (although the largest models can cost $50 or more), but have shortcomings. They flop around, banging into the backs of your legs (even those with antisway straps that attach to the seatpost). This isn't much of a problem, but some bags have a tendency of working themselves loose, which is a problem. Coming home from the grocery with a new saddlebag loaded with food one time, I suddenly felt like I couldn't move my bike another inch. I looked behind me and noticed that my bag had worked loose and dropped onto the rear tire. The friction had fretted a two-inch hole in the bag.

A backpack solves this problem, but has others. Instead of letting your bike carry the extra weight, a backpack makes you take the extra strain. If you keep the load light and the ride short, this is no problem. But if you overload the backpack, you're asking for pain. I used a backpack for about a year and found it worked well, but when I loaded it with more than five or ten pounds, it swung from side to side as I rode, chafing my back.

The best all-around choice is a sizable handlebar bag. These bags mount securely and hold as much as large backpacks or saddlebags. Most models have pockets to hold your keys, lock, toll fares and other necessities within reach. Many accept shoulder straps so that you can take the bag with you. The more expensive models also have clear, waterproof map pockets on top, so you can follow your map as you ride.

The map pocket also makes these bags handy for touring. In fact, most touring cyclists buy a handlebar bag before any other touring baggage. In addition to its convenience, it puts weight over the front wheel, adding stability. A handle-bar bag is not only great for cycling, but can come in handy as a camera bag and for a dozen other uses.

Cannondale, Eclipse, Kirtland and Touring Cyclist have been making well-designed handlebar bags for years. All but Touring Cyclist offer a range of bags with different features and capacities. Look for the models with an external steel frame, for support, and an internal metal or plastic stiffener, for stability.

If you have to carry large items, such as a briefcase, your best bet is to buy a rear rack. An inexpensive Pletscher rack and a couple of shock cords will hold your bag or packages in place. If you are considering cycle touring in the future, look into a stronger, more expensive triangular rack.

To keep your clothes from becoming wrinkled, roll them rather than fold them. And to keep them dry, put them in plastic bags before you pack them in the carrying bags.

Parking a Bike

All handlebar and saddlebags can be slipped on and off your bike in seconds, an advantage when it's time to park. But unless you're going to keep your bike next to your desk, you'll want to remove your bags, pump and quick-release front wheel before someone else has the chance to.

If you can get permission to park your bike in your office, by all means do so. It may look strange to others, but you'll be sure it will be there in one piece when you leave for the day.

If you work in cramped quarters, you may be able to find a place somewhere else in your building to store your bike. A basement, supply room or little-used conference room may be ideal. Unless you have the only key to the area, though, lock your bike securely.

More schools and offices are installing outdoor bike racks and lockers. The lockers fully enclose your bike and can be opened only with a key. Racks, however, are far less secure, even if you lock your bike and take the front wheel with you. I've seen bikes that have been stripped while locked to outdoor racks, and have even seen frames cut in two, with just the chained half still attached to the rack. If you have to park your bike at a rack, pick one that is well watched. Some parking garages, for example, have bike racks directly across from the tollbooths, where an attendant is always on duty.

In some areas, there are no bike parking facilities. Depending on the part of town, time of day and amount of traffic, parking your bike on the street can be either safe or a guarantee of theft. Only you can decide how risky an area is and how much of a chance you care to take. If you have to park in an unsafe area, it may be worth your while to scrounge around for an ugly, black battered bike to commute on.

If you do have to park outside, and there are no racks or lockers, find a solid post to lock your bike to. A parking meter is good, but I've seen a street sign cut down so that a thief could steal a bicycle that had been attached. Make sure there's no way to remove the chain or lock over top of the post. I once locked my bike to a parking meter and headed for a nearby store. As I left my bike, I saw a group of young men eyeing it. When I looked back, I noticed that the head of the parking meter was missing. All those fellows would have had to do was slide the lock over the top and the bike would have been theirs.

Good locks are, unfortunately, expensive—but not nearly as expensive as replacing a good bike. The least expensive types worth owning are chain locks. The thicker the links, the better. Look for case-hardened links (outside is treated to be hard, but inside isn't, so the chain isn't brittle) and pickproof locks. The flimsy combination locks with chains that sell for $10 or less can be broken through in seconds.

The only locks I trust, are the U-shape models made by Citadel and Kryptonite. These cost nearly $30, but are almost impossible to break. The manufacturers have such faith in these locks that they offer to pay if your bike is stolen while locked with one of their products.

Whatever lock you use, make sure you put it through the frame and the rear wheel when you lock your bike. To make it harder for thieves, take up any slack in the chains and keep

When locking your bike, make sure the lock goes through the frame and rear wheel, as high off the ground as possible. Take up all the slack you can. If you have a quick-release front wheel, remove it and secure it with the rear one, or take it with you.

all locks high off the ground so that a thief cannot get good leverage. If you cannot take your front wheel with you, run the chain through it, or remove and lock it up with the rear wheel and frame. I think that taking the wheel with you is the best deterrent: a bike with one wheel isn't as attractive to a thief as one with two wheels, and he surely cannot make his getaway on it.

If you have to park your bike outside on a regular basis, it's a good idea to make sure that your homeowner's or renter's insurance will pay for theft, and find out how the company expects you to prove theft. Some companies have low cutoff limits for "sporting goods" coverage. For instance, one company limits coverage of bike theft to a few hundred dollars, even if your bike is stolen from your home. While this is not a problem for most cyclists, I know many riders, especially racers, who own bikes that cost more than $1,000 each, or have three or four $200 bikes in one household.

Remember, too, that standard deductibles apply and most companies figure in depreciation—while most bikes actually grow in value every year. If you live or work in a high-crime area, check into supplemental insurance coverage as outlined in Chapter Nine.

Once all the details are taken care of, you can get down to riding. You'll inevitably draw the stares and snickers of your co-workers and neighbors, but eventually those people will probably be telling you how much they'd like to commute by bike. Ray Muia has practical advice for them: "Go ahead." Maybe you'll even be able to talk some of them into joining you on your rides.

CHAPTER TWELVE
CLUB
RIDES

Despite all the benefits and pleasures of cycle commuting, many find other forms of transportation more appealing for covering the long distances or dangerous roads that link them to offices, classrooms and shopping malls. Riding shoulder-to-shoulder with speeding rush-hour traffic is not every cyclist's idea of enjoyment, and enjoyment is, after all, what cycling is all about.

It's hard to find anyone, though, who does not enjoy riding with a cycling club. Club rides provide countless opportunities to meet people and explore new places away from the hustle and bustle of major highways. And they give you motivation to become a better cyclist, riding more often and longer.

Nancy Rosenberger, mentioned earlier, is a perfect example of an enthusiastic club cyclist. Nancy has cycled since she was a child, and never lost touch with the sport. Even after she was married, Nancy would often ride through Youngstown, Ohio's Mill Creek Park after a hard day at the office or at home. On warm weekend days, she needed little prodding to jump on her bike.

Nancy was never a distance rider, and didn't care to ride fast. Instead, she enjoyed relaxing while gently cruising through the park.

After Nancy divorced in her mid-twenties, she began to cycle more often, savoring the time cycling gave her to relax and collect her thoughts. At the same time, Nancy realized that she had fallen out of touch with many of her friends, and was hoping to meet new people and make new friends.

One afternoon in the park, Nancy met another cyclist who told her about a cycling club that had just started in the area. Nancy wasn't sure that she was a good-enough cyclist to join a club, but figured that joining would help her meet other cyclists and make friends.

Nancy went to the club's next meeting.

"I didn't know anyone there," she recalled, "and I didn't know how serious they were about cycling. But people came up to me and introduced themselves, asked questions, told me about their biking. They were all very friendly, and they gave me a super welcome. I joined that night.

"What appealed to me most was the way they acted. They didn't brag about how far or how fast they had ridden, but instead said, 'Pick your own pace and ride with us and enjoy it. We'll make a place for you to enjoy yourself.'"

Nancy went on to discover the joys of club cycling, riding her first 100-mile ride that summer, something she had never even thought of before.

Nancy's story is a common one. Club rides are probably the most important step between being an occasional rider and becoming a serious cyclist. Cycling clubs can open new doorways for you and can help you discover a whole new world of cycling.

As Nancy pointed out, it is people that make a club. I've met hundreds of club cyclists from across the country and they have all been great. Most club cyclists are warm, friendly people, ready to swap stories on a moment's notice and just as ready to help another cyclist in need. Without trying to be, these people are the sport's best evangelists: it's obvious that there's nothing they enjoy as much as cycling.

Club rides give you an excellent opportunity to improve your cycling skills and learn the easy way of doing things. Even if you don't ask a single question, you'll learn just by watching more skillful cyclists. And many club members will offer advice to help you along.

"That was one of the biggest advantages of riding with a club," Nancy said. "I learned all about safety, fitness and all kinds of things from others' experiences. On the rides they'd offer suggestions, but they didn't make me feel like a dummy."

John Forester, author of *Effective Cycling,* estimates that it takes about 10 to 20 years for a cyclist to learn safe cycling on his own, but less than 2 years with a club.

On just my first club ride, I learned about cadence, pacing and drinking enough replacement fluids for a long ride, and learned how to patch a flat better than I could before. And that's not counting the dozens of smaller hints I picked up on bike and gearing selection, clothing and a host of other topics.

But there's more to club cycling than good company and instruction. Even riding with our friends, most of us fall into a rut, riding the same routes over and over. Club rides span a wide area, and range in length from 5 to more than 100 miles. Many clubs also hold weekend outings once or twice a year, where members get together at a site away from the club's home base. The club I belong to meets every Father's Day weekend at one of three locations about 50 miles from the home base. In the fall, the club holds a cycle camping weekend, complete with cabins, cookouts and rides to see the changing leaves. Another club I once belonged to held rides in other towns in conjunction with cycle clubs there, providing a good way to meet new people while exploring a new town.

There's even more to joining a club. Most clubs hold monthly meetings that are part social, part informative. Besides giving members a chance to talk, club meetings are a convenient place to announce upcoming rides, handle club business and suggest changes. Many clubs also have guest speakers or show films on topics ranging from traffic safety to riding techniques to foot care. And members are always busy comparing notes on new routes they've ridden and equipment they've tried.

"It doesn't matter what kind of bike or equipment you have in my club," Nancy said. "But if you were looking to replace something, they'd say, 'Try this' or 'Try that.' You can get gobs of information from the club members' experience and knowledge."

More and more clubs are also planning noncycling activities. Nancy's club, the Out-Spokin' Wheelmen (OSW), is a classic example. OSW sponsors hayrides, Halloween parties and benefits to aid the handicapped. In the winter the club holds cross-country ski outings so that members can stay in shape and in touch throughout the year.

Despite all these incentives, few people join cycling clubs. There are all the usual reasons: not enough time, can't afford dues, and many others. But Ray Muia, past president of a large cycling club for three years, thinks that the biggest barrier is fear.

Ray and many other cyclists believe that novices think cycling clubs are just for superhumans with expensive equipment. But that's far from the truth. Clubs are constantly looking for new members to replace those who have moved or lost interest, as well as to enliven the club. The club Ray presided over has members from less than 1 year old (she rides in a trailer behind her parents) to more than 60 years old, and the club tries to plan rides for every member's tastes and abilities.

"People have to realize that no one's going to make fun of them or their bikes," Ray said. "All of us were beginners once."

Another barrier, Ray believes, is that most cyclists don't know how much potential they have.

"My wife and I lead a 20-mile ride for novice riders every Wednesday night," he said, "and people never believe they can do it until they try. Then they set even higher goals."

Even if you're a slow rider, you'll still be welcome. Nancy found that out on her first club ride.

"The ride was 25 miles, and I didn't know if I was ready for 25 miles. It was my first ride of the year, but no one else had been riding, either. Even though I was slower than the other riders, someone always stayed with me. Then I did the same when there was someone new who was a little slower."

It won't cost you anything to decide whether you like riding with a club. Newcomers are always welcome to try a club ride or two before joining, and they're just as welcome at the club's meetings.

And it doesn't cost much if you join. Yearly membership dues are usually less than ten dollars a person, with special family, student and senior citizen rates. One club I once belonged to charged a whopping two dollars a year for individuals, three dollars for families. And the membership dues are all you have to pay, unless you want commemorative ride patches or accommodations at out-of-town rides.

Finding a Club

The best way to find a club in your area is by visiting or calling a local bike shop. Clubs often leave application forms there, or the shop workers may know where you can reach the club. Most clubs are geared to recreational riders, but some are for racers only. Make sure you don't show up for a racing club's training ride if you're looking for a short, easy jaunt in the country.

If you live in a large city, or close to two or three large cities, you may have a choice of clubs. Unless one is more convenient than the others, try to check into them all. You may find one more suited to your tastes: it may offer more outside activities, or longer rides, or more family outings, whatever you find most appealing.

Most clubs will send you a complimentary copy of their monthly newsletter, listing rides for the month, including descriptions of terrain and food stops, and directions to the starting point. Pick a ride that looks good, and plan to be there about a half hour before the ride starts so that you can introduce yourself and find out a little about the club and its members, as well as about the ride.

Even though club members won't mind waiting for a slower newcomer, no one is going to be ecstatic if you burn out in the middle of the ride and have to be transported back to the starting point. If you have ridden only 5- or 10-mile rides, don't try a 100-mile ride on your first club outing. Pick something reasonable, maybe just slightly longer than you've already ridden.

Make sure you can handle the terrain, too. A 15-mile ride through the mountains may be far more difficult than the 25-mile rides you've taken on level ground. Typically, though, shorter club rides cover the easiest terrain, and longer ones are run over more difficult ground.

Be prepared for the weather, too. Most club rides are run rain or shine, so bring a rain jacket if there is a chance of storm or drizzle. If the ride starts on a cool spring or autumn morning, you should carry a saddlebag or handlebar bag to stow your extra clothes in as the day becomes warmer.

Even though you'll be riding with as many as a dozen or more other cyclists, never assume someone else will have the tools you need to fix a flat. Take your own patch kit, tire tools, spare tube and pump. You may become separated from the group, or may be riding behind the group with just one other cyclist who doesn't have those things. A friend of mine was separated from the rest of the group on a club ride, and his rear tire punctured. He didn't have a pump or patch kit, and so had to wait a half hour before someone circled back looking for him. And then that rider had a patch kit, but his pump wouldn't fit my friend's tire valves.

Unless you have a string of unbelievably bad luck, you'll be spending far more of your time riding than repairing your bike. A few, simple club riding techniques will help you get a lot more from your rides.

Riding in a Group

Riding with a group of cyclists is different from riding alone or riding with just one or two others in several important respects. First, when you ride in a group, it's especially vital that you don't move unexpectedly. If you jerk to miss a pothole, you may swing into another cyclist, causing him and everyone following to crash. Every rider has to work with every other one.

Charlie Pace, organizer of the country's largest weekend cycling outing, the Tour of the Sciota River Valley, once told me, "The greatest problem we have with the beginner cyclist or even the advanced one is his lack of group riding before he comes to TOSRV. Most cyclists just do not ride in packs, and then they attempt to participate in one and this sometimes results in sloppy cycling."

For this reason, it's not a good idea to go on a club ride until you have mastered the basics of bike handling. If you're still shaky, but want to ride with a club, have the courtesy to ride behind the others. Whatever you do, don't let yourself get in a situation where you feel like you are riding over your head.

Any time there are other riders behind you, it is your responsibility to let them know what is happening up front. Pay attention to how the other riders communicate to the cyclists in back. Some groups rely solely on hand signals to indicate stops (left arm out, palm facing flat forward); potholes (hand pointing down on appropriate side); need to slow down (moving palm up and down parallel to the ground); and right and left turns.

Other groups are more vocal, and will call out signals: "Holes right"; "Stop ahead"; "Slow!" When you pass another rider, you should let him know by announcing, "Passing on your right (or left)." If you are in the back of a group and see or hear a car or truck coming up from behind, yell "Car back" so the riders ahead know to move as far to the right as they can.

Riding with a group of riders also lets you draft. Drafting is the technique of sitting directly in another rider's wind shadow to let him break the wind for you. At speeds above ten mph, most of your energy is used to overcome wind resistance. So sitting close behind another rider makes cycling 15 to 20 percent easier than riding alone.

To draft, you have to stay close to the rider ahead of you. If your front wheel is more than six inches behind his rear wheel, you will not get the full benefits of drafting. Racers overlap wheels.

Drafting is not something for a rank novice to try. It takes skill and concentration to ride steadily just inches behind another rider. If your attention drifts for a second and the fellow ahead slows, your wheels will touch. He may not even notice, but you are bound to crash, possibly bringing down everyone behind you, too.

NEVER draft another rider without getting his permission. Just asking, "Mind if I sit in?" alerts him that you are inches behind, and lets him decide whether he wants the responsibility of riding so that he does not endanger you. If you don't ask permission, you're asking for trouble.

Even if he approves and you're confident in your abilities, drafting is not always the best way to go. Watching another cyclist's rear wheel—and peering over his shoulder to survey the road ahead—is not the best way to take in the scenery. Drafting can turn a ride through lush valleys and hills into a boring stretch of asphalt. But if you want to ride fast or need protection from a harrowing wind, drafting is a godsend.

Most of the time, sitting directly behind the rider ahead will give you a big advantage. But when the wind is coming in from the side, you want to move over to the side of the rider opposite the direction from which the wind is blowing. If the wind is howling from your left, you want to sit slightly to the right of the cyclist in front of you. The cyclist behind you will move slightly to your right, and so on down the line. This line of riders is called an echelon, and looks like this:

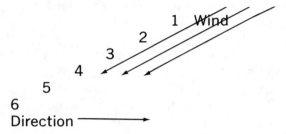

The amount of offset between each rider depends on how much room you have on the road. If you're riding on a little-used country road, your echelon might stretch across the entire lane. On a busy, high-speed interstate, though, you may not even be able to form an echelon. There, it may be best to ride single file, spaced far enough apart so that over-taking cars can pass one rider at a time.

Obviously, one person cannot stay at the front of an echelon and break the wind all day. So, in a highly organized group, the lead rider will drop back from the front when he becomes tired, and the next rider takes the lead for a while. When your turn comes, take over for as long as you can hold the pace without exhausting yourself. If you feel you cannot take the lead, just drop back with the leader when you are next in line. In the beginning, there will be many times when you'll just want to sit in for the whole ride. Go right ahead. If anyone asks you why you aren't taking the front, just explain that you're a newcomer and cannot hold the pace yet. They'll understand: they were new once, too. And sometimes even veteran riders and racers just feel like sitting in all day.

The chances are that on most club rides you'll take, the group will not be nearly as organized. Riders will clump to-gether in groups of two, three, five or more, riding two abreast wherever traffic permits. Most club cyclists don't care how fast they cover a distance; they ride to talk with other cyclists and to enjoy the scenery.

If the club bug bites you hard, it won't take long until

you'll start looking for new roads to explore, new people to meet and new challenges to conquer. Most club newsletters carry synopses of rides in other states that may interest their readers, and often a club member will help arrange car pools to the rides. By sharing gas and accommodations, you can explore a new area inexpensively: even with the entrance fee most invitational rides require, the whole weekend may not cost more than $10 or $20. You can explore someplace new every weekend.

The League of American Wheelmen's monthly bulletin, *American Wheelmen,* lists upcoming rides across the country. The listings usually give the length of the ride or rides planned (often, the agenda will include 25-, 50- and 100-mile rides on the same day for cyclists of varying skills), entrance fee, ride location, accommodations, and address and phone number for applications and further information. Some listings also include a capsule appraisal of the route ("moderately difficult," or "for strong cyclists with low gears," for example) and whether there are planned food stops. A subscription to the bulletin is included with membership in the League of American Wheelmen. Details are available from LAW, PO Box 988, Baltimore, MD 21203.

Most club rides last just one day, but some clubs offer weekend packages. Be careful in choosing the latter type. On some, you stay at one location, riding from there and back both days. If you overdo it the first day, you don't have to ride the second. But other rides, such as the Tour of the Sciota River Valley, require you to ride from one point to another the first day, then back the second. Even if you're exhausted the second day, you have to get back to the starting point, which may be more than 100 miles away. Fortunately, most of the bigger rides include sag wagons, cars or vans that carry cyclists' overnight gear and can shuttle riders who have been injured or whose bikes have been wrecked. But they have little sympathy for those who simply drop from exhaustion. You may have to take a bus back to the starting point if you're merely tired.

One of the few things that is as much fun as riding a club ride is leading one. If you have a favorite route that you think other cyclists would enjoy riding, talk to the club president to

find out how you can set up a ride. The Tour of the Sciota
River Valley, which now attracts about 4,000 riders a year,
was originally just a two-person trip.

Despite the growing popularity of TOSRV and club cycling in general, you may not find a cycling club in your area.
Many clubs have been forced to fold recently because of
dwindling membership. If there are no clubs where you live,
start your own. Photocopied announcements of meetings
and rides placed at local bike shops and universities should
generate interest, then you can decide what type of club
those responding are most interested in.

The *American Wheelmen* bulletin offers a wealth of suggestions for cycling clubs, and you could probably convince
the editors to run a query letter seeking information from
successful clubs on how they started.

If that sounds like too ambitious an undertaking, and
there are no clubs where you live, you owe it to yourself to at
least ride an out-of-town club's invitational ride. You'll meet
some of the friendliest people you'll ever know during the
hours you spend cycling there, and gain valuable knowledge
that will help you become an even better cyclist. And to help
you get started, many of the top club invitationals throughout the nation are listed in Appendix A.

CHAPTER THIRTEEN
LONGER RIDES

There comes a time when virtually every cyclist decides he must undertake a challenge. The challenge is usually to ride longer or faster than he has ridden before, as a test of his conditioning and, possibly, a stepping stone to the next higher performance level.

Most of the time, the challenge is to ride farther than ever before: to reach a town by noon or sunset, to cover 100 miles in one day. These goals, as lofty as they seem to beginners, are not difficult to meet. In fact, it's much easier to ride farther on your bike than it is to ride faster.

Still, there are steps you can take to make your first long rides as effortless as possible; steps that may make the difference between hours of pleasure and hours of pain.

The most vital step is proper training. To most, training conjures up images of long, boring and brutal hours of work. But that's hardly the truth. Every ride you take is a training ride. If you're just starting to ride but want to ride a 50-mile ride before the end of the year, you can easily work your way up by increasing the distance you ride every time you go out. Work on a 5-mile ride at first, then build up to a 10-mile ride. Next, shoot for 15 and work your way up until you reach your goal. If one of the rides along the way is particularly grueling, ride the same distance the next time out, rather than riding farther.

Nancy Rosenberger used this system to work her way up to her first century ride, 100 miles in one day. In June, she took a 25-mile ride. Two months later, after riding 25- and 30-milers to stay in shape, she pedaled her way through 60 miles. The next month, with more miles under her belt, Nancy was riding 110 miles.

"I felt great afterwards," she said. "My legs were a little sore, and the next day I was a little stiff, but I was ecstatic. I just couldn't believe that I had ridden 100 miles."

Charlie Pace, of TOSRV, recommends this training method for any long ride, but especially for centuries. "Condition yourself so you can enjoy the ride," he recommends, "and not suffer trying to make it. Each year we have a number of folks who attempt TOSRV when they have ridden a maximum of only 25 to 30 miles on any one day prior to the event. Then about 50 miles out they cramp up and have a difficult time of it."

But not everyone has the time to train this way—or even wants to ride that much in training—especially for rides such as the TOSRV, which fall early in the year. Fortunately, there is a way to train in less time—but you pay by working harder in training.

Let's say you want to prepare for a century but don't have much time. Instead of going out and slowly spinning your way through 25-, 50- and 75-mile training rides, you can train by riding much shorter, but faster rides.

One way to do this is by riding hard, fast 15-mile training rides. Then, when you ride your century, ride easier and rest and eat after every 10-mile segment. If you don't want to stop nine times during the ride, train hard and fast for 30 to 35 miles at a time. Then you can stop after every 25 miles, which is usually where the food stops are, and take only three breaks.

Remember, you have to give it everything you have on those training rides. If you just go out and meander, taking six or seven hours to ride the 30 miles, you'll never finish the century. And even if you do ride hard and fast in training, it's still a good idea to take at least one slower ride over a half to three-quarters of the distance to build your endurance.

All the training in the world will be useless unless you pace yourself properly. You want to pick a pace that you can hold all day, not one in which you leave the starting line in a burst of power only to collapse halfway through the ride. Riding at the proper pace keeps you from straining your muscles, and keeps the demands on your system consistent throughout the ride. The right pace will feel too easy in the morning when you are fresh, but should be just right when you're dragging 25, 50 or 100 miles down the road. If you pick too slow a pace, you can burn off your reserves in the last leg of the ride.

If you pick too fast a pace, though, you're going to have trouble. My cycling buddy Bob Snyder committed this classic mistake on his first century ride. We started out together with two friends, and Bob reaffirmed his vow to take it easy in the beginning. He kept that vow for about two miles, when a pair of racers flew past us. Bob took off after them.

Near the 25-mile mark, I saw Bob again. He was about a ¼ mile ahead, pounding down the road. I learned later that the only reason I caught sight of him was that he had lost time by making a wrong turn and backtracking 5 miles.

Bob was so engrossed in keeping up with his partners that just as he missed the turn marker earlier, he never saw the sign pointing out the first food and rest stop at the 27-mile point. I stopped there, stretched, ate fruit and cookies, talked to other riders and finally hit the road again.

Twenty-eight miles up the road, as I pulled into the lunch stop, I saw Bob leaning against a tree.

"I've been waiting long enough for you guys!" he said.

I told him that I couldn't hold the pace he'd been riding (and I knew he couldn't keep it up much longer, either). He said he was ready to go again with his newfound friends, but decided instead to wait for Brian, Mark and me, with whom he had started.

Pulling out of the lunch stop, Bob cranked hard, setting a rapid pace. The rest of us fell in behind him.

But about 3 miles up the road, Bob dropped off the front and pulled in behind me at the back of our four-man group. He looked terrible. He began yelling for us to hold down the pace, but Mark and Brian, apparently oblivious to his shouts, kept up the pace he had set, burning off the reserves they'd saved by riding at an easier pace earlier. Bob quieted down, and when I next looked back about ½ mile up the road, he was nowhere in sight.

Brian, Mark and I waited nearly a half hour at the third food stop for Bob. Finally he came slowly rolling in.

"I died back there! I had to take a nap in a cornfield," he said as he headed for the tables of fruit and cookies.

"I rode that first 50 miles too fast, and I haven't eaten anything all day. I never knew you had to eat on a ride like this."

A half hour of eating and drinking revitalized Bob, and we all rode the final 25 miles together. Bob's final time for the ride was an impressive 7½ hours, including all breaks and his nap. But his ride pointed out the need to keep a steady, conservative pace, as well as to eat and drink while riding.

Drinking fluids is vital for any ride longer than 10 or 15 miles, and even for shorter rides in hot weather. Water is a favorite, and can be poured over your head as well as drunk. But by mixing a powdered electrolyte-replacement drink with your water, you can also replenish vital minerals that you lose in your sweat. Most of these drinks are, however, too sweet and thick if mixed according to package directions; it's better to use double the water suggested.

Many European racers drink tea with honey or sugar, but the double boost of caffeine and sugar can backfire and leave you feeling like you've hit a wall. Warm tea is tempting, though, on cold mornings.

Don't drink carbonated drinks. Your stomach will become gassy and you'll feel terrible. And be careful with fruit juices: you may be courting diarrhea. Your drinks should be cool. Cool drinks leave your stomach quickly.

You should drink before you become thirsty. By the time thirst strikes, it's too late to bring your fluid level back to normal. Sip constantly as you ride, draining about one 16-ounce bottle every hour. Drinking a little at a time will keep your stomach from becoming full and sloshing.

For rides under 40 miles, you don't have to eat, unless the ride includes a lunch stop. But for longer rides, you should replenish your energy stores as you ride. As Bob's ordeal showed, by the time hunger strikes, it is too late. By then, you'll be too depleted to carry on.

Whatever you eat should be easily digestible and high in carbohydrates. Good choices are fresh and dried fruit, honey, peanut butter (with or without jelly) sandwiches on whole wheat bread, shredded wheat, nuts and rice pudding. Many cyclists like candy and cookies, which provide a quick burst of energy. They raise your blood sugar, but your body responds by producing insulin. The insulin, in turn, causes your blood sugar level to drop rapidly so that you end up feeling worse than when you began. Such foods also contain few nutrients to replace those you're burning off, and steal nutrients from other foods just to be digested.

The best way, of course, to learn what's best for you to

eat and drink, and what pace is most efficient is by riding often, and experimenting each time you ride. When you find a winning formula, stick with it.

As your skill improves, you may eventually want to try what many cyclists consider to be the ultimate: a century. A century is to cyclists what a marathon is to runners, but much more.

Unlike a marathon, a century is not just a test of speed or strength. You can ride a century to see how fast you can cover 100 miles, but then you're missing most of the point of riding it: to see new scenery, spark new friendships, share the joy of cycling with your family and friends. An entire family can ride a century together, or at least meet at the rest stops and finish line, savoring a day in the sunshine away from home.

The fact that anyone can ride a century does not mean that it is not a test of sorts: riding a century shows commitment, skill and perseverance that most cyclists and non-cyclists never will know.

The most important thing you need to ride a century is determination. For that determination, you get a day filled with some of the most memorable moments of your life and, usually, a commemorative patch to mark your accomplishment.

While you do have to meet a time requirement to qualify for some century patches (usually finishing the 100 miles in 9 to 12 hours), there is nothing strenuous about riding a century. In fact, the growing elite of touring and recreational cyclists are finding centuries so easy that they're riding double, triple and even quadruple centuries. They realize that cycling any of these super-rides entitles you to more than just memories and a patch: at the end, you can stand proud and look back at the miles you covered all by yourself.

PART IV
GETTING BETTER

CHAPTER FOURTEEN
CLOTHING

As you ride longer distances, little things will become more important to you, things such as the clothes you wear.

For short, leisurely rides, you can wear almost anything. But when you start pedaling 50 to 100 miles at a time, minor irritations that usually slip by unnoticed can become extremely obvious—and painful.

I learned my lesson during my first 50-mile ride. As we crawled up mountains for six hours, the temperature was well into the 90s, and the humidity level was not far behind.

By the middle of the ride, I was a mess. My T-shirt was soaked with sweat, my legs were chafed from rubbing against the saddle, and my feet and hands were numb.

I noticed that other cyclists, particularly the ones in the long, bright jerseys and the funny-looking black shorts, didn't seem to be having these problems. I knew that most of them were in better shape than I was, but felt there still had to be more to it.

Not many years later, I am addicted to riding in proper cycling clothing. Proper clothing is one of those things that you cannot understand the importance and comfort of until you try it. Then you won't want to be without it.

Good cycle clothing serves a multitude of functions. The most important one is to regulate your body temperature. When it's warm, your clothing should wick your sweat away from you to keep you dry and allow your natural cooling system to work efficiently. When the temperature drops, your clothing should hold a layer of radiated warm air next to your body, protecting it from passing outside air and rain that could chill it.

Proper clothing also keeps you from putting excessive pressure on the points that touch the bike: your feet, hands and crotch. By using proper padding and supports, cycle clothing keeps you from compressing the nerves in these areas, which causes numbness.

Cycle clothing is also cut long to keep your lower back covered as you lean forward and keep your thighs from rubbing on the saddle as you pedal.

And cycle clothing helps protect you in a crash.

Despite these benefits, most cyclists do not ride in proper clothing and consequently suffer needlessly on long rides. Even those who don't hesitate to spend $600 on a custom bike or $50 for a drilled-out titanium water bottle that will lower the bike's weight by 1.7 grams, usually ride in tattered cutoffs and sneakers.

Yet the proper clothes will make far more of a difference in your cycling enjoyment than will making any other changes or additions to your bike. Street clothes just are not suitable for riding long distances on a bike.

The Proper Shoes

Nowhere is this clearer than with shoes. Most cyclists ride in sneakers, running shoes or other soft-soled shoes. These are, unfortunately, the worst type of shoe for cycling. Most are cut too wide to slip easily in and out of toe straps; in fact, just removing and inserting your feet in the clips can quickly chew up a pair of running shoes.

The soles of the shoes can quickly become ruined, too, because you have to press down harder on the soft soles to transmit your force to the pedals. This ruins your shoes and wastes your energy.

Shoes that may be OK for walking a block or two may not be so comfortable after a few thousand pedal strokes. If your shoes are too loose or too tight, the constant pedaling movements can cause painful blisters. And a tight fit can make your feet sweaty, perfect for breeding athlete's foot fungi.

Street or running shoes also let your feet move around on the pedals, throwing your legs out of line. This not only wastes your energy by making your muscles work improperly, but can cause serious knee and ligament injuries.

Cycling shoes are designed to prevent these problems. They are cut narrower than running shoes, so they hug your feet and slide easily in and out of the clips. Most cycling shoes are ventilated to let your sweat escape. Better cycling shoes also have thin, reinforced rigid soles to keep your feet from flexing while transmitting all your energy. And most models have grooved soles or accept slotted cleats to hold your feet correctly in line on the pedals. As a bonus, cycle racing shoes weigh less than other shoes. Since your shoes rotate, the lighter they are, the less work you have to do.

Virtually all cycling shoes are of the traditional racing

design: light, stiff, ventilated black leather models with steel stiffeners in the soles. These shoes cost from $15–$60, and vary greatly in width, stiffness and leather quality.

If possible, you should try on cycling shoes before you buy them, wearing the socks you'll wear cycling. Initially, the shoes should fit snugly; the leather will soon stretch. Make sure the shoes are wide enough for your feet, though: many European brands are infamous for their narrow cut that does not fit American feet well.

If you plan to race or go on long recreational rides or tours where you won't be walking much, this type of shoe is probably your best choice. A pair that fits you properly will be so comfortable that you won't realize you have shoes on.

For best performance and care of your legs, your cycling shoes should have cleats. Not only do properly mounted cleats hold your feet in line so that you ride efficiently and avoid painful injuries, but they also let you apply power evenly throughout the entire pedal revolution and keep your feet from slipping off the pedals under stress. Until I began wearing cleated shoes, my feet would often slip off the pedals as I shifted into a higher, faster gear. Sometimes I banged my shins on the crankarms or seat tube, and nearly always I lost so much momentum that I had to shift down.

I once read a terrible book on cycling, probably the worst ever written. In it, the author warns cyclists not to ride with toe clips and straps because you may not be able to free your feet in emergencies.

But you can always pull free of even the tightest strap, even if you're wearing cleats. Still, it's a good idea to take your first few rides away from traffic, in case you do have problems adjusting. After a few attempts, you'll have mastered the escape process.

The most expensive cycling shoes include premounted cleats. These are highly popular for two reasons: people are lazy and they believe that manufacturers should know more than cyclists about how to properly mount cleats.

In many cases, the premounted cleats can be set up to position your feet properly. But, far too often, the range of adjustment is not wide enough, so you have to compromise.

And many premounted cleats cannot be tightened securely enough to keep them from slipping while you're riding.

Mounting your own cleats overcomes this problem: you find the correct spot and nail the little buggers on securely. But finding that correct spot can be difficult, especially if you follow conventional cycling wisdom.

The traditional way to mount your cleats is to first ride about 50 miles in your new shoes without cleats. Then line up the cleats with the marks the pedals made on your soles. The problem with this method seems obvious, but generations of "expert" cyclists managed to overlook it: if you cycle with your feet placed incorrectly, then your cleats will be mounted in the wrong spots.

After years of riding with cleats, I still have not found a foolproof mounting procedure. The best I know is one suggested by Harlan Meyer of Hi-E Engineering, a small company specializing in top-grade bicycle components. Harlan's method is covered in Appendix B.

A new breed of cycling shoes developed during the late 1970s offers most of the advantages of cleated cycling shoes without requiring you to find the right spot for your cleats or lock your feet tightly to the pedals. These shoes are called touring shoes. They have stiff soles, usually reinforced with nylon or metal shanks, and molded with grooves that act as cleats to hold your feet straight on the pedals. (But again, as with premounted cleats, these grooves may not hold your feet exactly where they should be.) And they are attractive and comfortable for walking as well as cycling, whereas you can ruin the sole of a racing shoe by walking on it.

Shorts for the Sport

Another important point of contact with your bike is the spot where you hit the saddle. There is nothing like a comfortable saddle to help the miles fly by. But you can increase the comfort of even the best saddle by wearing good cycling shorts.

The biggest problem caused by wearing conventional

shorts and cutoffs is skin irritation. When you cycle in regular shorts and underwear, you usually end up sitting on a seam. After miles in the saddle, this becomes irritating. If you sweat, your shorts will also become soaked. This is not only uncomfortable, but can cause agonizing boils and abrasions.

Cycling shorts solve this problem with a chamois pad in the crotch area. The pad is seamless and wicks your sweat away from your body. On a hot or wet day the chamois will still become wet (the "clammy chamois" syndrome), but at least you won't slide around on seams.

Of course, you won't sweat only in the crotch area. So cycling shorts are usually made of wool or a blend of wool and polyester. Unlike wool shirts, these wools are soft and gentle to the skin. More importantly, wool is an amazing material: it slowly moves your perspiration away from the body to be absorbed by the outside air; can hold nearly a third of its weight in water without feeling damp; and is thermostatic, so it regulates your body temperature, shielding you from the hot outside air in summer, and cold outside air in winter.

Cycling shorts are cut to be more comfortable than other shorts, too. The best models have long legs to keep your thighs from chafing the saddle, and are cut low in the front to make breathing easy and high in the back to keep your lower back warm and covered as you lean forward. And they have either elastic or drawstring waists, which expand as you breathe.

Finally, good cycling shorts also have a reinforcing outer seat of nylon or polyester. While wool alone would soon wear out under the stress, these synthetic materials will last for years, and then can be replaced.

During the past few years, in an effort to solve these problems, some of the touring shorts on the market are no more than chamois-lined hiking shorts which are no good for cycling. But others combine comfortable stretch material with absorbing, quick-drying seat inserts for a near-perfect combination. All include plenty of pocket space, which racing shorts lack.

As comfortable as chamois-lined shorts are, they have two problems. The first is cost. As the prices of wool and chamois rise, so does the price of cycling shorts. Virtually all chamois-lined shorts now sell for more than $25. The few, less expensive models available use a thinner, less expensive chamois, which quickly loses its softness and can easily tear.

The other problem is that chamois retains moisture too well. By holding your perspiration, chamois becomes a perfect breeding ground for bacteria that can cause infection. You can prevent this by washing chamois-lined shorts after each wearing. Unfortunately, wool shorts must usually be hand-laundered and air-dried, and chamois takes two days to dry completely. Some manufacturers have partially solved the problem by using wool that is machine-washable and -dryable, but the heat of machine dryers removes the natural oils in chamois, making it harsh and tough. You can partially restore the pliability by rubbing the nap of the chamois against itself after it dries, or by rubbing cold cream or chamois fat (a combination of fish oil and vitamins A and D) into the dry chamois.

Shirts are far simpler. You can wear virtually any shirt for cycling in warm weather. Inexpensive cotton/polyester T-shirts work well. But for the utmost in comfort and design, you cannot beat a cycling jersey.

A Choice of Jerseys

Cycling jerseys are cut long and lean, to keep your lower back covered and to keep wind resistance down. They hug your body to wick away your sweat, and usually have a zipper at the neck for ventilation.

For cool-weather riding, wool is again the best material. In hot, humid climates, a cotton/polyester blend is the most comfortable, wicking your sweat away before it can soak you. Unfortunately, the vast majority of cycling jerseys are made of acrylic and polyester. Both have limited wicking ability so that you may end up feeling clammy instead of cool.

As with any kind of shirt, cycling jerseys are made in long- and short-sleeved models, and some companies offer wool T-shirts and turtlenecks, too. Most jerseys have two or three pockets sewn across the back to hold food, keys, tools and a wallet. These pockets keep your possessions handy, but out of the wind stream, where they would slow you down.

You should always wear a shirt that covers your shoulders while cycling, if only to protect them should you crash. For the same reason, you should also wear cycling gloves. It's natural to stick your arms out to try to break your fall in a crash, and that's a perfect way to skin your palms. Even a minor spill could scar you for life.

Cycling gloves also pad your palms so that you do not press down as hard on the handlebars. This prevents numbness and possible nerve damage.

Cycling gloves are cut off at the knuckles, allowing a good grip on the handlebars. They have double leather palms for padding and sweat absorption, and open netting on the backs for ventilation. You can find a pair of comfortable cycling gloves for less than ten dollars, and there's no cheaper way to increase your riding comfort as drastically.

Other Protective Clothing

Being caught in a rainstorm can cause an unprepared cyclist to feel uncomfortable; how uncomfortable depends on the temperature and your disposition.

If you are caught in a shower on a warm day, it's best just to let the rain fall on you and cool you. But if the weather is cold, or the storm heavy, or if you have to stay dry for work or school, you'll be much more comfortable and safer if wearing protective clothing.

There are as many types of rain gear as there are people. At a recent Tour of the Sciota River Valley, I was caught in a sudden, violent hailstorm just two miles before a rest stop. Even before the first drops of rain began to fall, the shoulders of the road were covered with hundreds of cyclists digging into handlebar bags and saddlebags for rain protection. Soon, cyclists were covered with tight nylon windbreakers, billowing rain capes, hooded parkas and even trash-can liners.

By the time we reached the rest stop, virtually everyone was soaked. The 40-mph winds had torn the trash bags and rain capes to shreds; the cyclists in rainproof parkas and windbreakers were soaked in their own sweat.

Gore-Tex is the only one waterproof material worth wearing in the rain. Fortunately, I was wearing it that day. Every time I talk to an experienced cyclist and the topic turns to rain, I hear the same words: "Only Gore-Tex is worth a damn."

Gore-Tex is a membrane (part of a three-part laminate) that has been used to make rainwear and tents since the mid-1970s. Gore-Tex works like a strainer: if you rinse peas in a strainer, water will pass through the holes but the peas will remain. With Gore-Tex laminates, water vapor (your sweat) will pass through microscopic holes, but water droplets (rain) are too large and remain on the outside. In contrast, all other materials either let rain in or trap your sweat inside.

At least a half-dozen companies now make Gore-Tex shells that fit close, keep your back covered and have underarm zippers for additional ventilation. Also, the shells are available in yellow, which increases visibility. The jackets are expensive and prices are rising about 25 percent a year, but I wouldn't ride in the wind or rain wearing anything else.

You can also find Gore-Tex and coated-nylon rain pants and chaps (covering the legs only), but I don't think they're worth the expense. Chaps still allow rain to splash up from the road, and both chaps and rain pants make it harder to move unhindered and increase your wind resistance. Also, the constant rubbing against the saddle quickly wears out this expensive material.

Still, you must keep your legs warm and dry in cold, wet weather. I find unlined wool tights over chamois-lined shorts work best; wool is water-repellent and keeps you warm even when wet. Polyester and acrylic warm-up pants also will repel water, but won't keep you as warm.

Tights are by no means the only solution. A less expensive option is a pair of leg warmers. These are separate wool or wool-blend leg coverings that protect you from your ankles to your thighs, and are held in place by elastic. They are inexpensive and warm, but many have a tendency to slip down your legs. Similarly, arm warmers have the same sag problem.

Nylon dance tights are also inexpensive and warm. Wool tights and leg warmers keep you warm even as they absorb water; nylon tights simply don't absorb water. Another foul-weather option, popular with Europeans and cross-country ski tourers, is knickers. These pants, typically of wool or wool blends, come down to below your knees; you wear long wool socks to keep your lower legs warm. They're attractive enough to wear off the bike as well as on.

Keeping your feet warm and dry calls for more ingenuity. Nylon shoes are more water-resistant than cotton or leather ones, but even these leave much to be desired. The best protection is waterproof shoe covers, preferably made of Gore-Tex, but they cost a fortune.

If you're on a limited budget, you can keep your feet reasonably warm and dry with combinations of plastic bags, wool socks and thin boot-liner socks. I wear liner socks, plastic bags and outer socks, but know of others who wear the bags under the inner socks. Leigh Phoenix wears heavy wool socks under and over his shoes.

A warning: If your leather shoes or gloves become wet, let them air-dry. Heat will make them brittle.

Just as cold feet are no fun, neither are cold hands. Fortunately, the solution is not elaborate or expensive: thin wool gloves under your cycling gloves, or a nylon or Gore-Tex shell over wool gloves or mittens. You can find expensive, lined full-fingered cycling gloves, but rain soaks the leather in seconds and they leave your wrists uncovered.

I've seen cyclists wear covers on their helmets, but I don't like them. Little rain can get through the ventilating holes in good helmets, and cutting off your ventilation can be even more uncomfortable. If you want partial protection with some ventilation, you can plug only the holes in the top of your helmet with Styrofoam, cut to fit.

Keeping Warm

As the temperature drops, cycling becomes riskier for a number of reasons. The most serious risk is a drop in body core heat. If your body core temperature falls just a few degrees, you can become ill or die.

Bundling up in bulky clothes is not a solution to the problem, though. As you exercise, you produce up to ten times the amount of heat you produce standing still. If you dress so you're warm while standing still, you will sweat when you start rolling. The sweat will then cool you and will lower the insulating value of your clothing.

The best way around this problem is to wear clothes that let your perspiration escape and to dress in layers that can be removed one at a time if you become too warm. For this reason, long underwear is not good for cold-weather cycling: if you become too hot, you cannot take your pants off.

What you should wear depends not only on the temperature but also on the wind speed (including your cycling speed) and how hard you ride. Wearing the same clothes, you may be as warm riding at 20 mph on a 10°F. day as you would at 10 mph on a 35°F. day.

Racer Leigh Phoenix piles on wool jerseys and T-shirts to keep riding even when the temperature drops to zero. Wool tights and wool socks pulled over his shoes keep his lower body warm. At the same temperatures, touring cyclist Holland Peterson wears long underwear, a sweater, a down-filled ski jacket with hood, snowmobile gauntlets, wool gloves and fleece-lined curling boots.

There are dozens of other pieces of clothing you can mix and match: insulated vests, wool arm and leg warmers, wool shirts and stocking caps. It will take you a while to find what's best for you; in the beginning, dress conservatively and carry a bag to stow away extra layers as you warm up.

Whatever you wear, keep this in mind: your body's priority is to keep your head and torso warm to protect your brain and other vital organs. It will shut off the blood supply to your extremities (hands and feet) to do this. If you keep your head and torso warm, though, blood will be channeled to your extremities, keeping them warm too. It's said that if you want to keep your feet warm, wear a hat, and with good reason: an uncovered head can release up to half your body's total heat output at 40°F.

As the temperature drops below 10°F., it's a good idea to cover your face: riding at 20 mph, your flesh can freeze within a minute. The best way to cover up is with a silk or wool ski mask or balaclava. Cover your eyes with plastic-framed sunglasses (metal will freeze to your face) or, better yet, wear ski or bicycle motocross goggles.

Dressing for the weather can keep you rolling comfortably all year long. As a Scandinavian saying notes: "There is no bad weather, only inadequate clothing."

CHAPTER FIFTEEN
RIDING WITH MOTHER NATURE

It takes more than the right clothes to safely and en-
joyably cycle year-round. A basic knowledge of the hazards of
weather, and the correct attitude for coping with Mother
Nature's moods will keep you spinning day after day.

During the first years that I cycled, I suffered from a
perverse fear of bad weather. If there was even a chance of
rain, I'd sit inside all day—even if the sky stayed blue and the
temperature stayed in the 80s.

But then came my first century ride. I had trained for
months and had begun to eat better. I was ecstatic with the
prospect of breaking that magic barrier.

When I awoke that last Saturday morning in September,
the sky was gray and packed full of brooding clouds. The
temperature hovered around 50, and the forecast called for
rain.

For the first time, I didn't give a damn. I *had* to ride that
century, and there wouldn't be another chance that year.

I arrived at the starting point about 15 minutes early. As
departure time neared, a man arrived in a Jeep. He was the
ride leader, and said he had decided to cancel the ride
because of the imminent rain.

I was crushed, but decided to wait to see if anyone else
would show up. Sure enough, another rider rolled in about
ten minutes after 8 A.M., just as I was about to leave. Joe
wanted to ride, he said, and it didn't matter that we had no
maps or leader—he knew the way.

Twenty miles from the starting point, the rains came.
First, a drizzle, then, by the halfway point, torrents. Joe and
I took an hour-and-a-half lunch break in a small restaurant,
eating hot sandwiches and drinking tea while the rain poured
down heavier by the minute.

By the time we reached the finish line, Joe and I were
drenched and covered with mud. I was cold, but otherwise
felt great. I had never experienced such a sense of accomplishment in my life.

As I drove back home, I realized that while most of the
thrill came from riding 100 miles, at least part was from doing
it under less-than-ideal conditions. And I realized that those
conditions were not really so bad.

I know I'll never become a poor-weather fanatic like the
cyclists who ride in snowstorms or compete for patches

awarded for riding 50 miles in a day when the temperature doesn't rise above zero. But I've learned that sometimes you have to put up with less-than-ideal conditions, and being prepared mentally and physically makes all the difference.

The key to mastering the weather is your attitude. If you believe that it has to be sunny and 70°F. for you to enjoy a ride, then it will be impossible for you to enjoy riding any other time. If you start a ride under those ideal conditions and find yourself caught in a storm 20 miles up the road, you'll be miserable, and make your companions just as miserable.

The best attitude to adopt is one of cautious optimism: hope for the best, expect the worst, and take whatever comes. This way, you're prepared for changes, so quirks in the weather cannot ruin your ride.

Many cyclists won't ride, however, unless the sky is clear and the temperature is in the 70s or 80s. Any other weather, they figure, is too risky or uncomfortable.

Heat-Related Problems

Unfortunately, cycling in hot summer weather may be riskier than riding at any other time of year. When the temperature soars into the 80s and above, your body's thermal balance can be upset by exercising, which in turn can lead to dehydration, heat stroke or heat exhaustion. And, of course, there is always the possibility of heat cramps and sunburn.

Sunburn is the most common hazard of hot-weather riding. The threat is at its worst between 11 A.M. and 1 P.M.; experienced cyclists avoid riding during this time.

If you have to or want to ride during those hours, cover up. You should always wear a shirt, not just a tube top or tank top. A light-colored, cotton or cotton/polyester shirt will reflect the sun's rays and wick your sweat away, so you'll be more comfortable than riding shirtless. Your helmet will keep the sun from boiling your brain; a tennis or helmet visor will help shield your face. To protect your neck, turn up your shirt collar or wear a bandanna.

Some cyclists recommend wearing long-sleeved shirts and long pants for summer cycling to shield you from the sun. This is hardly comfortable, though. A better alternative is to coat yourself liberally with a good sunscreen. Sunscreens are rated with Sun Protection Factors of 2 to 15: the higher the number, the more protection it gives you from the sun. If you want a tan, take the sun in small doses, then cover yourself with a strong sunscreen.

The sun can not only dry out your skin, but your body fluids, too. As you lose those fluids through perspiration, you also lose vital minerals. Thus, the rule of drinking before you are thirsty is extremely important when it is hot. There are no hard-and-fast rules on how much you need to drink, but try to take in at least one bottleful of water or an electrolyte-replacement fluid every 45 minutes on hot days. Drinking a bottle or two before and after each ride is also a good idea.

If you don't drink enough, you are courting heat exhaustion and heatstroke. Heat exhaustion occurs when you do not replace all the fluids you lose. You feel generally lousy and, if you continue to lose fluids day after day, as on a long tour or race, your blood volume and pressure will drop. You can go into shock, and may suffer heatstroke.

Heatstroke occurs when your body core temperature becomes too high, and can take place even if you are not dehydrated. Your body's thermostat becomes confused and stops trying to cool you. You then stop sweating, and your core temperature can soar as high as 110°F. This literally poaches your brain, and quickly leads to loss of consciousness and death.

You'll know when heatstroke is coming. You'll become painfully hot—or even cold, as your thermostat goes haywire—your head will throb; skin temperature will rise; and thinking, vision and breathing will deteriorate.

If this happens to you or a friend, stop what you're doing immediately and go to a hospital. If you cannot get to one quickly, apply ice and water to the skin and drink plenty of fluids. Stop the treatment when the victim is alert and out of pain. Continuing to lower his body temperature can kill him.

Ernst van Aaken, M.D., advises giving the victim a mild salt solution during the recovery period. This is important, he says, because as an athlete nears heat prostration, his body dumps sodium rapidly. Drinking plain water dilutes the already-low levels of body electrolytes, and may cause death. If you only have water available during the recovery stage, encourage the victim to drink plenty of fruit juices and other potassium-rich drinks as soon as possible.

The best way to prevent such problems is by training for hot-weather riding. Doing so helps your body adapt to the heat. The blood vessels in your cooling system enlarge, as will your sweat glands. And your heart will become used to the extra work. You will also be able to find the right pace that you can maintain without becoming overheated. Ride a little longer each time you go out, and you'll soon be heatproofed. This is especially helpful if you're planning to ride a long tour in an area that's warmer than your hometown.

High humidity can compound the effects of heat. When the humidity nears 100 percent, not much sweat can be evaporated from your body into the air when you're standing still or moving slowly. This can cause you to heat up rapidly. As it becomes more difficult to eliminate the heat your body is generating, more blood is diverted from your muscles to your skin, reducing your performance.

The Other Elements

While being soaked by high humidity is never pleasant, being cooled by an unexpected summer shower can be. After hours of sweating, a cool shower can be a gift from heaven.

In fact, as long as the temperature is above 50, riding in the rain can be an enjoyable, if not the cleanest, form of recreation, provided you dress to stay warm and dry and ride cautiously.

But when it rains, there is always a chance of lightning, too. Lightning is a serious hazard: more people are killed by lightning in the United States every year than by all other natural catastrophes combined.

Although the rubber in your bike tires insulates you from the ground, the metal in your frame and wheels and your upright body make fine conductors of electricity. When you see lightning, the best thing to do is to get off your bike. If you can, get inside a building or car. Stay away from solitary trees and water. If you cannot find shelter, the International Commission on Atmospheric Electricity recommends that you kneel down, press your knees and feet together, put your hands on your knees and bend forward.

Another frequent companion of rain is the wind. Wind is the cyclist's worst adversary. Hills always end, but winds can last for days, and can completely demoralize you.

The best way to cope with winds is to take them into account when you go out for a ride. The air is calmest in the morning and evening, so riding then will help you avoid them. And wind patterns are predictable so that you can make a good guess as to how the wind will be blowing next week or next month.

On all but the shortest rides, it's a good idea to ride out into the wind and have it at your back on the way home. If you ride out with a strong tail wind, you may misjudge and exhaust yourself before starting your much more difficult return trip against the wind.

On longer tours, wind becomes an even more important factor. Making the mistake of riding the final leg of a 30-mile ride into a head wind can be painful and demoralizing, but at worst you'll be late for dinner or have to call a friend to pick you up. But on rides of longer than one day, unforeseen winds can throw you off schedule and may keep you from reaching your destinations in time. It's a good idea to check maps that show the prevailing winds for the area and time of year you'll be riding. A good series with detailed maps for all regions in the United States is the "Local Climatical Data" pamphlets. Write for specific maps to: National Climate Center, Federal Building, Asheville, NC 28801.

Of course, not all winds are bad. I've been blown along at 30 mph by some beautiful gusts. When the wind blows from behind, I just sit up, gear up and take advantage of it.

On the other hand, I'm often convinced that there's a yet-undiscovered law of physics that says if you ride 30 miles into a head wind and turn around, the next 30 miles will also be into a head wind. (And, of course, there's the corollary: if you ride 30 miles uphill and turn around, the next 30 miles will also be uphill.)

I've climbed hills so steep that I could barely walk up them, yet on the descent, have had to pedal to go downhill because a head wind was so strong. When facing a wind such as that, the only thing you can do is gear down and bear it. Winds present a challenge, a way to increase your strength and skill. Like hills, they can slow you down—and often for hours on end—but if you can accept that, riding into the wind will be no harder than riding on a still day. Use a lower gear than normal so that you can maintain your normal cadence, and ride in a crouched position if your bike has dropped handlebars. When you ride with others, you can draft each other to cut down the wind resistance.

There's a third type of wind that cyclists rarely talk about, yet it can be the most dangerous: the crosswind. A steady crosswind can be as hard to ride into and as demoralizing as a strong head wind; maybe even more so, because you know there's no way to beat a head wind.

But it's the gusty crosswinds that are dangerous. When a gust hits you, you have to quickly compensate for it or tumble to the ground. If it stops suddenly, your overcompensation can also cause you to fall.

Crashing is not the only danger. I was cycling through the countryside in upstate New York on a warm, still afternoon when a crosswind blew in from my right just as I was making a sweeping, downhill left turn. The wind blew me from the far-right side of the righthand lane all the way across and into the oncoming lane, even though I fought against the wind as hard as I could. Just as I managed to move back into my own lane, a garbage truck came barreling over the crest of a hill in the oncoming lane.

As demoralizing and dangerous as the wind can be, there is a far more serious, hidden danger. While a steady wind may actually feel refreshing on a hot and muggy day, as the temperature drops the wind can become a deadly enemy.

As air moves past your body, it cools the warm-air layer between your clothes and your body. In warm weather, this is a blessing. Your speed cools you, so you'll be more comfortable cycling through Death Valley than standing in it.

But in colder weather, windchill can lower the effective temperature to dangerously low levels. Cycling at just 15 mph on a 40°F. fall day is the same as standing still when the temperature is 25, 7 degrees below freezing. And if it's a windy day, the effective temperature will be even lower.

The only way to prevent losing flesh and, possibly, your life is by dressing properly for all conditions, including windchill. The consequences of cycling while improperly dressed can be severe.

Frostbite is the least severe. It damages the tissues of the exposed skin. Even though you generate many times the amount of heat through cycling than you would while standing still, that heat does little to warm your nose, ears and cheeks. These are, unfortunately, the same areas left exposed to the chilling wind. Consequently, they are the first areas to develop frostbite.

The first sign of frostbite is prolonged numbness, followed by a tingling sensation. The area will look white and hard. As soon as you notice this, warm the area by placing your hand over it or soaking it in warm water until it looks flushed. In most cases, frostbite will cause only peeling or blistering. But the consequences of hypothermia include death.

Hypothermia is the opposite of heatstroke, the lowering of your body core temperature through long exposure to cold air or water. If the prolonged exposure causes your core temperature to drop by as little as five Fahrenheit degrees, you could die.

The most frightening aspect of hypothermia is that most cases occur in temperatures between 30° and 50°F., not in extreme temperatures. I've seen a cyclist fall prey to hypothermia after riding 12 hours of a 24-hour marathon in 40°F. rain.

The first sign of hypothermia is cold and clammy skin. Shivering follows, then a loss of dexterity and, finally, violent shaking. At that stage, your brain is in danger: it can become numb. Within 90 minutes, your heartbeat and respiration can stop.

If you have any of these symptoms, get off your bike and move to someplace warm. Get out of your wet clothes, and into a bed or sleeping bag. These should be preheated with hot water bottles or warm bodies. Drink plenty of warm fluids, but avoid hot ones. Rewarming has to be done slowly, only about one Fahrenheit degree an hour, and preferably under a doctor's supervision in the hospital. Rapid rewarming can be fatal.

If you dress properly and drink enough fluids, you shouldn't have any of these problems. But if you do, or are with someone else who does, you may be able to save a life. And now that you know how to cope with Mother Nature, you can meet her on her terms year-round and enjoy every minute of it.

CHAPTER SIXTEEN
THE FITNESS CYCLE

Not long after I began cycling regularly, I noticed that I was moving into a sort of fitness cycle. As I rode longer and more frequently, I could feel myself growing stronger and healthier. After years of marginal health, this new feeling was great: I felt alive, in control of my body and my life.

At the same time, I began to realize that if I wanted to become even more fit, I would also have to take a closer look at what I was eating to make sure I was getting the fuel and nutrition I needed—but without thousands of unnecessary calories. As I began to eat better, I reached new levels of fitness and endurance, and the cycle has been ongoing.

Undeniably, one of the most important things that cycling makes you better aware of is your own body. And being aware of and taking care of it will ensure that it takes care of you.

There are essentially just two parts to the path to better fitness: exercising and eating right. Unfortunately, both are shrouded in myths and misconceptions.

The most common misconception is that there is a quick and easy way to become and stay fit. There isn't. Doing five minutes of isometric exercises at your desk every day is not going to significantly improve your fitness; jettisoning 30 pounds on a one-week miracle diet is not going to stabilize your weight; eating a cup of yogurt with your greasy burger and fries is not the best way to keep your body going and growing.

This "overnight wonder" myth is as prevalent in the field of exercise as it is in the "fad diet of the week" world of weight control. Researchers are always looking for a shorter, easier way to become fit—not because it is the best way, or even a good way, but because most of us are lazy.

John Marino wrote, in *Wheels of Life,* "Considering that most people today are trying to find the least laborious methods of accomplishing tasks substantiates our laziness."

What we've come to view as "the good life" isn't really good for us, for many reasons. The most important one is that when your life-style places no regular demands on your heart, it uses all its power just to keep you alive. The sedentary person's heart is weak, and has to beat an average of 72 times a minute just to keep him alive.

Cycling will make your heart stronger and more efficient. Instead of having to beat 72 times a minute just to keep you going, a regularly exercised heart may only need to beat as few as 40 times a minute. Since your maximum heart rate is still the same (about 220 minus your age), it's like having a high-performance engine in a compact car: your heart has no trouble keeping you humming along, and has plenty of reserves for coping with physical and emotional shocks.

You'll have to cycle regularly to build up your heart, just as the weight lifter works out several times a week to build up his other muscles. When you push or pull slightly harder than you have before, the muscles involved become just a little stronger than necessary to meet the resistance. If you regularly push or pull at the same resistance, you will maintain your strength; if you increase the resistance, the muscles will grow stronger.

Your heart is a muscle, and the blood it pumps has weight, or resistance. The harder you regularly make it work, the stronger your heart will become. The stronger your heart becomes, the more blood it can push out to the blood vessels in your muscles. The more blood it can pump with each stroke, the fewer strokes it needs to make each minute, so your reserve increases.

While your heart is improving, so are your lungs. The tiny air pockets in your lungs become more efficient at taking in oxygen and getting rid of carbon dioxide as you improve your fitness. The fitter you are, the more air pockets will be used and the better your lungs will be able to extract oxygen from each breath you take, so you won't have to breathe as hard or fast for a given activity.

Minimum Program for Health

The key to accomplishing these changes is training regularly against increasing resistance. Unless you routinely make your cardiovascular system work harder, it will not become stronger or more efficient.

No one is sure how much exercise is the minimum needed to maintain or improve fitness. But it's generally accepted that you have to stress your system for at least a half hour on three nonconsecutive days each week to at least hold your ground. Five or six workouts a week will give better results, provided you alternate hard and easy workouts to let your muscles repair and rebuild their fuel stores.

A half hour is not a long time, but riding just that long at the proper intensity will bring far better results than meandering along for hours.

You'll get best results if you train at about 60 to 85 percent of your maximum heart rate. Any less, and your fitness will not improve. If you push harder, you will quickly run out of oxygen and become exhausted.

Pushing too hard is as bad as not pushing hard enough. While many novices feel they aren't getting exercise unless they're struggling for their breath, just the opposite is often true. Pushing too hard makes you run out of breath after too short a workout, so you do not get a long enough workout to gain any real benefits. If you cannot carry on a conversation while you're riding, you're pushing too hard. Slow down. Working at a level where you are not quite out of breath ensures that you won't tire early and have to end your workout, and that you are stressing your system enough to increase its performance.

If you are interested in improving your overall fitness, you should combine at least one other sport with cycling. Running, swimming, cross-country skiing and weight lifting are all good for developing the upper body, which cycling ignores, and will give you added flexibility by requiring your muscles to move differently. Ozdemar Karatun, M.D., vice-president of the Cardiac Treatment Centers in Pennsylvania, combines cycling with running and swimming. "Each exercise will improve some muscle groups, but make others dormant," he said. "It's best to combine them to hit all the groups."

Still, if you plan to race, tour or ride long recreational rides, it's best to follow the advice of Eddy Merckx, five-time winner of the Tour de France, the most grueling and prestigious cycling event in the world: "Ride lots." Even though swimming, running and cross-country skiing will improve your fitness, they will not improve it in exactly the way cycling does. Muscles, including the heart, are task-specific. What-ever task they are trained to do, they do best.

For general recreational cycling or commuting, a ride over the terrain you normally cycle is the best training. But if you want to be able to ride longer, faster or over hillier ter-rain, you should spend at least one training session a week concentrating on your specific goal or goals.

A Typical Schedule

I've adopted a three-ride-a-week schedule that seems best all-around for improving my performance. On Wednes-day, I ride 20 to 35 miles of the hilliest terrain I can find, to improve my hill-climbing ability. On Friday, I ride the same distance over mostly level terrain, pushing harder to improve my speed. On Sunday, I ride 50 to 100 miles at a slower pace, to improve my endurance. That way, I stress each system only once during the week, even though I exercise three times. This not only ensures that I stay strong all-around, but keeps me interested in riding by giving me something dif-ferent to look forward to each time I go out.

This schedule also includes all of the three types of train-ing that are beneficial to the cyclist: interval, steady state and long steady distance (LSD).

Interval training is, as the name implies, an on–off train-ing method that allows you to stress your systems to near maximum for short periods. Interval training can increase your power quickly, but you pay a price: it hurts. If you are interested in racing, intervals are essential.

A typical interval is 30 seconds at almost maximum power followed by 30 seconds at cruising speed—not coast-ing. Then you push at almost full power again for another 30 seconds, ease off and repeat until you cannot do another.

The best place to ride intervals is a flat road with a tail wind. There, you can hold a decent pace in the off periods. Short hills are also good for interval training: work hard going up, then cruise on the way down.

On your first intervals, keep your gears low. A 52 × 20 is about the highest you'll need. Pushing higher gears will only wear you out quicker. You can use a gear in this range in both the on and off periods—spinning as fast as you can in the on periods, then holding normal cadence in the off periods.

Don't worry about how long your on and off periods last the first few times you try interval training. Push yourself at close to maximum, and hold for as long as you can. Then ease off until your heart rate drops back to a comfortable point, and push again. If you decide to train by clocking yourself, keep your interval periods to less than 60 seconds on and 60 seconds off.

As you ride more intervals, you should need progressively less time to recover after an on period. This is a sign that your cardiovascular system is improving.

Most cyclists don't have to ride intervals. But if you hope to ride 50- to 100-mile rides or take long tours, you will have to do some steady-state training. Instead of working near your maximum limits, in steady-state training you ride at a pace that you will be able to hold over the entire ride. An hour of steady-state riding is a good workout.

Long-steady-distance training lasts longer than two hours, and is ridden at a slightly slower pace, the highest you can hold over the entire ride. If you want to ride far, ride plenty of LSD rides for training; if you're more interested in riding fast, concentrate on steady-state and interval training.

However you decide to train, make a point of riding at least three times a week. There will be times when it's hard to fit in those 90 minutes of riding (plus warm-ups and cool-offs), and you may think you can make up for it with one long ride on the weekend. But that may do more harm than good. William Bell, M.D., a physiologist at the University of Nebraska's college of medicine at Omaha, told *Parade* magazine that people who exercise only sporadically suffer more chronic injuries and fatigue than those who work out regularly.

"Vigorous physical activity during the weekend is not frequent enough to provide significant physiological improvement," Dr. Bell added. "In fact, it isn't even likely to maintain one's level of physical fitness."

Nor will you be able to maintain your physical fitness if you make a habit of taking off a week here or a month there.

John Holloszy, M.D., of Washington University in Saint Louis, has shown that muscles quickly lose their ability to use oxygen efficiently when they are not regularly stressed. Aerobic sports such as cycling require your muscles to use oxygen over an extended period of time, so a reversal will set in quickly. In three to four weeks, your body can lose its conditioning, even if you've been training all your life.

Ernst van Aaken, M.D., reports that German distance-running champion Herbert Schade provided a startling example of reversibility. After a two-month layoff, Schade's heart volume had shrunk from 1,200 cc. to 890 cc., and he had to struggle to run 5,000 meters in 18:02 seconds, even though he had previously set the Federal Republic of Germanys' national record at that distance in 14:06 seconds.

That's not to say that you should never take a break. On the contrary, overtraining is just as serious a threat to your fitness level. If you are always tired and have frequent colds and injuries, you are probably training too much. Overtraining can lead to depression, loss of interest in training, nervousness, loss of weight and many other symptoms, including a marked drop in your performance. When you notice any of these signs, slow down. Either take it easier on your workouts or take a day or two off. Your renewed vigor may surprise you.

One good way to make sure you don't overtrain is to never lose sight of the fact that cycling should be fun. Don't become wrapped up in trying to see how many miles you can ride in a month or how many hours on the road you can squeeze into each day. Unless you're training to race, your prime objective should be to have a good time. If you make sure you're enjoying each and every training ride, the miles and miles per hour will take care of themselves.

It used to be that women planned their cycling around their menstrual cycles, but things are changing. While some women still feel that cramps make exercising impossible during their periods, others find that exercise actually lessens cramps. A study by G. J. Erdelyi, M.D., of Cleveland, found that female athletes had fewer symptoms of premenstrual tension, including headaches and painful menstruation. The best advice, then, is to try cycling during your period, even if you don't feel like it. If it makes you feel better, fine. If not, stop.

The cyclist also has to cope with Mother Nature's cycles. If you live in an area such as the Northeast, there will be two or three months of the year that are too cold, rainy or snowy to cycle. From December through March, roads are often covered with ice and snow, and temperatures hover at zero or below.

When it's too cold, wet or dangerous to cycle, it's perfectly all right to hang up your bike—as long as you remain active. John Howard advises, "Do something to keep your energy level up. Don't allow yourself to vegetate. If the only thing you do is get up from your desk twice, that's all the exercise you'll get. Run, ski, speed skate, play a fast team sport like basketball: your body doesn't care, as long as you're active."

If you choose to do nothing during the cold months, you'll pay in the spring. You can quickly lose an entire season's worth of training by slacking off for a few months. And, when you get back on the bike in spring, you'll be more susceptible to injuries than if you had stayed active.

Alternate Sports

Fortunately, there are many things you can do during the winter to stay fit for cycling, and one exercise actually lets you stay on your bike.

Riding rollers indoors is one way to stay on your bike in the winter. Stationary rollers are an apparatus with three rotating rollers on which your bike's tires spin as you pedal. It takes a few tries to keep your balance. You'll work up a sweat within minutes, and unless you have a television nearby, roller riding can be extremely boring. "If anyone ever feels their life is passing by too fast," a local racer said, "he should try riding rollers. Every minute feels like an eternity."

Still, roller riding does have good points. A set of rollers is less expensive than all but the cheapest exercycles, and it keeps you familiar with shifting and balancing. And it also keeps your backside in shape. Since you ride in your living room or basement, it's easy to monitor your pulse to make sure that you're training at a proper rate. And you can enliven your winter training by joining in on or helping to set up roller races in your area.

Leigh Phoenix recommends a specific type of roller training to increase strength. Let some of the air out of your tires, he advises, then alternate one minute of hard effort at 120 rpm in your top gear with two minutes at an easy rate in your middle gear. Do sets of ten. You can set up a big fan to cool yourself. "Three sets of ten will do a job on your legs and improve your breakaway strength," he says.

Unfortunately, roller riding offers little enjoyment compared to that of cycling outdoors. If being outside is an important part of cycling for you, then you would probably be happier—and more apt to train regularly—running, swimming or cross-country skiing.

Cross-country skiing is the closest sport to cycling. It exercises most of the same muscles as cycling, and is as gentle and rhythmic. National champion cyclists ski during the winter, while their skiing counterparts cycle during the summer. A good book to help you get started is John Caldwell's *Cross-Country Skiing Today*.

If you want to try running, get a good pair of shoes and make sure you keep your knees warm. James Fixx's *The Complete Book of Running* is the bible of the sport, and *Runner's World* magazine is packed with information helpful to the novice.

Activities such as squash, racquetball, basketball and swimming can also keep you supple and help you maintain your cardiovascular fitness, but they won't do much to improve your strength. If you want to do that (you'll have to if you plan to try racing), you'll need some weight training. Bill Reynolds' *Complete Weight Training Book* will give you a good start. While a simple set of barbells is OK for training, it's better to work out with a Universal Gym setup (not as dangerous as barbells) that allows you to gradually increase resistance.

"The single most important exercise for all of us—and

the one known for hundreds of years—is pushing ourselves away from the table when we're not quite full," nationally renowned cardiologist Herman K. Hellerstein, M.D., told a meeting of the American College of Chest Physicians. John Howard agrees: "Keeping your weight down is important, regardless of age."

Unfortunately, an estimated 80 percent of all Americans are overweight. One problem, Creig Hoyt, M.D., points out in *Food for Fitness*, is that life-insurance-company figures, the usual norm, "are nothing more than an averaging of a large group of Americans examined upon application for insurance policies. This type of 'ideal' weight table is obviously an average of what people weigh, not necessarily what they should ideally weigh." As a consequence of these foolish standards and our poor eating habits and lack of exercise, one out of every two women in the United States is obese (having more than 25 percent body fat) by the age of 50, as is one out of every three men. This is a more severe health problem, Dr. Hoyt and many others agree, than any other.

Even if you are a mere ten pounds heavier than the insurance-company norm, you're still taking an unnecessary risk—and a big one. People over age 45 who are ten pounds overweight have a death rate 8 percent higher than that for normal or underweight people. If you are heavier than that, and the odds really stack up against you: those who are 10 percent overweight have twice the risk of developing high blood pressure as those at normal weight, three times the risk of diabetes, and five times the risk of gallbladder disease. And obese people run three times the risk of developing heart disease, vascular disease and heart attacks as their thinner relatives, and have higher chances of developing high blood pressure, arthritis, joint diseases, cirrhosis of the liver and intestinal problems.

As a cyclist, you have even more reason to shed every pound you can: every excess pound means more work for you. A rider who weighs 160 pounds has to lift 10 more pounds on every pedal revolution than his 150-pound partner as they cycle up a hill. If the climb takes 300 revolutions, the heavier cyclist has to lift the equivalent of 3,000 extra pounds on the way up.

Weight Loss by Cycling

The only way to lose weight is by burning off more calories than you take in. You can do this by dieting or exercise, but the most effective method is a combination of the two.

Food is measured in calories, the amount of energy it gives off as it burns. One calorie unit (actually, one kilocalorie) is the energy required to raise the temperature of one kilogram of water by one Celsius degree.

The National Academy of Sciences has compiled a list of daily caloric requirements for men and women. For a man between the ages of 23 and 50, the academy recommends an intake of 2,700 calories a day; for a woman, about 2,000 calories a day.

Many people find it hard to stick to those limits. Just a single cheeseburger, small soft drink and french fries for lunch contain nearly 700 calories; a piece of pie can add another 300 to 600 calories.

To make matters worse, those calorie "requirements" are far too high for some, if not most, people. Some nutritionists contend that sedentary people do not need more than 1,200 to 1,500 calories a day. Even cycling several thousand miles a year, I eat less than 1,500 calories a day on days I don't ride, and have not gained or lost a pound in ten years.

On the other hand, an athlete in training needs as much as 4,000 to 5,000 calories a day to maintain his fitness. But he burns the excess off during his next training session.

Each of us has an appetite control center that is supposed to make sure we don't eat more than we use. But as *Bicycling* magazine contributing editor David Smith, M.D., pointed out in an article, the center doesn't always work: many of us eat when we are not hungry, and for social or emotional reasons. And since the lower limit on the appetite control is about 2,500 calories, most people will be hungry with an intake of less than 2,500 calories—even if their output is far less. Since most people don't have the willpower to stay hungry all the time, dieting alone usually fails.

Losing weight solely by dieting has another pitfall, too. About a quarter of the weight lost through dieting is muscle tissue. As you lose weight, you will also lose muscle. But if you take in more calories than you burn, the added weight will all be fat. Consequently, you'll have more fat on your body than you originally had. There's a good chance you'll become even less active and gain more weight.

Combining exercise and dieting will help you lose fat without losing muscle. A 150-pound cyclist riding at 15 mph will burn off up to 600 calories an hour; if he picks up the pace to 20 mph, he'll burn up to 1,000 calories an hour. At 10 mph, though, the cyclist will burn off only about 300 calories an hour.

A pound of fat contains about 3,500 calories. So to lose that pound, you either have to eat 3,500 calories less, exercise off 3,500 calories or work a combination of the two. A 30-year-old man who has been eating the recommended 2,700 calories a day can ride an hour each day six days a week or cut his daily intake to 2,200 calories to lose 1 pound a week, or do both and lose 2 pounds a week. While this might not seem like much of a loss, a 1- or 2-pound loss per week is considered stable and medically safe, and it's weight you'll keep off if you follow your program—not just water weight that will come right back. And over the course of a year, that loss adds up to 50 to 100 pounds.

Any of the dozens of diet guides on the market will give you an idea of how many calories are in the food you eat, and an inexpensive scale will help you precisely count your calories. You'll probably be amazed to find out how much you've been eating.

One way to help lower your intake is by switching to water instead of other beverages. Not only is it better for you than virtually any other drink, but it is also calorie-free. A 12-ounce soft drink contains between 115 and 170 calories, as does the same amount of beer or fruit juice. Even the sugar and cream in your coffee or tea can add up to hundreds of calories a day.

You'll lose weight fast at first, then reach a holding level. The chances are that you can still go down from there. The only way to do that, though, is by eating even less or cycling more. This stage requires caution: there is little known about optimum weight, and an athlete's best weight often hovers near the breakdown point. Take it easy, and watch for signs that you've gone too far.

Whether you're trying to lose weight or not, it's important to eat properly. Top national cyclists Dale and Wayne Stetina are vegetarians. Transcontinental record holder John Marino eats mostly fruits and vegetables, rice, nuts, cheese, seeds and sprouts. But national champions John Howard and John Allis have been seen wolfing down their hot dogs and, gulp, even raw ground meat.

Howard has a simple, rational outlook on diet: "Theories about exotic diets correspond to fascination with exotic equipment. Fuel is just not that important. You need to avoid fast foods, fried foods, nonfoods, but you don't have to be a vegie, or a carbo-loader, or a fanatic. Just eat a good, solid diet. Use your own common sense.

"True, the better the fuel, the more efficient your body will run. But I think diet is overemphasized. I soft-pedal the dietary requirements."

Jerry Simpson, who has run a race training camp and is the operator of Bike Tour France (Box 32814, Charlotte, NC 28232), has similar feelings:

Instead of all this dietary faddism, I think we should be guided by, or at least take a look at, what the top-rank European racing cyclists eat while they are on an extended stage race such as the Tour de France. Surely, as cyclists, these are the supreme physical organisms. We are not likely to subject ourselves to such stress as they endure, but the fact that they can and do endure it makes valid and of general interest their regimen.

And lo! They eat more or less normally! A typical dinner during the Tour de France consists of shredded raw carrots in a vinaigrette sauce for hors d'oeuvre; a cream of leek and potato soup; a fish (like sole) poached in white wine and butter and topped with lemon and parsley; boiled potatoes; a grilled veal cutlet with green beans and butter; green salad; cheese and fruit; lots of bread; and red and white wine and mineral water.

Whatever you eat, make sure you get everything you need: protein, plenty of carbohydrates and a little fat. This can be tricky with special diets; a vegetarian, for example, has to make up for the protein he doesn't get through meat.

No one needs as much protein as most people think. The protein myth is one of the hardest to kill. Despite what you have heard, athletes simply don't need a great deal of protein. Although protein is vital to health and to build muscles, it is of little use during physical activity. Carbohydrates are much more important then. For that reason, the traditional pregame steak is being replaced on many training tables with spaghetti. And a peanut butter sandwich is a much better cycling lunch than a hamburger.

Avoid salt as much as possible. There is no proven link between salt and better performance, even in hot weather, but salt has been linked to high blood pressure.

Avoid sugary snacks, too. Sugar can give you a quick lift, but lets you down just as fast. The natural sugars in fruit are distributed to your system more slowly and contain other necessary nutrients that you need.

Try to stay away from processed foods as much as possible. Eat raw or lightly processed foods, and a wide range of them.

It should be obvious that there is no place for smoking on the way to fitness. Smoking can easily offset any gains you make in improving your oxygen uptake, as well as cause a host of diseases.

Smoking increases breathing resistance by limiting the expansion of the lungs and by robbing them of surface area needed to exchange carbon dioxide for oxygen. While the sedentary smoker may not notice this, the consequences will quickly become apparent when he starts to exercise and the demand for oxygen sharply increases. Even mild exertion will make the smoker short of breath.

Smoking also has a detrimental effect on the heart and blood circulation. The carbon monoxide in smoke combines with hemoglobin in the red blood cells much more readily than with oxygen. This lowers the ability of the red blood cells to transfer oxygen to the tissues by 10 percent or more. The smoker's heart therefore has to pump more blood over a given time to supply body tissues with the oxygen they need, in turn raising the work load of the heart.

These changes have a definite, adverse effect on performance and physical condition. But far more importantly, smoking also has been linked to cancer, lung and cardio-vascular diseases, and peptic ulcers. A 35-year-old who smokes two packs a day can expect to live 8 or 9 years less than a nonsmoker of the same age. Remember that in 6 years of working with a cycling program for postcoronary patients, Dr. John Camp reported only one death due to cardiovascular problems: a man who refused to stop smoking.

Cycling makes the effects of smoking painfully obvious and discourages smokers from continuing their deadly habit. Few serious cyclists smoke; indeed, one of the pleasures of club cycling is enjoying dinner afterward with several hundred people in a smoke-free room. Smoking has no redeeming value, and has no place in the life of anyone who is serious about cycling—or about living.

Just as your body will show you the bad effects of smoking, so too will it alert you to other problems. It's a surprisingly intelligent machine that will let you know when you need a specific type of food, more rest or a lighter training program. Above any other rules, listen to what your body tells you. If it responds well to a regimen or diet, stick with it. Otherwise, adjust until your body approves. If you take care of it, your body will take care of you, for a long time.

CHAPTER SEVENTEEN
WHEN THINGS GO WRONG

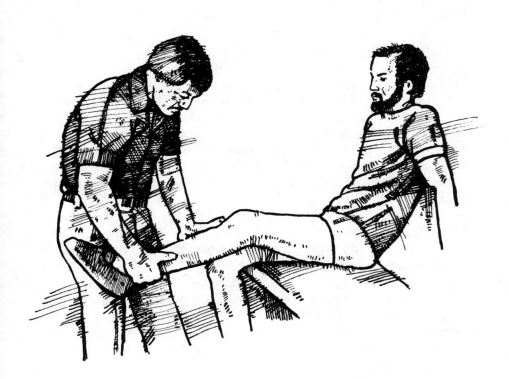

Sometimes in the course of building up, something breaks down. This is especially likely if you push too hard or try to accomplish too much too soon.

Most of the problems are minor: sprains, aches and pains. Many are the result of using muscles that have long been dormant: on your first ride of the spring, there's a good chance your neck and backside are going to ache.

Other problems are the result of hard effort. When your legs ache, this is simply the result of the products of fatigue building up faster than your body can dump them.

If you continue to push too hard, you'll collapse. But if you can stabilize your effort, your body will eventually be able to catch up with the work load, removing the lactate from the muscles and, with it, most of the pain. This is what happens when an athlete "breaks through the wall of pain." If you ease off when you feel the pain is too much to bear, you'll be able to make it.

Fatigue is never serious. It is just your body rebelling against the work you're asking it to do. But there are other pains that are serious. Ignoring them or trying to push through the wall may keep you off your bike, or even off your feet, for a year or longer.

Knee Problems

One of the cyclist's nemeses is knee problems. Your knees are the most complicated and vulnerable joints in your body. The knee was not designed to bear the full weight of an upright person, let alone the abnormally high stresses of cycling.

The bones of the knee do not form a true joint. Instead, they prop against each other, with the kneecap held on by skin to protect them. Synovial fluid flows through the joint to lubricate and aid movement.

The joint surfaces of the thigh bone, lower leg bone, and smaller bone of the leg are covered with smooth cartilage to reduce friction. But the stress of pedaling, particularly in high gears and if your knees are out of line, can wear away the cartilage and cause calcium deposits to form on the backs of

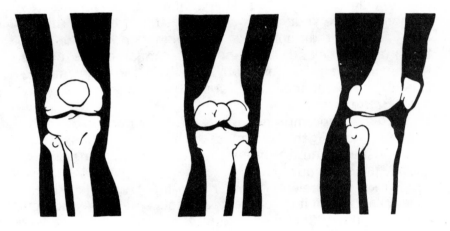

Three views of the knee. From left to right: front, rear and side views.

the kneecaps. This condition is known as chondromalacia.

The first sign of chondromalacia is pain in the back of your kneecap (either one or both knees can be affected) when you forcefully straighten your knee. You should be able to elicit the pain by grasping your kneecap and moving it from side to side while pressing it against the underlying bone. Chondromalacia can make climbing stairs, standing up from a chair or pedaling a bike painful and difficult.

There is no treatment for chondromalacia other than stopping the process that caused the injury. If you stop cycling at the first sign of pain, and do everything you can to keep excess pressure from your knee joints, the condition will improve. When the pain diminishes enough for you to ride again, use only your lowest gears.

Tendinitis is another problem that can affect the knee area, as well as the tendons that attach to the heel bone and calf muscles.

Exercise physiologist Ed Burke details the types of tendinitis in *Inside the Cyclist:*

Patellar tendinitis affects the tendon that connects the kneecap to the lower leg bone (tibia) and is caused by over-using the quadriceps muscles on the front of the thigh.

Popliteal tendinitis is caused by the continuous locking

and unlocking of the knee. This action causes the popliteal tendon, to the rear and outside of the knee, to rub on the ligament that connects the thigh bone (femur) and the smaller bone of the leg (fibula). This inflames the tendon, the ligament and, occasionally, the fluid sacs (bursae) between them. This is usually caused by having your seat too high, Burke says.

Achilles tendinitis occurs in the tendon that connects the calf muscle (gastrocnemius) to the lower leg bone (tibia) and is usually caused by improper seat height or pedaling action.

Burke recommends similar treatment for all three injuries: "application of ice, rest, and local massage and heat after inflammation has subsided." Since tendinitis is caused by tight muscles, smooth, gentle stretching will also help.

The forces of pedaling, especially when pushing the large gears, can also strain the quadriceps tendon, which inserts into the leg just below the knee. When this happens, you'll feel pain or tenderness just above or below the knee. If your feet are improperly positioned, you can also tear the lateral ligaments on the inside and outside of the knee.

These injuries can be disabling, and take a long time to heal. At the first sign, ease off. Don't push hard enough to cause pain: the pain may well mean that you are doing more damage to the tendon or ligament. If the pain is on the inside or outside of your knee, change the position of your foot so that it is straighter on the pedal. Better yet, stay off the bike until the injury heals. If you don't, and tear a ligament, it will have to be surgically replaced.

Repeated strains or abuse of your knees, or even exposure to cold or a direct blow to your knee in a crash, can cause bursitis. Bursitis is inflammation of one or more of the bursae, the sacs of lubricant that act as bearings at friction points in your knees and elsewhere in your body. Acute bursitis causes severe pain, often of short duration. I developed bursitis for a short period after crashing hard on my right shoulder: some days it hurt terribly to raise my right arm. If you don't aggravate bursitis by repeatedly irritating the bursae, the condition will disappear. But if you aggravate it, bursitis can become chronic, with persistent pain that is much more difficult to treat. Burke recommends the same treatment as for tendinitis. But chronic bursitis may require removing bursa fluid by needle, or injecting cortisone, which may ultimately weaken the surrounding tendons and cause them to rupture.

When your leg problems don't just disappear under home treatment, it's a good idea to visit a sports podiatrist, orthopedist or physiotherapist. Knee injuries in particular can become disabling, ending your cycling days and making even walking miserable in later years. Sports physicians are used to treating injuries of health, not illness, and recognize that standard treatments may not work for the athlete. Ed Burke gives an example: It's common practice to treat tendon inflammation with cortisone. But cortisone reduces blood supply to the tendons, making it much easier for the athlete to tear them when training or competing.

Of course, the best way to deal with injuries is to prevent them. If you keep your knees warm and straight, and pedal rapidly in low gears, there will be little chance of your developing such problems.

Lesser Aches and Pains

Most other cycling aches and pains are not nearly as worrisome as knee problems, even though they may be excruciatingly painful. Leg cramps are one of the most painful examples.

Leg cramps occur at the least expected times, and no one is sure why. A popular theory is that they are caused by salt depletion, but experiments have shown that athletes deprived of salt had no more cramps than those who ate salt liberally. Other researchers suspect deficiencies of calcium, magnesium, potassium and vitamin B.

Some people's cramps disappear after drinking salt-water or quinine (a prescription drug also found in tonic water). The best treatment is usually to stretch the muscle involved, pulling the cramp out. Kneading or stretching may work. There is a good chance that the muscle will try to cramp again, though, so don't hop right back on your bike.

A side stitch is a milder form of cramp. Stitches are sudden, sharp pains that strike in the upper abdomen area. Stitches are as mysterious as leg cramps, but seem to become less likely as fitness improves. Slowing down, breathing more deeply or bending and stretching on the side of the stitch may relieve the pain. Avoiding food for two hours before beginning a ride may also help prevent stitches, as may avoiding milk and wheat products.

Painful feet are another problem that is much more uncomfortable than serious. Foot pains are caused by pushing too hard on the pedals. With soft-soled shoes, such as the running shoes and sneakers the majority of recreational and touring cyclists wear, the pedal cages dig into your feet as you press hard on the downstroke. Pressing hard also flattens the transverse arch of your foot, putting pressure on bones that are not designed to take it. The solution to the first problem is to wear hard-soled shoes, preferably with metal sole plates. The second problem may require metatarsal arch supports. Both problems can be alleviated by spinning in lower gears.

Constant excessive pressure on the pedals can also cause numb feet. As you push hard against the pedals, you compress the nerves in your feet. This can damage them and cause permanent injury. Lifting your feet from the pedals on the upstroke, pushing easier in lower gears, and wearing stiffer shoes should help. If you severely damage the nerves, stay off your bike until they recover.

By gripping the handlebars too hard, you can also damage the ulnar nerves in your hands, causing them to become numb. Leigh Phoenix said that his hands take weeks to recover after a 24-hour ride; in the interim, just buttoning his shirts is virtually impossible. I find that even a much shorter ride can cause numbness if the roads are bumpy.

To alleviate the problem, try not to grasp your handlebars so much as to lay your hands on them. Padded cycling gloves (or regular full-fingered gloves in cooler weather) will help. The most helpful remedy, though, is to add extra padding to your handlebars. You can devise your own padding from insulation foam, then tape over top with regular handlebar tape, or buy preformed, slide-on foam grips. These are preventive measures; once the symptoms strike, ride as little as possible until feeling returns.

Nearly as common, but not often discussed, is the problem of numb crotch. This is caused by compressing nerves in the area between your pelvic bones and the saddle.

When men sit on a bike saddle, their genitals are pushed up out of the way of the saddle, and the worst resulting problem is numbness. Switching the angle of the saddle or using a padded saddle will relieve most of the problem.

But for women, there is another, less easily remedied problem. A woman's genitals are not pushed out of the way of the saddle, but are crushed against the nose of the saddle by her pelvic bones. This is not a problem when sitting upright, which is why many women prefer that position to the inclined position required by the 10-speed bike.

Some recent saddle designs for women have employed raised bumps to cushion the sit bones, with a groove between to relieve pressure on the genitals. But the groove is too far back to relieve the pressure for most women.

Possibly the best solution to the problem is to buy an inexpensive plastic saddle and cut a hole at the spot where the irritation occurs. You can cover the saddle with soft leather for even greater comfort.

A more serious problem is saddle soreness. There is a mild type that you may have when you first begin cycling or get back in the saddle after a lengthy layoff. This soreness is the result of sitting on tissues that are not "hardened" to such use, and should disappear after riding for a while.

But sores and boils are more serious. These can be especially miserable for long-distance tourists or professional racers who ride day after day. This type of saddle soreness is the result of chafing and is aggravated by sweat and any discharge from the skin. The friction irritates the skin and damages hair follicles, leading to boils and infections.

Prevention is the best cure for saddle sores. Wear chamois-lined cycling shorts, which have no seams where you touch the saddle. Wash the shorts after every ride, and apply plenty of chamois fat to soften them after they're dry.

If you develop minor soreness, wash the affected area

well after each ride. Use medicated soap, followed by rubbing alcohol. Cornstarch or petroleum jelly will keep the area from chafing.

If the soreness is a major problem, or if a boil develops, get off your bike and see a doctor.

Many saddle sores are the result of incorrect saddle positions. If the saddle is too high, you'll slide from side to side as you pedal. The wrong saddle angle can also cause irritation.

Cycling can also be a pain in the neck, and in the lower back. Muscle aches in these areas are usually the result of using unconditioned muscles, or of having the bike set up wrong. If your bike is set up properly, a few hundred miles in the saddle will train these muscles for their chores. The aches may reappear when you take longer rides than you are used to, but should disappear with training over the longer distance. Leigh Phoenix says his biggest problem in 24-hour time trials is neck pain: his neck muscles aren't used to being held in the racing position for 24 hours at a time.

Until your neck and back become used to their chores, you can make riding more comfortable by making sure you stretch before every ride, as outlined in Chapter Ten. If pains persist or become worse after weeks of riding, your bike is undoubtedly set up wrong. Cycle commuter Mike Kane recalled having severe shoulder pain when he started cycling. When he raised the handlebars and took weight off his shoulders, the pain disappeared.

There's a final type of injury that virtually every cyclist will someday encounter: road rash, or scraping off your skin in a crash.

When the inevitable happens, clean the abrasions with soap and water, using a brush if necessary to remove dirt. If the area is extremely dirty, rinse with hydrogen peroxide.

After the area (or, more likely, areas) is well cleaned, cover it with Neosporin or Bacitracin antibiotic ointment to keep it moist and free from infection. Recent studies have shown that it's best to keep abrasions moist while they heal from the inside; a scab can rub off too easily if you remain active.

Cover the medicated area with a nonstick sterile pad, and change the bandage daily.

Watch for signs of infection. If the area becomes red, swollen, hot or tender, see a doctor. And if you haven't had a tetanus shot within the past five years, get one within 24 hours of the injury.

By the way: you'll probably hear many theories about why racers shave their legs. The real reason is that it's easier to change bandages on smooth skin.

If you stay alert to the warning signals of common cycling problems, and take care of any injuries as soon as they crop up, you need never worry about serious problems. Sometimes you may have to give up cycling for a week or two, as devastating as that might seem. But it's much more devastating to find out months later that you injured yourself so badly that you will never be able to ride again. While you heal from cycling injuries, you can usually keep in shape with another sport: running, swimming, skiing or skating, for example. But if you heed the warning signals, and waste no time in treating your injuries, you should be able to stay on your bike virtually every day of the year, building up to longer, faster and more exciting rides.

CHAPTER EIGHTEEN
LONG-DISTANCE TOURING

One of the most exciting ways to use your bike is by touring with it. Cycle touring lets you wheel your way to and through virtually any spot on the globe:

...You and your partner speed through a quiet back lane near Paris, riding in the cool shade of trees. A light breeze urges you on; red-faced men and women smile and wave as you ride by.

Around midday, you cycle into a village full of tiny shops, pick up a loaf of bread, a liter of wine and a half-pound of cheese, and wheel on down the road to find a warm, grassy spot on which to share them...

...You stand quietly atop the highest of the Rocky Mountains, cool and worn, but filled with the beauty of the blue sky, the crystal white caps of the neighboring mountains, the sheer distance to the ground below—and your accomplishment of cycling to the top...

...Ending a long day's ride, you join an Asian family for dinner in their village. You don't understand a word of their language, yet they treat you just like one of the family, offering you their best dinner and a warm place to spend the night...

...You come home Friday afternoon at the end of a hard week's work. Instead of heading for the hammock in the backyard, you hop on your bike and pedal up the road. By dusk, you are in a quiet town miles out in the country, water boiling for tea as you listen to the chirping of crickets and feel the golden warmth of the sunset...

These and an infinite variety of other experiences await the cycle tourist. Cyclists have ridden from Cape Horn, South America, to Alaska; have crossed Death Valley; have climbed many of the highest mountains of the world. And they've done so as a part of the world they were exploring, not shielded from it by steel and glass.

The world is yours for the taking, and cycling is one of the best ways to take your part of it. No other form of transportation allows you to see so much, yet cover so much ground, with the freedom of traveling as light or as heavy as you want.

Traveling by bike makes you open and appealing to others. In many parts of the world, the bicycle is the primary source of transportation. Even in other places, William Quinn wrote in *American Wheelmen,* the bike "is a letter of introduction to people everywhere: the hitchhiker along the road, the truck driver in a restaurant, the fellow biker met along the highway, or the campers encountered at the end of the day. . .There was an immediate bond of mutual interest, of companionship, that was very much appreciated." And while cycle touring makes you more appealing to others, it also allows you to explore any roads that appeal to you—or even places where there are no roads.

Cycle touring is one of the least expensive ways to travel. Lloyd Sumner began his 28,478-mile, four-year bicycle tour of the world with only $200 in his pocket. By giving lectures and writing articles on his travels in the 34 countries he visited in Europe, Africa and Asia, he managed to return home richer, in every sense of the word.

Cycle tourist Tim Wilhelm, after riding more than 3,000 miles across the United States with his wife and two children, reflected in *Bicycling* magazine: "To cross the country is a poor reason to bicycle, but crossing the country riding day after day while taking the time to really experience what the land and the people have to offer is what bicycle touring is all about—to us, anyway."

Planning Your Tour

Probably the most difficult decision in planning a bike tour is picking where to tour. Any place is fair game, and only your time and finances limit your choice.

Still, there are other factors to consider. Time of year is one. If you can tour only during August, for example, you probably won't want to go to a place where it rains for the entire month. And if you're looking for a quiet, relaxing trip, you'll want to avoid towns during prime tourist season.

After you have a general idea of when and where you'd like to go, you should decide whether you want to plan your own tour or ride with an organized group. If you want to visit a specific area and can go only at a certain time, you may not be able to find an organized tour. For many areas, though, you'll be able to find organized rides throughout most of the year—though not necessarily at the pace or as long as you would like.

For the utmost in freedom, there's nothing like planning your own tour. Aside from general guidelines, you need never be at a specific place at a given time. If you fall in love with a quaint town, you can spend an extra day there. If you decide to take a side road or explore a neighboring area, you're free to do so. You can plan a tour that lasts three days or three years, and covers 10 miles or 210 miles a day.

Costs are lower, too. You need not pay a guide, and can find cheaper facilities and meals than a guided tour might offer.

But those guides can come in handy. You cannot possibly know an area as well as an experienced tour leader. Unless you plan your route carefully, you just might miss the most beautiful spots. And beginning cycle tourists usually have no idea of how far they can realistically hope to ride in a day.

Jerry Simpson of Bike Tour France once told me about two girls he met in the middle of a bike trip. They had planned to cycle between 80 to 120 miles a day from Holland to Italy.

"They made it through Belgium and into northern France," Jerry recalled, "and then they began to cry. All their hotel reservations were based on this 100-mile-a-day average, and they couldn't keep it up, so all their reservations were down the drain."

It is, indeed, the efficiency and simplicity of the organized tour that is so attractive. For the most part, you sit back and leave the planning to someone more experienced. Your decisions are limited to what to take, how to get to the starting point, and what ride category—novice, intermediate or advanced—you should pick if there is a choice.

Many organized tours are advertised in *Bicycling* magazine, but the majority are not. The best listing of organized tours that I know of appears in Tim and Glenda Wilhelm's *The*

Bicycle Touring Book, which is also packed with useful touring advice. Raymond Bridge's *Bike Touring: The Sierra Club Guide to Outings on Wheels* is another excellent cycle-touring source book.

Doing It Yourself

Ironically, a more carefree, spontaneous, self-planned tour takes longer to plan.

The first step is to decide who you'll be touring with. Other riders can greatly add to your enjoyment, but can also hold you back from covering the distance you are able to ride—or set a pace that's too fast for you.

The simplest solution is to go alone. Mark Winer, who toured Ireland a few summers ago, would go no other way:

"When you ride alone," he said, "you have your own choice of where you want to go. Come a hill, I could decide to get to the top no matter how long it took. Someone else might have wanted to stop and rest along the way. If you want to do something when you're riding alone, you do it."

When you ride with others, you trade off that control for moral and social support, for predictability and companionship.

If you don't want to ride alone, a group of four to six is best for cycle touring. With more, meals and accommodations can become a problem, as can simply keeping track of everybody.

With a larger group, there also may be a wide disparity in cycling abilities. You always have to consider the weakest cyclist in a group when deciding how far to ride. If you force weaker or less experienced riders to keep up with more advanced cyclists, the novices will not enjoy the tour. And once the tour is ruined for one of your group, it's ruined for everyone.

"Touring companionships," Bridge writes in *Bike Touring,* "are not really made in heaven, any more than marriages are. The primary ingredient in any successful tour has to be a mutual understanding of the general objectives and spirit of the trip. Even if you are riding with friends and lovers of long standing, things can go sour in a hurry if part of the group thinks the object of the trip is to sightsee at a leisurely pace while another contingent intends to *ride,* perhaps for 12 to 14 hours a day."

Bridge suggests that you plan to cover half the mileage per day that the weakest rider can manage. This seems terribly conservative at first, but there are several factors that make it a good rule.

In particular, you have to allow for bad weather and rough terrain. Most cyclists I know take their recreational and training rides only on good days and over flat courses. If they overextend themselves on a century ride, they can always spend the next day recuperating.

On tour, though, you may have to ride for days on end into strong head winds or in severe rainstorms. You'll find the steepest mountains and roughest roads just when you're most fatigued. And mechanical problems, sight-seeing stops and weaving through heavily populated cities will also slow you down.

Jerry Simpson keeps the average daily ride of his tours to 35 miles. "That's enough," he says, "if you're enjoying the scenery, stopping to look at things, stopping to talk to people, stopping to explore villages. That's about three hours on the bike, at the rate we usually ride, two hours for those who like to tootle along, and four hours for those who poke. That leaves plenty of time to SEE and EXPLORE, and to wash out clothes."

Thirty-five miles is far from the upper limit, though. When John Potter rode the 7,100-mile "continental triangle" from Washington, D.C., to San Francisco to Portland to Rehobeth Beach, Delaware, in 65 days, he covered as much as 250 miles a day. There's no doubt that an experienced rider can consistently cover 100 miles a day, but, Jerry Simpson says, "That's not really touring."

After you decide who to ride with and how far you want to go, you'll have to choose a route. This is not as easy as it is for auto touring. In a car, you want the fastest, most direct route between two points. For cycle touring, though, you are more concerned with finding back roads, which have better scenery and fewer motor vehicles.

If you're riding through desolate areas, you could tour with just a map and compass, stopping in major cities along the way to pick up detailed city maps to guide you. Most of us aren't that adventuresome, though, and need a more stable course.

Most oil companies and auto clubs offer maps of major routes, and the clubs will map out routes for their members. But the only routes these maps show are the largest, busiest ones. State tourist bureaus and county governments can usually furnish more desirable maps detailing secondary roads.

Bikecentennial (PO Box 8308, Missoula, MT 59807) publishes exquisite maps of its transAmerica and other trails, offers a routing service and publishes *The Cyclists' Yellow Pages,* which, among other things, includes excellent information on finding maps for cycling in the United States and Canada.

When you cannot find a map for an area you want to tour, or if you want to know how hilly your route is going to be, you should get topographical maps for the area in 1:250,000 scale. These maps cover an area of about 70 by 110 miles in detail. Unfortunately, many of the details are out-of-date, so you should use topo maps in conjunction with up-to-date road maps. Topo maps are available from the addresses listed in Chapter Eleven.

Dr. Clifford Graves, president of the International Bicycle Touring Society (2115 Paseo Dorado, La Jolla, CA 92037), recommends the Bartholomew series of maps for England, Michelin maps for France, the Shell Deutsche Generalkarte series for Germany, and the Dutch cycle touring organization Koninklijke Nederlandsche Toeristenbond's maps for Holland. A good bookstore should be able to get these for you. Many are expensive (five dollars or more for each map), but they are well worth the price.

Even if you can find good maps, it's still best to talk with other cyclists before mapping your route and beginning your tour. If you cannot find an American who has explored the area, try to find a native of the area through a bike club there. You may have to visit the international student center at a large university to solicit a name (and, possibly, an interpreter), but the time spent will pay off in a pleasurable tour.

In addition to choosing which roads you should take, you also have to decide whether you want to ride a loop or ride point to point. You don't want to drive to the Midwest, then cycle to Mexico if you don't have a way back to your car or home. You can usually find a fairly quick way back from the end of a point-to-point trip, but this can add tremendously to the cost of the tour. On certain tours, you simply have no choice: most cyclists don't pedal back to Oregon from Virginia after a cross-country trek.

If you decide to finish your ride at the same point you begin, try to make a loop—don't just ride back on the same roads you cycled out on. If you plan a circular route, you'll see the most possible.

The next step is to count your pennies and decide whether you want to travel in class, slum it, or something in between. Actually, money is not the only consideration: how independent you want to be also plays a big role.

For the fastest, most luxurious independent touring, you stay in motels and hotels, eating all your meals in restaurants. This way, you carry little gear, just a change or two of clothing and your tools. On the most luxurious organized tours, sag wagons follow the routes to carry even these essentials. Having guaranteed accommodations with running water every night lets you wash your clothes nightly, so you can get by with just a few changes of socks and underwear or riding shorts. And you rarely have to worry about finding a place to stay, since you can make reservations months in advance.

A sag wagon also allows you the luxury of taking along dress clothes and other items that would be a burden if you had to carry them on your bike. And if a rider falls sick or fatigues, the wagon can pick him up. This type of travel is costly, of course, and is dependent on a motor vehicle. Still, if you like comfort, and money is no object, it's the way to go.

For both financial and aesthetic reasons, most cycle tourists prefer to carry more gear so that they can have more freedom. Carrying your own supplies, you can stay in hotels or motels or, if pressed for funds, hostels. Depending on whom you talk with, hostels are either the budget tourist's best friend—or pure hell.

Hostels are an international chain of buildings that provide low-cost dormitory-style accommodations. They are cheaper than motels, but a tour group may find a motel's group rate a better deal.

Most hostels have showers; some charge for hot water, and there may not be enough to go around. Some provide meals; others require you to buy the meals, which may not be cheap. Others provide cooking facilities.

Hostels are great places to meet people, but those people can be loud, and the crowded conditions noisy and disturbing. Most have separate accommodations for men and women.

To get a bunk, you usually have to arrive at the hostel by 4 P.M., then wait until check-in time at 4:30 or 5:00 P.M. Lights are turned out at 10 P.M. and checkout time may be as early as 8 A.M.

To stay at a hostel, you must be a member of American Youth Hostels (despite the name, it is open to people of all ages). In addition, you must have, or rent, a sheet sleeping sack—not a sleeping bag—and may have to help with the chores.

Still, hosteling is an inexpensive way to travel self-sufficiently. American Youth Hostels (National Campus, Delaplane, VA 22025) publishes handbooks that will help you locate hostels around the world.

In Europe, you'll also find bread-and-breakfast establishments, usually private homes where you can sleep and eat breakfast for a reasonable price.

But some cycle tourists are happy only when they carry their accommodations and cooking facilities with them. These riders carry a sleeping bag and, depending on weather and personal temperment, tarps and bivouac sacks or tents. The purist also carries a small stove and cookware, and anything else he might need.

Although the camping tourist has to haul along the extra weight of his equipment, he is the freest of all cycle tourists. He has to do more work on and off the bike, and has a higher initial outlay for equipment, but he is prepared for any circumstance. The camper has the option of eating in restaurants and sleeping in the plushest hotels, but he need never worry about meeting room reservations, getting into town early enough to find a place to sleep, or cutting his day's ride short because there are no accommodations in the next town.

The primary rule of enjoyable cycle camping is: travel light. There are two parts to this rule: take as little as you can, and take the lightest equipment you can afford.

Some cycle tourists have made an art of traveling light. When Jerry Simpson and his wife, Janie, rode from France to Spain a few years back, they carried the lightest, cheapest sleeping bags they could find and a six-by-ten-foot piece of waterproof material. They used the sheet as a ground cloth or, when it rained, as an improvised tent, tying the grommeted ends to trees and staking others to the ground.

Other camping tourists skip even such makeshift shelter. They sleep in fields, forests, on stream banks, or in church pews and jail cells. John Potter slept in the back of a pickup truck once on his "continental triangle" expedition. You may have to get permission to sleep on a porch or in a barn, but you should always be able to find a place to sleep, even if the weather's bad.

Likewise, even if you are never going to eat at a restaurant, you can get along without a stove and cookware in warm weather. Fruits, vegetables, cheeses, breads and many other foods can be eaten raw; in a pinch, you can build a fire for cooking.

If you don't mind living a spartan life, you can travel with just a foam sleeping pad, one change of clothes, and a few tools and spare parts. This adds less than ten pounds to your bike, so you can cover as much ground as you would on your unloaded bike.

Most cycle tourists prefer a little more luxury, though. And if you plan to see the area you're touring, the slower pace and lower daily mileage is not a hindrance, especially since you don't have to waste time looking for a place to sleep: virtually anywhere will do.

Basic Equipment Needs

No two cycle tourists agree on what is necessary for a tour. Still, there are generally agreed-upon items that no camping cycle tourist should leave home without.

First is a sleeping bag. Like everything else, this should be as lightweight as possible. Down bags are still the lightest, with models weighing as little as 1 pound, 14 ounces.

But there are some problems with down bags. First, they are very expensive. In the past five years prices have doubled on many models. It is virtually impossible to find a good-quality down bag for less than $150.

When down becomes wet, it loses its loft, and with it, its ability to keep you warm. Synthetic-filled bags, made with materials such as Hollofil and PolarGuard, lose little of their insulating abilities when wet.

Few down bags are intended for warm-weather use. Since down is so light, this is OK if the bag can be zipped open at the foot for ventilation; if it can't, you'll bake on warm nights.

While good three-season synthetic bags start at about $40, they are much heavier than down-filled bags; typically, a synthetic bag is 1½ to 2 pounds heavier than a down bag with the same insulating value.

Whichever kind of bag you choose, you may also want to buy a pad, especially if you plan to travel without a tent. A closed-cell foam pad will cushion you from the hard, cold ground, keeping you warmer and more comfortable, and will protect your bag from wear and tear.

Since a good sleeping bag can cost as much or more than your bike, it pays to shop around. As with most things, you usually get what you pay for. By talking with people in mountaineering shops, reading outdoors magazines and catalogs and watching for sales, you can make sure you get the most for your money.

Those same people, magazines and catalogs can also help you choose a shelter. If you're going to be riding through an area with a dry climate where there are motels for sanctuary on unexpected stormy nights, then your sleeping bag is all you need. Even under such conditions, though, a tarp will protect your sleeping bag from the ground, and can be rigged to protect you from the rain.

Tube tents do essentially the same. A tube tent is nothing more than a tubular piece of fabric, open at the ends. You hang it on a cord tied between two trees, and your weight keeps the bottom on the ground.

Both of these setups leave you partially exposed to wind, rain and bugs, though. One more private alternative is a bivy sack. A bivy sack (bivouac sack) is a breathable shell, usually made of Gore-Tex, that fits around one or two sleeping bags. It's like a cocoon. On warm nights, you can leave the hood open, or zip mosquito netting shut over your head. On cooler or rainy nights, you close the Gore-Tex hood over your head. If you're claustrophobic, you won't like most bivy sacks. But a bivy sack is a useful lightweight shelter and bag protector that will keep the rain, wind and bugs out.

The next step up is a tent. A tent can be the costliest and heaviest piece of cycle camping gear, which is why many tourists go without one. I've seen "lightweight" two-man tents that weigh close to ten pounds and cost $400.

There are so many types of tents available that I can offer only the most general suggestions. For warm, dry weather, look for single-wall, uncoated-nylon (inexpensive) or Gore-Tex (very expensive) models. Single-wall, coated-nylon tents are acceptable, but only if you can vent the tent at both ends to allow your perspiration to escape.

For cool or wet weather, Gore-Tex or double-wall nylon tents (just as expensive) are best. The inner wall of a double-wall nylon tent is uncoated so that your perspiration can escape. The outer wall is coated to keep rain and snow out. On some models, the two walls are attached; on others, the outer wall is a separate fly sheet, which you attach only during bad weather.

Few lightweight tents will sleep more than two or three people. For some reason, larger tents are disproportionately heavier: you can find a good three-man tent that weighs less than four pounds, but the lightest four-man models typically weigh nine pounds or more. Two- or three-man tents are, therefore, the best buy: a group can carry several, at a lesser total weight than one big tent, yet each tent is light enough for one or two campers to use alone.

The next heaviest piece of equipment is a stove. If you're content to eat only cold meals or to gather wood at campgrounds (which is devastating to forests and, increasingly, prohibited), you can get along without the weight and expense. But after three days of riding in 40°F. drizzle, it's nice to have the comfort of a warm meal or a cup of tea back at camp.

As with tents and sleeping bags, stoves are available in a bewildering array of types, weights, and prices. Again, I can offer only the most general suggestions. Your decision will have to be based on how often you plan to cook, how many you have to cook for and how much you want to spend.

The lightest and least expensive stoves are those that use liquefied petroleum (butane or propane) cartridges. These typically have a low heat output, though, and cartridges may be hard to find—and expensive when you do find them. On some, the cartridges cannot be removed until completely empty, yet they produce little heat when they are nearly drained.

White gas, kerosene and multifuel stoves are more expensive and heavier, but burn hotter and cook faster. Fuel may be easier to find, but you may have to buy a gallon of white gas to fill your ten-ounce tank reservoir.

Cookware ranges from expensive, imported Teflon-coated cooking sets to cheap toy mess kits. Again, meal plans, size of the group and cost will determine what's best for you.

One or two pots, a lid and a skillet are sufficient for virtually all cooking. In addition, you'll probably also need:

    Salt and pepper shakers
    Cups
    Plates
    Utensils
    Knife
    Can opener
    Spatula

Waterproof matches
Pot cleaner
Biodegradable detergent
Collapsible water container
Spare fuel bottle
Water purification tablets

Proper clothing depends as much on your style of riding as on the time of year. For general spring through fall use, you might take:

Cycling helmet
Sunglasses
Long and short cycling gloves
1 long-sleeved cycling jersey
2 short-sleeved cycling jerseys or T-shirts
1 drip-dry dress shirt
2 or 3 pairs cycling shorts
1 pair slacks or knickers
3 pairs socks
Cycling shoes and sneakers, or touring shoes
Light wool sweater
Windbreaker or rain jacket
Handkerchiefs
Needle and thread
Nylon line and clothespins

That includes what you'll be wearing as well as carrying. If you'll be riding only in warm weather, forget the long gloves and jersey, and the sweater, but take a swimsuit. For cooler weather, you might want to add a down vest and riding tights and substitute another long-sleeved jersey, possibly a turtle-neck, for one of the short-sleeved ones.

Toiletries and personal items are also important. Jerry Simpson suggests:

Toothbrush
Dental floss
Shampoo

Alcohol (as disinfectant)
Tissues (also used as toilet paper)
Comb
Razor
Murine eyewash
Band-Aids
Sunscreen
Insect repellent

Simpson uses the shampoo for shaving cream, laundry detergent, soap and even dentifrice. I'll take my toothpaste, thank
you. In place of the eyewash and razor, I pack insect repellent, lip salve and a mirror. Be sure to take a towel, too, if
you'll be washing in streams or at campgrounds.

Simpson also suggests carrying about 40 medicated
Rantex cloth wipes, available in drugstores. These are like
Wash 'n' Dri towelettes, but are intended for your backside.
Without these, on extended tours you may run into problems
with hemorrhoids and itching. This is a bigger problem in
Europe than in America, because toilet paper over there is
often similar to sandpaper.

You may want to carry more first-aid supplies than just
Band-Aids and alcohol. Some touring cyclists load their
saddlebags with splints, Ace bandages, gauze and adhesive
tape. In years of cycling, though, most riders have never
required anything more than large Band-Aids and antiseptic.
It's probably more valuable to know first-aid techniques than
to carry every possible medical supply. You can usually get to
a hospital quickly if an injury is severe enough to require
treatment.

Don't forget your medications. Take enough prescription
medicines to last the length of the trip. For trips outside the
United States, Creig Hoyt, M.D., suggests asking your doctor
for 10 or 20 Lomotil tablets to cure diarrhea. If you've ever
had bad reactions to bee or wasp stings, you should also take
medication for them. Dr. Hoyt also suggests getting a
tetanus shot before your trip if you have not had one in two
years or more, just in case you scrape yourself. It will save the
time of looking for a doctor during your tour, and you can let
the aftereffects wear off at home.

There are also dozens of miscellaneous items you might want to take. Typical ones are:

Notebook and pen
Address book
Maps
Flashlight
Book
Needle/thread
Camera and film
Swiss army knife
Fishing gear
Bike light
Nylon cord (at least 8 feet)

and don't forget:

Wallet
Money
Credit cards
Identification
Keys
Traveler's checks

You'll need tools and spare parts, too. Hartley Alley of the Touring Cyclist Shop suggests having your bike over-hauled before your tour—replacing the tires, tubes, cables and brake blocks. Then, he says, take along:

Bike lock/cable
2 inner tubes
Tire irons
Patch kit
6 spokes
Spoke wrench
Freewheel remover
2 brake blocks
1 rear derailleur cable
1 rear brake cable
Small screwdriver

Chain tool
4- and 6-inch crescent wrenches
Allen wrenches to fit all allen bolts

If you ride with toe clips, carry a spare. If your bike has 700C tires, take a spare.

This may sound like a lot, but it isn't. You should be able to keep the total weight down to 25 pounds or less, including carriers and racks. If you're not sure you'll need an item, don't take it. You can always get it later, unless you're touring the Black Forest. It helps to make a list of everything you take on your first tour, then check off the items you actually use. Next time, leave the unchecked items at home.

If you'll be preparing your own meals, you can pick up food for dinner and breakfast just before stopping for the night. It's OK to carry staples, such as honey, peanut butter and bread, but don't overdo it. You'll pay for your excesses on every hill.

Packing for a Tour

Packing for a tour is an art in itself. The first step is to package all the items, or groups of items, in plastic bags. This will keep everything dry and clean. You can compress bulky items, such as clothing, with rubber bands.

How much you carry depends on how you carry it. For light loads, such as John Potter's ten pounds of tools and clothes, you can get by with just a saddlebag. If you want to carry a sleeping bag or tent, you'll also need a rear rack.

Make sure the rack is sturdy, or it will slip while you're riding. For loads up to 10 or 15 pounds, a Pletscher-type (single leg, with spring clamp on top) will suffice—but only if you use a brake-mounting brace. For heavier loads, a sturdier triangular-leg rack is essential.

If you're not carrying a stove, cookware and a camera, you can probably get by with small panniers that attach to the rear rack. These have a lower center of gravity than a saddlebag so that your bike is more stable. However, they usually cost far more.

Most panniers were at one time made of canvas because its fibers swell when wet, keeping water out. Then coated nylon panniers were introduced; these are virtually waterproof, yet lightweight. They have replaced canvas models almost completely.

Even nylon panniers, though, are not totally waterproof. Water can enter through the holes in the seam stitching. To prevent this, you'll either need rain covers or you'll have to seal the seams of your panniers with seam sealant, sold in most backpacking stores.

If small rear panniers aren't big enough to carry everything you'll need, you might want to complement them with a handlebar bag. A handlebar bag will help to more evenly distribute the weight on your bike. And you can retrieve items easily, even as you are riding. The clear map cases that come with most handlebar bags also allow you to keep your map in view while you pedal.

For the utmost in carrying capacity, choose large rear panniers and a handlebar bag. Some cycle tourists prefer small front and rear panniers to large rear ones, but front racks can decrease the flex of your fork, making your bike unstable.

The larger a pannier, the more pockets it should have. Individual pockets allow you to find things quickly without having to dump everything on the ground, but these raise the price substantially.

With panniers, it's important to pack your load low and evenly. The heaviest items should go in the bottom of the panniers, and the weight on the right pannier should balance that on the left. Otherwise your bike will be unstable. Keep the weight toward the center of the bike, too. If you have a five-pound tent and a three-pound sleeping bag to put on the rear rack, put the sleeping bag at the rear.

Improper packing can greatly increase your chances of having an accident. A study conducted between 1976 and 1977 by Dan Burden and Bruce Burgess for the U.S. National Highway Safety Administration looked into the dangers of cycling. The survey was based on accidents that took place along the 4,500-mile Bikecentennial transAmerica bicycle trail. One of the key findings was that riders who

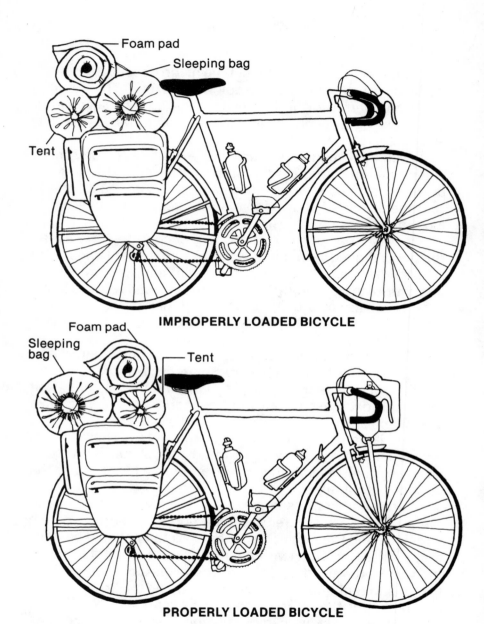

IMPROPERLY LOADED BICYCLE

PROPERLY LOADED BICYCLE

Properly and improperly loaded bicycles. The bike on the top is improperly loaded. All the weight is over the rear wheel, with a heavy tent at the rear edge of the rack. The bike on the bottom is properly loaded, with the weight distributed over the front and rear wheels. The heaviest items are placed on the front of the rear rack, near the frame, and to the bottom and inside of the packs.

carried their own luggage had three times as many accidents as cyclists riding without equipment on board.

A bicycle loaded with 30 or 40 pounds of equipment—and cyclists carried as much as 100 pounds on the transAmerica trail—handles much differently than a bare bike. Going down hills, you can easily reach speeds of more than 40 mph. The panniers and other bags catch more of the wind, so gusts are potentially more harmful. And carrying those bags may also mean that you need more room to maneuver the bike.

A skilled rider can deal with these problems. But the task is made easier if the bike is loaded evenly so that it doesn't fight the rider. Proper loading also eliminates constantly having to correct your bike to keep it upright.

There's only one way to learn to ride a fully loaded bike: by doing it. It's good to work up to it in steps. First, ride with your bags attached, but stuffed with paper. After you are accustomed to the feel of riding with the difference in wind resistance, put heavier items in your packs. Before your tour, load everything you plan to take. This test will let you see if you can carry everything. It's better to find out ahead of time than on the morning you start your tour.

If you're going to tour overseas, there are other details you should check in advance to make sure your tour goes smoothly. If you'll need a passport or visa, take care of the requirements months before you plan to leave. While you generally won't need to get shots to tour Europe, you might need to be inoculated to travel in places with disease outbreaks, as well as for touring in many parts of Asia. Many vaccines will make you feel weak or have other side effects that can last as long as two weeks, so it's best to get them well ahead of time.

Make hotel and motel reservations early, too, and check on them before leaving home. A reservation isn't worth much if it's been lost.

Spend a little time studying the history and culture of the places you plan to tour. This will give you a better appreciation of the areas, and may help you find special points of interest. Read articles in travel magazines, and try to talk with people who have recently visited the area where you'll be touring.

Try to find out what the roads are like. If you'll be riding on gravel and dirt roads, you may want to put heavier tires on your bike. If you do, or if you make any other equipment changes, road test the new items before you leave home, with the load you'll be carrying.

Even in Europe, you may find yourself in a small town where no one speaks English. In *International Bicycle Touring,* transworld cycle tourist Lloyd Sumner writes:

> Language is not such a big problem. One can get along with just English more easily in Asia and Africa than in much of rural Europe. Even so, it's worth learning a few key words. Especially learn to count and ask the prices of various items. Sign language or drawing a picture will usually get you what you want if all else fails. But not always. In one remote part of Indonesia, the local people don't even speak Indonesian. Sign language left them much amused and my drawn picture was accepted as a present and rushed off to show the neighbors. The more you know of the language of the area, the more you will get out of the trip.

Hartley Alley said that the most important phrase to learn in any language is, "What do you call this in your language?" When you get an answer, you can add it to your growing vocabulary.

If you're touring overseas, decide early whether you want to take your bike or rent or buy one once you reach the starting point. I have heard cyclists swear by each method.

The advantage of taking your own bike is that you are intimately familiar with it, and it is already set up to fit you perfectly. Unfortunately, it may not survive a transoceanic flight in the same condition. And if your bike is damaged en route, your entire trip may be spoiled.

Renting a bike at the starting point is one way around this potential problem, but other problems can arise. Rental bike quality varies from excellent to barely rideable. Jerry Simpson has found good bikes in Belgium and France for less than $25 a week; but the bike Mark Winer rented in Ireland was totally out of adjustment, with the components smothered in grease. If you do rent a bike, you may still want to take your own saddle and luggage rack. Some bike-rental shops advertise in the cycling magazines.

Contrary to popular belief, you cannot buy a bike in Europe for less than it costs in America. Moreover, if you do buy a bike overseas, you still have to go through hassles in order to ship it back home, and will have to pay an import duty. And in many parts of Europe, it's not even easy to find a good bike or even spare parts: most European bike shops sell single- and 3-speed utility machines. It's wise to place an order well in advance if you do decide to buy a bicycle overseas, and to take along spare parts.

If you take your own bike, carry a receipt so that you won't have to pay duty coming back into the United States. And check well in advance to see how your bike must be packaged for air travel. Certain airlines will let you ship your bike virtually assembled, without a carton. Some touring cyclists feel this is the best method: if it looks like a bike, they reason, it will be treated like one. But other cyclists prefer to ship their bikes disassembled in sturdy cartons. Some airlines insist on this procedure.

An important part of your preparation for any tour is training. It's a good idea to ride twice your projected daily distance at least once a week in training, with shorter rides on at least one or two other days. Dr. Hoyt rode 30 to 35 miles a day with a 100-mile ride once a week to prepare for his first European tour, on which he averaged 75 to 100 miles a day. But before his transAmerica ride, Alan Abrahamson rode only 20 to 30 miles three times a week, then worked his way up to 70 miles a day as he toured.

Whatever your training plan, don't overdo it, or you'll lose some of the fun of cycle touring. And when you finally hit the road, don't worry about your mileage or about rushing to the next town by a certain time. Take your time basking in the world around you, letting it fill your senses. If you do that, your tour will be one you'll never forget, and an inspiration to ride many more.

CHAPTER NINETEEN
BREAKING INTO RACING

For some cyclists, inching up a mountain with your home on your back is not an appealing thought. They would rather sprint up, working as hard as they can to break free of 30 other cyclists, then career down the other side at 50 mph.

Even if you're not attracted by the thrill of cycle racing, it may still have much to offer you, if only as a spectator. Cycle racing is a blend of raw strength and refined tactics that is second only to soccer as the world's largest spectator sport.

After I rode in my first club rides, I was eager to see just how good I was compared with cyclists who had been at it for years. I began to pay more attention to the racing articles in the cycling magazines, but for a long time felt that I didn't have a chance. The prospects of crashing at 50 mph left me shaking.

But then one day, I entered a local time trial, where cyclists race individually against the clock over a given distance. While I didn't set the world on fire (I finished next to last), I still had fun, and had a standard with which to measure my progress.

Cycle racing appealed to me because it gave me a chance to prove myself, a chance to find out just what I could do. It is one of the most demanding of all sports—in no other sport do the participants work at such high intensity for such long periods—and therefore challenges even the fittest.

Others enjoy cycle racing because it gives them a sense of community with other riders and satisfies their competitive urges in a healthy, productive way. Through racing, you become healthier, and can even win equipment and cash to offset your expenses.

Since cycle racing improves your fitness, some tourists and recreational riders take it up just to make their routine rides easier. When it's easier to ride, you can pay more attention to the scenery, the weather and your companions.

For the most part, cycle racing is an individual, not team effort. John Howard was attracted to cycling for just this reason: "I was playing football and was fed up with being part of the team. In cycling, if you make a mistake, it's your fault. You don't have to rely on someone else. In other sports, it gets to the point where you blame other people when it's actually your performance that's lacking."

There's plenty of room for women in cycle racing. Not only are women's classes being filled with good riders, but some of them are demolishing all the myths by regularly beating good male cyclists in mixed races. Of all sports, cycling and swimming are the two where women's performance records are closest to men's.

Just as cycling is a sport that you can pursue throughout your lifetime, so is cycle racing. There are separate categories for riders from age 8 to 80, so racers always compete with those of nearly the same age and ability.

Despite all these positive points, cycle racing is not without drawbacks, and it's definitely not for everyone. A demanding sport, it can often be grueling, even for riders who have been competing for years. Most racers retire by their early- to mid-thirties; if they continue to race, they're relegated to the veterans' category at age 35.

It takes a total commitment to make it at the national or international competition level. The best racers ride hundreds of miles every week in training, giving up school and careers to have the time to do so.

You don't have to be particularly strong to try racing. Tactics are just as important, and the weaker of two riders will often win a race just by making the right moves. And you don't have to be young, either. Cornell professor Leigh Phoenix started racing at the age of 29, and moved up to national class within two years, where he defeated top national riders.

But Phoenix's performance is not typical; it was undoubtedly helped by the fact that he kept in shape with other sports throughout his life. In addition, he has an astounding amount of the determination needed to win.

Most racers have to start much earlier to match his performance at the national level, or to reach world-class caliber. Most top racers start in their teens or earlier, and spend years moving up through the ranks.

If you'd like to compete nationally or internationally, try to find a coach or trainer immediately. These people, usually ex-champions, know how best to channel a rider's time and energy to produce winning results. They can help you avoid doing the wrong things, and show you the way to the top.

But not even the best coach will be of much help to the cyclist who has little natural ability. John Howard suggests that beginning racers who aspire to become world-class athletes should find a kinesiology or physical-education lab to measure their oxygen uptake and see if they are otherwise suited for the sport. Howard feels that it doesn't make sense for the serious athlete to plug away at a sport if he lacks the natural abilities required to excel. A good lab will help you find what you do best.

Training for Racing

Unless you merely want to explore the thrill of competition and don't care if you ever win a race, it's important to begin a thorough training program. A coach will help you devise the best program for your goals, but until you find one, or if you don't want to find one, you should work out a routine of your own.*

The principles discussed in Chapter Sixteen apply to racing schedules. But your training should emphasize certain types of training during different times of the year to build you to the greatest level of fitness.

The racing cyclist's training season begins around mid-November. For the next few months, the emphasis is on developing a spin and suppleness. The best way to train during this period is on a bike with a single fixed gear, not a freewheel. This makes you pedal constantly, and gives you good sprint training by forcing you to pedal down hills.

Some racers buy track bicycles for this training, or put together "trashmo" bikes from spare parts. The least expensive way to try fixed-gear riding is by mounting a fixed sprocket on the rear hub in place of the freewheel on your 10-speed. You can lock it in place with a spare bottom-bracket adjustable-cup lockring. Remove your derailleurs,

---

* Ed Burke's *Inside the Cyclist: Physiology for the Two-Wheeled Athlete* is a good reference for establishing a training program.

and shorten the chain so that it just covers the small front sprocket and the fixed rear sprocket. A 42 × 18 combination is perfect, although you may want to use an even larger rear cog if the weather or terrain is bad.

The only alternative to riding a fixed gear is shifting into a similar gear and leaving it there while you ride, making a constant effort never to freewheel.

Take it easy during these rides. Push only hard enough so that you feel slight resistance. Ride a maximum of 50 to 65 miles per workout. On exceptionally cold days, limit your workouts to about an hour.

If the weather is too cold or the road conditions too bad for you to ride during the winter months, you should do something else that will strengthen your legs and cardiovascular system. Roller riding is good for maintaining your conditioning, but is virtually worthless for improving your strength. Only if you combine roller riding with a good weight-training plan can you hope to improve your overall fitness. The Nautilus program is highly recommended.

By late February, the blizzards should have stopped and the temperatures have risen enough for you to hit the road. Use a gear within the same range as you've been riding, but you can ride your 10-speed, shifting when necessary. Six 90-minute rides a week are sufficient.

By March, you should be taking longer rides and picking up your pace. You should be using a higher gear, and be ready to begin occasional interval training.

By the start of racing season, your training should be rigorous. Coach Jack Simes, in *Winning Bicycle Racing*, recommends following a schedule such as this one for a national-class racer:

Monday: 50 to 65 miles in 42 × 15, flat terrain;
Tuesday: 90 minutes of very fast riding in the same gear.
Wednesday: up to 100 miles in low gears, with possibly a half hour in your top gears;
Thursday: same as Tuesday;
Friday: about 80 miles, not too hard unless you feel great;
Saturday, before Sunday race: easy 40 miles.

If you're not racing on Sunday, train that day as close to a racing pace as possible.

If you're going to become competitive, you have to go out and work at it every day. "You have to make riding as vital as eating," Leigh Phoenix once told me. Every day you miss, or every day you goof off on a ride is a day's training lost. The only time you shouldn't ride is when you have injured yourself or are physically worn out.

If you don't have time to follow a schedule such as the one Simes prescribes, or don't have such grand aspirations, ride as much as you can, following the same hard-easy-hard pattern. This will keep you from wearing down. Make sure that you get enough rest and enough variety in your training so that you don't go stale. And never stop listening to your body. As Leigh Phoenix pointed out, "There's a fine line between building up and tearing down."

Many national-class racers keep a careful record of their resting pulse rate, weight and general mental outlook every day. Drastic changes signal that something is wrong.

"Even if you're not interested in racing, but only in improving yourself," John Howard suggested, "keep a diary of your performance. You have to know yourself. It sounds easy, but it takes many years."

Of course, you don't have to wait until November to begin race training. If you want to start in the middle of the year, begin by looking for novice-class races in your area. These are often sponsored by racing clubs to attract new members and give older members training for riding in packs. A club in my hometown holds a series of races every Thursday evening. There are separate classes for novice and advanced cyclists, but a newcomer is allowed to enter the upper classes. Anyone who shows up with a bike can enter. The races are advertised in the club's newsletter and in local bike shops.

Another good way to train is by riding in time trials. Time trials are races over a fixed distance against the clock. Riders leave the starting line at one-minute intervals and are not permitted to pace each other or ride together. Early in the season, many clubs hold 10-mile time trials, adding 25- to 100-mile races later.

While some racers find time trials painful and boring, I think they're the best introduction to racing. Since you ride alone, you don't have to worry about your handling or tactics. And while it's thrilling to be one of the fastest riders at a time trial, the real thrill comes from bettering your own time, no matter how slow it is compared to the other riders'.

"If you enjoy playing with the relationships of the mind and body," John Howard said, "if you enjoy pushing yourself to the limit, you'll enjoy time trialing. I think runners would enjoy it. Even if you tour, you need to know your limits, strengths and weaknesses. Time trialing helps you learn them, and gives you a good, fast workout."

As soon as the racing season opens, you should start entering races sanctioned by the United States Cycling Federation (USCF). These are the races that count, and the ones where the top racers meet.

To enter a USCF race, you must have a license. This costs $15 a year for riders 15 years or older, $10 for those under 15. You can get an application form from USCF at PO Box 480, East Detroit, MI 48021.

You will be classified by your age as of the first of the year in one of five categories: midget (8–11), intermediate (12–14), junior (15–17), senior (18–34) and veteran (35 and up). Men and women are classified separately.

You'll also be placed in a category according to your ability and experience. You start in category 4, and stay there while you learn the basics. To move up into the next category (3, regional competition), you must place among the top three in three sanctioned races or the top six in six, and must submit proof to your local USCF representative. Alternately, after at least eight sanctioned races, you can ask to be upgraded, based on your experience and competence.

The procedure for moving up to category 2 (state competition) and category 1 (national competition) is the same. If you find you've graduated before you were ready for the next category, you can ask to be downgraded to a lower category.

"Don't get into a hurry," Leigh Phoenix advises. "Experience gained in the lower categories is vital."

The USCF publishes a rule book for racers, which covers

everything from rules of the road to clothing. You must follow the rules, or you will be disqualified from any USCF-sanctioned race you enter. Black racing shorts and a helmet are among the requirements.

A Variety of Events

When you start racing, look for a local racing club. In addition to holding weekly races and time trials, good clubs also hold training rides, offer coaching and hold informative meetings. Many clubs have sponsors who help pay for the club's activities, including sending a team to distant races. In return, the cyclists wear jerseys emblazoned with their sponsor's name.

In the beginning, it's best to try as many different kinds of races as you can so that you can find what event you're best at. USCF sponsors a host of different events, one of which just might be your forte.

The most popular races in this country are criteriums. These are held on level courses, measuring less than 2 miles. Criteriums are often staged on a rectangular circuit around one or two city blocks. Senior races run from 25 miles to 100 kilometers (about 62 miles) with as many as 100 laps on the circuit.

Since the course is flat and the race short compared to other events, a criterium is fast. Speeds average more than 25 mph, and occasionally hit 30 mph. There are no hills to break up the pack, so riders stay bunched together until the final sprint. And there are the inevitable crashes as the pack narrows through the tight corners, along with a hair-raising sprint for the finish line. You have to be fast, have good concentration, and be good at handling and sprinting to make it as a criterium racer.

Road races are run over longer, hillier courses. A road race may consist of just one or a few laps on a large circuit, or may start at one point and end at another. Distances range from less than 10 miles to more than 100 miles, with most senior races falling closer to the longer distance. Depending on terrain, weather and wind speed, the winning speed may range between 20 and 30 mph.

Because road races cover a variety of terrain, they give every rider a chance to exploit his strengths. Time trialists will try to wear down the other riders by pushing the pace as fast as they can. Sprinters sit back and wait until the end, when they try to blast free of the pack and over the finish line. Climbers wait until the hills, then work as hard as they can to break away.

Sanctioned time trials are run under the same rules as club time trials. The skilled time trialist knows exactly how much effort he can sustain over the distance, and allots it so he is totally depleted as he crosses the finish line—and not a second sooner. It takes determination to stay hunched over in a streamlined position for an hour or more at a time, pedaling as hard as you can.

Two types of time trials don't require great speed and strength: the 12- and 24-hour time trials. Unlike the other events, which are run over a preset distance, these events are run by the clock. The person who covers the longest distance in the allotted time wins. The world record for the 24-hour time trial is just under 510 miles, or a little better than 21 mph for a complete day. Endurance is obviously the key to these events; they may be for you if you are better at riding far than fast.

Another type is the team time trial. The classic is 100 kilometers (62 miles), although shorter and longer ones are run. Usually, four riders form a team, with each one taking the lead for a short burst of speed, then dropping back. A winning team has to run like clockwork.

Stage racing, while nearly a century old in Europe, is still in its infancy in the United States. A stage race consists of a series of races, including criteriums, time trials and road races, over a period of several days. The classic stage race is the Tour de France, a three-week-long ordeal that is the most prestigious race in the cycling world. The Red Zinger Classic, held yearly in Colorado, is the premier stage race in the United States and draws top-class cyclists from around the world.

Stage race placings are determined by adding the times of each rider over all the stages, with the lowest time winning, or by awarding points for the top places in each race, with points or time bonuses given to the first to the top of a mountain or the first to finish a lap of a criterium. There is big money in stage racing, but only the best international riders see it—or even receive an invitation to the races.

Cyclocross races are run outdoors, but not on paved roads. Instead, cyclocross courses run through forests, down unpaved hills, across streams. Cyclocross consists as much of running as cycling, and requires the skill to know when each will be most advantageous.

Cyclocross events are held during the winter, and many racing cyclists ride them to stay in shape. Sanctioned cyclocross races are grueling, perhaps the most brutal type of cycle racing, and can quickly destroy a bike. Still, the event's popularity is growing, and it may even become an Olympic event.

There is yet another category of racing, track racing. These events are run on paved or wooden indoor and outdoor oval tracks, using superlight bikes with a single fixed gear and no brakes. Events include:

. . . *The Pursuit.* Two cyclists take off from points on opposite sides of the track, and chase each other over a given distance. The first rider to catch the other or to complete the distance is the winner.

. . . *The Team Pursuit.* Groups of four riders race the pursuit. This race requires precise teamwork.

. . . *The 1,000-Meter Time Trial.* This is also known as the kilo. The object is to ride the distance alone as fast as possible. While simple in execution, it is one of the most demanding races. Even the best kilo riders ride the event no more than twice a year because it is so brutal.

. . . *Match Sprints.* These are also run a distance of 1,000 meters. Two riders start together. The first one over the finish line wins, no matter how long it takes. This event is based on tactics. Cyclists spend the better part of the race just jockeying for position. Only the rare rider will try to go for it from the start: his opponent will then be able to draft behind him until they near the finish line, where he can zip by. Sometimes being able to hold your bike at a standstill is as vital as being able to ride at full speed.

. . . *Tandem Sprints.* A rarer form of sprint, in which two or more tandem teams compete over a 1,500-meter course.

. . . *Points Race.* This is a massed-start race of five to ten miles. It includes a series of sprints, with points being awarded to the top riders in each sprint. The rider who finishes with the most points wins.

. . . *Miss-and-Out.* Another massed-start race where the last rider over the line after each lap or every other lap is dropped, until just two or three riders are left. They then sprint for the win. This is a fast, exciting race.

There are other track events, including the Madison, where team riders take turns racing; handicap races, where cyclists ride different distances proportional to their abilities; and motorpacing, where cyclists on special bikes draft motorcycles around the track at speeds up to 50 mph.

Your First Race

No matter what type of race you enter, there are preparatory steps you should take. Make sure you're feeling well and have been getting enough rest. Sometimes a cyclist will drive all day Saturday to enter a race on Sunday, then collapse in the middle of the race.

It's good to have someone along to help with the driving chores, as well as for other reasons. In longer races, a support person can hand you food and water and have a replacement wheel ready in case your tire punctures. A support person can also help rub out your kinks after the race, and share your victory or soften your defeat.

Make sure you take everything you will need. Your racing kit should include: shorts, socks, jersey, shoes, gloves, helmet and, if the weather is cool, a warm-up suit. If there will be a place to clean up after the race, take a towel and soap, and a brush for your hair. Pack a tool for everything on your bike, and spare cables, tires and, if you own or can borrow them, a spare set of wheels.

Eat your last meal at least two to three hours before the race. Arrive at the track at least an hour early. Register, then ride a few practice laps around the course to size it up and make sure your bike is in top condition. Twenty minutes at a moderate pace will warm you up and loosen your muscles. But don't overdo it, and don't finish your warm-up too long before the race begins or you'll cool down again.

Your warm-up ride will help you size up the course; by checking the program, you should also be able to size up the competition. By the time you leave the starting line, you should have a race plan.

In the beginning, you'll just want to try to stick with the field. But as you gain experience, you'll learn other riders' traits, and be able to pinpoint racers who are just a little better than yourself. The next step is to stay with them, then to beat them. If things go well, you'll eventually be planning to beat the best riders.

It won't be easy in the beginning, unless you're incredibly lucky or strong. The other racers are going to do everything they can to drop you; to them, you're just a dangerous new rider who may cause them to crash and lose the race and prizes. Be prepared for an onslaught of insults, or to crash or be dropped from the pack.

Through it all, just try to hold on. Ride as smoothly and strongly as you can, and accept failures. Maybe ten years ago a kid in sneakers on a $50 bike could come out of nowhere and win a race, but as the caliber of racing has improved, this has become virtually unheard of. It takes time to become good at anything; if you expect to set the world on fire in your first few races, you're only in for disappointment.

"To do badly at first can be extremely disappointing," John Howard said. "You have to keep an open mind, and don't take it too seriously at first. Don't feel that you're going to conquer the world in your first few months.

"You have to watch for a sign of some sort. By the end of your first year, you'll know if you are competitive. You won't be riding in category 3 and 4 events for long if you have any ability."

During those first few months, you should work on your weak points and try to exploit your strong ones. If you're a good climber, you'll want to ride hilly races. But at the same time, riding criteriums and time trials will help you develop your other abilities.

Whatever else you do, don't blame your failures on your equipment. This is easy to do when you see the winning racers sitting atop $1,500 exotic beauties. But equipment is the least important factor in racing: your mind and body are far more vital. One racer I know became despondent when his $1,000 Italian racing bike was stolen. But after he started racing on a $200 Schwinn, he became stronger and faster by trying to compensate for the differences in the bikes. "Bad equipment may cause you to lose a race," Leigh Phoenix says, "but good equipment won't be the reason for winning."

Sometimes when I look at some "racers" I know—people who own seven bikes but race only once or twice a year, and then with dismal results—I wonder how many of them race so that they can own all that equipment, rather than the other way around. It's especially easy for cycle racers to fall into this trap, looking at the bike as an end in itself, rather than a means to an end.

And it is those ends, after all, that are important: enjoyment and fulfillment. Cycle racing should be just one more way to reach them.

CHAPTER TWENTY
THE CUSTOM BIKE

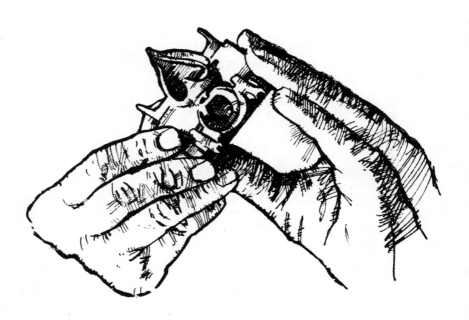

While it's not a good idea to become obsessed with bicycles rather than cycling, a poor bike, or one not designed for your needs, can interfere with your cycling enjoyment.

After my cycling pal Brian Karger had pedaled his first several hundred miles, he became painfully aware of the limitations of his 50-pound, trusty-rusty 10-speed and, at the same time, began to notice the more exotic bikes that other cyclists were riding.

While Brian managed to push his bike through several long, hard rides, including his first half-century, it hadn't been sheer pleasure. The bearings and cones on his bike were constantly working out of adjustment, almost locking the hubs, headset and bottom bracket. The bike's weight made it difficult to accelerate, as well as hard to drag up the hills around our western Pennsylvania homes. The bike's gearing didn't help the climbs: it was set up for flat Kansas roads.

Not everyone starts cycling on a cut-rate trusty-rusty like Brian's. But sooner or later, every cyclist who becomes addicted to the joy of cycling decides to upgrade his equipment for similar reasons: to cut weight, make maintenance easier, get a better fit for himself or his style of cycling or just for the sheer joy of ownership.

There are two ways to accomplish these goals: by putting better equipment on your bike or by buying a new one.

Building Your Own Bike

Replacing components is the least expensive method—sometimes. If you just want lighter wheels, different gearing or a more comfortable saddle, it makes sense to buy only those parts and add them to the bike you own.

But if your plans are wider in scope—such as outfitting your bike for touring or cutting a 30-pound bike down to 20—replacing components can be costly and unproductive. I speak from experience: I once modified a $150 bike by adding $250 worth of parts. Unfortunately, the end result was not nearly as good as a $400 bike would have been.

There's a good reason why this happened. Manufacturers buy components by the thousand, or even million, at costs far lower than what you have to pay for a single unit. Building a $250 bike from scratch can cost $350 or more.

Still, in some cases it is actually less expensive to build your bike from parts, particularly if you don't want the exact accessories that are standard equipment on most bikes. After shopping for weeks, Brian finally fell in love with a $600 bike that was on sale for $450. But as he looked it over carefully, he noticed that the gearing was designed for racing, not touring; that the wheels were too light for traveling over the potholed roads he rode every day on his way to work; that the handlebar stem was too long for him to reach the bars; and a host of other problems. We tallied up what it would cost to replace those items, and the price came out to about $150, for a total of $600 for a 24-pound bike. Then we sat down and figured out how much it would cost to build a bike from scratch with all the things he wanted. The total came to $500, for a 19-pound bike.

You don't have to be an ace mechanic to build your own bike, and you don't need a large cash outlay either. You can get all the information you need from other riders or a good maintenance book, such as *Richard's Bike Book* by Richard Ballantine. And if you know a racer or shop owner, you might be able to borrow the special tools you'll need.

You cannot build a bike from scratch for much less than $500. But if you watch for bargains and sales, especially those advertised by mail-order firms in the cycling magazines, you can build an excellent bike for that price. Also watch for package deals: some mail-order firms offer discounts if you buy a group of components at the same time, or offer a discount on the components when you buy a frame. A few years ago, one of my friends built a bike this way for about $300. When she took it into a bike repair shop to buy a spare part and told the salesman she had built it herself, he said, "That's really dumb. It always costs about 40 percent more to do it that way."

My friend had looked at dozens of bikes before deciding to build her own, and knew she had the best deal. But she played along: "Really? Then how much would it cost for an assembled bike like this one?"

The clerk looked the bike over carefully, then said, "about $400."

Whether you're buying a new bike or replacing just a part or two on your old one, you'll be able to make a much better choice if you study different components before you buy.

Undoubtedly, the most-often-replaced bike part is the saddle. In Chapter Four, we looked at the differences in saddles that can make one model sheer heaven and another sheer hell.

Your Gearing Needs

Bad gearing can also take the fun out of cycling. If your low is not low enough, your high not high enough, or you don't have the proper middle gears, you should change your gearing setup. But if you do not have these problems, leave your gearing alone. Don't change your freewheel cluster just because the silver one you saw at the store looks prettier than the black one on your bike.

If you have a 3-speed bike, you can change your gearing by substituting a larger or smaller rear sprocket or by changing chainwheels. The only problem is that doing so changes all your gears. This, then, is a change you'll want to make only if all your gears are too high or too low.

You can be much more precise in changing the gearing on a 10-speed. There are two ways to get the gearing you want: by replacing the front chainwheels or the rear cluster. Replacing a chainwheel is like replacing the rear cog on a 3-speed: doing so will change five of your gears. And chainrings are expensive, costing as much as $30 each.

Most freewheels, however, sell for far less, and you can lower your outlay even more by simply replacing the individual cogs on your freewheel (at about $2–$4 each), provided you buy or borrow special cog removers (less than $10 a pair).

The first thing you have to do is decide where your gearing is deficient: lows, highs, middle, everywhere? For a long time, I rode a 50–38 × 13–15–17–20–24 combination. While the middle gears were good, it was a strain to climb the

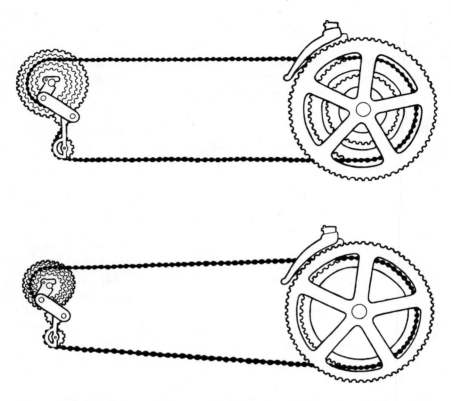

Note the differences between the touring and racing drive trains. The touring drive train on the top has wide-range triple front chain-wheels, a 14–34-tooth rear freewheel and a long-reach derailleur. The racing drive train (bottom) has double chainwheels of just a few teeth difference, a 13–17 rear freewheel and a small-capacity derailleur.

longest and steepest hills around my home in the 38 × 24. And even when I came down those mountains I never used my 50 × 13: the roads were too bad to ride that fast.

So I changed my freewheel to 14–17–20–24–28. I still have the same middle gears (38 × 17, 38 × 20, 50 × 17, 50 × 20, 50 × 24), but now have a lower low gear and a high gear that I use more often.

While this setup works for me, I know cyclists who think it is worthless. They point out the duplicated gears and large jumps between gears, but these don't bother me. I have five or six gears that I like, and don't have to double-shift (shift both the front and rear gears at the same time) every time I want to change gears.

Unfortunately, the setups that give the best range, least duplicated gears and closest steps between gears require double-shifting. The shift sequence goes:

Gear	Chainwheel	Freewheel Cog
1 (low)	small	1 (largest)
2	large	1
		double-shift
3	small	2
4	large	2
		double-shift
5	small	3
6	large	3
		double-shift
7	small	4
8	large	4
		double-shift
9	small	5
10 (high)	large	5 (smallest)

As you can see, to go from second to third gear requires you to shift both front and rear sprockets at once. Double-shifts are also needed between fourth and fifth, sixth and seventh, and eighth and ninth gears. As complicated as this seems, this is still an easily remembered shift pattern.

To set up your gears like this, you will probably have to replace one or both of the chainrings as well as freewheel cogs. Good examples of chainwheel and freewheel combinations are:

52–49 × 14–16–18–20–22   52–48 × 13–15–17–20–23
50–45 × 14–17–20–24–29   50–46 × 14–17–22–28–34

For lower lows or higher highs, you can use different chainrings as long as you keep the same ratio between the chainrings. (For example, there's a 10 percent difference between the 50 and 45 chainrings, so you can also use 46–42 or 44–40, or any other combination with the same difference.)

Alternately, you can change to a crossover shift sequence. There are no double-shifts with this setup, but it restricts your range and choice of gears. A good example of the crossover sequence is a racing setup, 55–50 × 13–14–15–16–18. You use the 50 sprocket with only the 18, 16 and 15 cogs, then shift over to the 55 sprocket, and move up to the 14 and 13 cogs. This limits you to six gears and results in a high low gear, but for racing or riding on the flats, it's a simple system.

For touring, unless you're taking a tail-wind tour of Kansas, you won't need huge gears. It's harder to pedal a loaded bike than an empty one, so the only chance you'll have to use high gears is coming down steep hills or mountains. And that's when most everyone uses his brakes instead.

Most cyclists probably will never need a top gear higher than 47 × 14 or, more likely, 42 × 14. One of the most avid touring cyclists I've known, a man who often rode 200 miles in a day and could knock off 100 miles in six hours, had a 42 × 14 high gear.

Cyclists have made it through the Rockies and the Alps with low gears of 42 × 24. But I doubt that they had much fun. When you're touring, pushing on day after day, up unexpected hills, through unexpected rain, over the extra miles to hunt food or shelter, it's good to have superlow gears. Even though you may grow stronger on your tour, those gears can come in handy in your weakest moments.

As a rough guide, figure that you'll need a low gear of about 42 × 34 for cruising with a light load in hilly country;

about 32 × 34 for heavier loads or steep hills; and about a 26 × 34 for mountain touring with heavy loads. These may be too low for your style of riding, but I'd rather have a low gear that I end up not using than not have one I need.

I hesitate to mention 15-speed setups, because their high prices are often not justified. As of this writing, you can put together an inexpensive 10-speed combination with a low gear of about 28 × 34. That will just about get you up the sides of the World Trade Centers, or up the steepest mountains with a fully loaded bike. Alpine tourists use only 28 × 28 or 28 × 32 to climb mountains such as the Col du Galibier, which, in 11 miles, rises from an altitude of 3,986 feet to an altitude of 8,684 feet.

The most expensive 15-speed setups offer only marginally lower lows, with inner chainrings of 26 and 24 teeth. But they do offer a wide range of gears. Dr. Clifford Graves, president of the International Bicycle Touring Society, has traveled thousands of miles with 50–45–30 × 14–16–20–25–31 and 50–40–30 × 14–17–21–25–31 setups. Sumner White of S. F. White Touring Components recommends a 52–42–26 × 16–18–20–24–31 for touring with a load.

One reason that such wide-range setups are exceptionally expensive is that they also require wide-range derailleurs. Standard front derailleurs can only handle chainrings that are no more than 15 or 16 teeth apart (52–36, for instance). When there is a 20-tooth or larger difference, you may need a wide-range touring derailleur.

Likewise, the typical rear derailleur is hard-pressed to take up the slack between the lowest and highest gears of wide-range setups. Even though you use only the two or three smallest rear cogs with the inner chainring and the two or three largest cogs with the outer chainring on a 15-speed, your rear derailleur may have to take up as many as 26 chain links of slack, something even some "touring" derailleurs cannot do well. Those that can do the job tend to be costly.

Revamping your gearing to match your style of riding will greatly increase your performance and enjoyment. Another way to better performance and more enjoyment is by switching to lighter wheels.

Lighten Your Wheels

As mentioned in Chapter Four, the wheels of your bike determine how easily you can accelerate, climb hills, turn and stop. The lighter the wheels, the better, up to a point.

While many cyclists buy new wheels for increased performance, some want wheels that are more rugged. As heavy as they are, the wheels on many standard bikes are not sturdy enough to support heavy riders or touring loads. Often, the spokes and rims are too weak for the loads, so the spokes break or the rims dent easily.

Even more important than the components is the skill with which the wheels are built. If you find that you're regularly breaking spokes, but don't want to spend $50–$100 for new wheels, take your wheels to a shop that sells top-line equipment and ask the mechanic to rebuild your wheels with heavy-gauge spokes. Expect to pay about $20.

Ironically, the mechanic may suggest that you change to lighter alloy rims if you're using steel ones now. The ultra-light, box-section alloy rims that have become popular recently are often stronger than their steel counterparts. If you

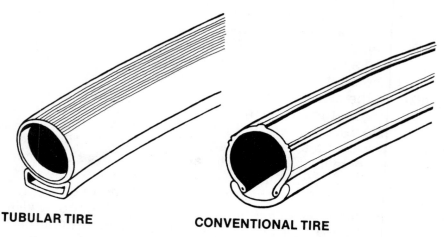

TUBULAR TIRE   **CONVENTIONAL TIRE**

Tubular vs. conventional tire. Note in the cutaway view that the one-piece casing of the tubular does not have steel beads as a conventional tire does.

Compare the low-flange hub on the left with the high-flange hub on the right. The smaller hub uses longer spokes, which are more flexible and shock absorbent, while the larger hub uses shorter spokes that are not as flexible. With large-flange hubs more power is delivered to the ground, but the ride is stiffer. Small-flange hubs are the overwhelming choice of cycle racers, tourists and commuters. Large-flange hubs are only practical on smooth roads and tracks.

don't care about working a little harder, and don't ride in the rain (remember, steel rims are virtually impossible to stop when wet), stick with your original rims. But if you want to substantially increase your bike's performance, or if your steel rims are badly banged up, change to alloy rims.

A heavy-duty steel rim, tire and tube combination weighs about 1,300 grams per wheel. An equally strong setup with alloy rims and lighter tires and tubes weighs only about 700 grams per wheel, more than 2½ pounds less per pair. Because they are made of costlier materials that are exceptionally strong for their weight, alloy wheels may actually be sturdier than steel ones, and will weigh far less but cost more. A third type of setup, using a different type of tire and rim, can tip the scale at less than 500 grams per wheel, almost another pound lighter.

This third setup uses the tubular, or sew-up tire. Conventional tires consist of three parts: tire, tube and rim. The tire has wire or fiberglass beads in its edge that rest inside the lips of the rim. The pressure inside the tire holds it in place.

Tubular tires are sewn closed around the tubes. The rims have no lips, only a smooth, top surface to which the tire is glued. Because there are no beads or lips, and because the tire casings are made of lighter fabrics, tubular tires are lighter, more expensive and often more fragile than standard wired-on tires. They are easier to change than wired-ons, but are much harder to patch.

Until the mid-1970s, if you wanted to ride fast and easily, you rode on tubulars. But with the development of lightweight wired-on tires, this has changed. While the lightest wired-ons are still as much as a ½-pound heavier than good tubulars, they are usually less expensive and sturdier.

For all cycling except advanced racing, lightweight wired-ons are the best bet. I have ridden thousands of miles on the lightest wired-ons made with virtually no problems, even on chewed-up, glass-littered roads with 20 pounds of groceries on board. Used with puncture-resistance latex tubes, these tires give a quick, responsive ride and are great for climbing and novice racing, yet perform equally as well under touring loads.

If you are beyond novice racing, or want your recreational rides to be as easy as possible, tubulars are the best choice. But there is a wide disparity between the best and the worst tubulars, both in quality and price. Generally, you get what you pay for. I know recreational riders who have ridden 5,000 miles on a silk tubular without a single flat, and others who haven't been able to ride 10 miles without puncturing their inexpensive tubulars.

The least expensive tubulars are made by vulcanization, as are all wired-on tires. A strip of rubber compound molded into a tread pattern is partially melted into the casing cords.

The best tubulars are cold-processed. In cold-processing a tire, the tread strip is attached by hand to the casing and glued in place with a latex solution. The process is more expensive and time-consuming than vulcanization, but avoids heat that softens the tread and makes the sidewalls brittle. In addition, the treads on cold-processed tires are straighter and track better.

Cold-processed tubulars have casings made of cotton or silk. Cotton is less expensive, but is too stiff for riding on most roads. Silk absorbs road shocks better, but is more expensive: up to $50 a tire.

The most-often-used tubular for racing and touring is the Clement Criterium 250-gram Seta (silk). Lighter riders can get by on 220 Setas, but heavier cyclists should stick with the 275-gram Paris–Roubaix Setas or the 290-gram Campionato del Mundo Setas. Vittoria makes a line of silk tubulars comparable to the Clements, just as good and outrageously priced. These tubulars are the only ones worth buying; they are in a class by themselves.

If you decide to try good tubulars—and more people are deciding not to, since lighter weight wired-ons are less troublesome and almost as responsive at a lower cost—it's a wise idea to age your tires before you use them. This strengthens the threads of cold-processed tires so that they won't tear or puncture as easily.

To age a tubular tire, mount it on a rim and inflate to about 50 psi. Then cover it with a garbage bag, add a little talcum, and hang in a dark, dry corner for about a year. Don't try to age vulcanized tires: aging only makes them more brittle and fragile.

Switching to tubulars also requires buying new rims, of course. Tubular rims weigh between 200 and 400 grams each. The best ones for medium-weight riders are those in the 290- to 350-gram range. Check with a local racer or club cyclist to see what rims are best suited for the roads in your area.

The other major element of a wheel is the hub. Most mid-priced bicycles include good hubs. As long as you're sure you're not going to need your old set of wheels, you can use your original hubs as the center of your new lightweight wired-ons or tubulars.

Even though you can have tubular wheels built up around your present hubs, it's probably a better idea to keep your set of wired-ons. Good tubular tires are too fragile to use all the time; use wired-on tires for training and riding in bad weather.

Most mail-order bicycle shops sell preassembled tubular wheels. Typically, the cost of the wheels is about the cost of the individual parts, so the wheel building, normally a $15–$25 job, is free. As an alternative, you can pick the rims, hubs and spokes you want and pay a local shop to assemble them.

Hubs are simple, but come in a staggering array of models and prices, from less than $20 a pair to more than $100. Generally, the more expensive hubs work slightly more smoothly, will last longer and are better polished than the less expensive models.

The most expensive hubs also have one other important difference over typical models: they use sealed bearings. In a typical hub, pedal, bottom bracket or headset, ball bearings run against tapered cones, and are bathed in grease or oil to limit friction. This is inexpensive, but leaves something to be desired.

For one thing, loose bearings must be kept clean, lubricated and in proper adjustment. This is messy and requires skill and special tools to maintain. When the cones work their way out of adjustment, excess friction is created and you have to work harder.

Sealed bearings are shielded from outside dirt and water, and also keep grease from running out. The bearings and races are assembled in one piece so that they are always in adjustment. Since the bearings are not wedged into place under pressure, they create less friction. If the bearings do fail, or if they wear out after five or ten years of use, you merely replace the entire sealed assembly for a few dollars.

While car designers have been using sealed bearings for years, sealed bicycle components are still in their infancy, with new manufacturers popping up and disappearing every month. But if you take the time to track down sealed components made by established manufacturers, it will save you time and money. You can replace your hubs, pedals, bottom bracket, headset (the bearings around which the front fork rotates), and even derailleur pulleys (the wheels in the rear derailleur that the chain rides on) with sealed units.

Custom Frames

It would cost much more to replace your frame, but that is what many cyclists do first, even if there is no reason to. The frames on most mid-quality bikes are excellent, and serve a variety of uses: light touring, novice racing, commuting and general recreational riding. Only if you become hooked on a specialized type of cycling is it worth your while to look for a better frame.

If you're in the market for a racing frame, it would be hard to beat the ones that are standard equipment on top-line stock bikes such as the Schwinn Paramount and the Raleigh Record. These bikes include frames that are rigid, so they transfer most of your power directly to the ground, but are resilient enough to absorb road shocks. And the frames weigh between four and seven pounds, substantially less than the eight- to ten-pound frames found on most mid-priced 10-speeds.

Most of these stock racing frames are built of Reynolds' alloy 531 tubing. This brand, as well as Columbus and Champion, is suitable for most hard riding, including touring and racing. The tubing used in these top-line frames is double-butted: the ends of the tubes are thicker than the middles, to put extra material at the stress points while holding overall

Double-butted tubing construction. The ends of the tube are thicker than the middle. This keeps the weight of the tube low while putting extra material at the joints, where there is more stress.

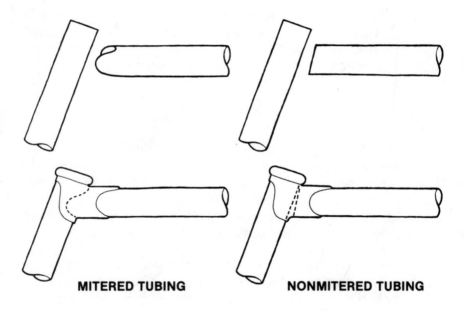

MITERED TUBING   **NONMITERED TUBING**

Top-quality bikes have mitered tubing which enables the separate tubes to act as a single piece of metal.

weight down. In addition, the tubes are precisely mitered, or fishmouthed, where they join so that after they are brazed together the tubes act as a single piece of metal. In less expensive frames, the mitering is not as precise and the tubes can flex inside the lugs at the joints. Contrary to what many novices believe, lugs are not meant to hold the tubes together, but merely to distribute the stress at the joints over a wider area.

For the racer of average build, these stock frames offer a good combination of strength and lightness. But it's difficult to buy the frames alone, and complete bikes cost $1,000 and up. If you cannot afford a complete bike, are not of average build, or want a frame designed for touring or commuting instead of racing, you'll have to buy a separate frame.

Although bike prices have soared during the past decade, you can still buy a good separate frame for as little as $150. At the other end of the scale, it's possible to spend more than $1,000 for a frame.

Unless you've been riding for years, it's best to stick to the models at the lower end of the scale. Most of them are made of Reynolds, Columbus or Champion tubing, which are uniformly good and can easily be repaired.

More expensive models are often made of exotic materials, usually titanium or reinforced aluminum alloys. These frames are remarkably light and, the manufacturers claim, unbelievably rigid.

Unfortunately, such designs are often far from perfect. Should an exotic frame break, only the manufacturer can repair it, and then at high cost and often only after indeterminable delays. One of my friends had to wait two years for a replacement for an Italian aluminum frame that broke within months after he bought it.

While all of these exotic frames, and most of the stock steel models, are produced only in standard dimensions, there are dozens of frame builders who will custom-build a frame to fit your body.

When you buy a standard bicycle or frame, you pick your frame size by matching the seat tube length to your inseam. The frames come in a variety of seat tube lengths, but the manufacturers build them for average-size torsos and arm lengths. Unfortunately, virtually no one is average. While many cyclists can comfortably ride standard frames, short men and women especially have problems: many manufacturers shorten the seat tubes of their small frames but leave the top tubes as long as the ones on the largest models.

Much of this mismatch can be corrected with stem and seat adjustments. But then the cyclist may not be able to ride in the proper position.

A custom frame builder will measure his client's arms,

legs, thighs, torso and even feet, and will tailor a frame to fit. And, of course, the custom builder's workmanship and finish may well be far better than that of the assembly line.

A custom frame can be designed for specific uses. Rather than being built for general racing, touring or track use, it can be designed for the specific race, tour or track event the customer will participate in.

For example, a criterium racer wants a bike that is, above all, quick and responsive around corners. The geometry and materials of that bike will be different than the time trialist's bike, which would be lighter and less upright. A production racing frame would be a compromise of the needs of the criterium rider, the time trialist, the climber, the sprinter and the general road racer, and it would be less than ideal for any of those uses.

The custom-frame builder can vary more than frame angles and tube lengths. He can use different tubing gauges for heavy or lightweight riders, and can offer an attractive choice of custom-finished lugs, bottom brackets, fork crowns and seat clusters.

Good lugwork sets a custom frame apart from a stock frame in strength, beauty and difficulty of manufacture. A good frame builder tapers his lugs with a file so that stresses extend smoothly from one tube to the next. Many builders make decorative cutouts in the lugs; these cutouts also provide a window to monitor solder flow during the brazing process.

The custom-frame builder can also offer a wide range of finishes and braze-on accessories. Braze-ons replace frame-marring clamps that hold shift levers, cable stops, water bottles, pumps and racks. Braze-on reinforcements are used on fork blades, seatstays, chainstays and bottom brackets.

Whether you choose a custom or stock frame depends on several factors. If you have little experience with a particular type of riding and are more interested in having, for example, a general racing frame rather than a frame designed for a specific racing event, a stock model may well fill the bill, assuming you are not of extremely odd proportions. A stock model will not give you as varied a choice of braze-ons and finishes, but will not take the eight months to a year in waiting that many frame builders demand, and will not tie you down to a frame designed for a specific purpose. A general racing frame may not be the ultimate frame for time trialing, but it will be better for that purpose than a criterium frame would be.

Still, most stock and custom frames cost about the same, $350–$1,000, and if you are sure of your needs or are willing to trust a builder's judgment, the wait for delivery of that one-of-a-kind frame may well be worth it. In either case, if you are thinking about buying a new frame, you should take the time to test ride every frame you can to see what dimensions suit you best.

For the ultimate in togetherness, you can build a tandem. A few companies still market the famous bicycles built for two, but to make sure that your tandem is fitted to your and your partner's physiques and riding styles, it's best to build your own from parts.

A good tandem is expensive, running at least $1,000. But you get a lot of bike for the money: heavy-duty frame and wheels, double brakes, special fittings for everything from racks to lights. And tandeming is a wonderful way to go: two well-matched cyclists can roar down the road at 30 mph while holding a quiet conversation. Faster friends, lovers and spouses don't have to wait for their slower companions, and if one finishes the ride so does the other.

Not every pair of riders, though, makes compatible tandem partners. Since the cost is so high, it pays to test ride a store's or friend's tandem before you buy. And if you decide to buy one, expect to wait at least six months to a year after you place an order.

The Right Brakeset

About the only component that cyclists don't pay much attention to is their brakes. That's ironic, because your brakes can mean the difference between life and death.

For the past decade, sidepull brakes have been popular with status-seeking racing and recreational cyclists. They've been popular not because they are inherently better than centerpulls—as I pointed out in Chapter Four, the least expensive sidepulls barely work—but because top racers use them. Few status seekers realize, though, that those racers use them because they are paid to or were given the brakes free of charge.

Not long ago, those same top racers used centerpull brakes. Centerpulls are still widely used, and sell for as little as a tenth of the cost of status sidepulls. The differences lie mainly in appearance, ease of operation and degree of control. In a pinch, the difference between the most expensive sidepulls and the less costly centerpulls is virtually nil. And you can decrease even that tiny edge for a small investment.

A brakeset is only as good as the cables and shoes used. Putting the best cables and shoes on the cheapest, flimsiest brakes available won't make them comparable to a $125 set, but good cables and shoes will minimize the differences between good and excellent brakesets.

Most brakesets include good blocks. The pads are made of hard material that won't compress under braking force to give a mushy feeling; have a smooth surface that acts as a squeegee to wipe water from the rim; and have a large surface area that gives good contact with the rim.

Of the conventional brake blocks, Campagnolo, Shimano's Dura-Ace and Dia-Compe are excellent. Even better, though, are the finned Scott/Mathauser blocks. Many tandem riders, seeking more braking power than conventional blocks provide, have used Mathausers successfully. One tandemist told me that his rear disc brake has faded under hard use, while the Mathausers kept working.

Stiff brake cables, too, can make a big difference in your stopping power. One racer told me, "The best way to get stiff brakes is by using stiff cables." Flimsy cables, like flimsy caliper arms, stretch under hard use, waste your energy and require constant adjustment.

Campagnolo brake cables are in a class by themselves. They are thicker than most other brands, and have an outer layer wrapped in reverse around an inner core to prevent unwinding. To further reduce the chance of fraying,

"Campy" cables are soldered several inches near the ends. And the cables come prelubricated from the factory so that they will not bind and fray in the housings.

To make your cables even more slippery, you can replace the standard cable housing with an Elephant Brand housing. This housing is available to match or complement most bike colors, and is lined with a slippery plastic. Beware of imitations, though: other types of lubricated cable-housing combinations include flimsier, not-as-safe cables.

Campagnolo, the company that makes the great cables, is a name you'll probably hear often. Since the late 1960s, Campy has dominated the high-class (and high-price) component scene. Campy produces high-priced but excellent brakes, derailleurs, hubs, headsets, shift levers, cranksets, seatposts, pedals and bottom brackets. The finish on Campy's top-line components is flawless, as is their performance. The hubs and bottom brackets spin like silk; the derailleurs shift crisply.

Campy products are loaded with refinements, many of which have been copied by other manufacturers. Campy brakes, for example, introduced a host of engineering breakthroughs including:

. . . A brake-lever mounting bolt that does not pass through the brake-lever pivot bolt, ensuring the bolt won't bind the pivot.

. . . A quick-release on the calipers that works at any position between fully open and closed, making it possible to ride with a broken spoke or bent rim without losing all of your braking power.

. . . A rubber protector on the cable-tension adjuster that keeps it from scratching the frame if the fork is suddenly turned.

. . . Adjusting flats on the brake center bolts that allow you to easily center the brakes with just a 13-mm cone wrench. Other brakes require two or more wrenches, or the not-so-subtle use of hammer and screwdriver.

. . . A slot in the brake-lever body that allows you to quickly remove or insert the brake cable without threading it up from underneath.

As with any other products, the innovator has to recoup the high costs of design engineering, so Campy products are among the most expensive. But they are also among the most durable, and even the smallest spare parts are readily available; with other products, a damaged ten-cent part may be the end of the component.

As I've noted, virtually every other company has borrowed Campy's design innovations. So now there are many close copies on the market at more reasonable prices. In some cases, the copies are excellent; in others, the performance, durability and refinements are sometimes lacking. It's always best to check with someone who has used a product before you buy. There are less expensive, lighter and prettier components, some with sealed bearings. Some are as good as Campy products, but few are better. The Campy "myth" is well deserved.

Like the best components from which they are built, bicycles are simple and elegant machines. And it's easy to fall in love with the stark functional beauty of bicycles. But to do so is to miss the entire point of their existence: when you find yourself spending more time talking about bikes and looking at equipment than riding, it's time to hop in the saddle and take a long ride while reevaluating your priorities.

PART V
STAYING ON THE ROAD

CHAPTER TWENTY-ONE
FLAT TIRES

No matter how good or how expensive your bicycle, it will occasionally have minor problems: flat tires, gears and brakes going out of adjustment, chain slipping off the chain-wheels.

You can avoid most of these problems by following simple, routine maintenance procedures. A few minutes of your time every week or two will keep your bike running smoothly year after year.

Of course, you could instead ignore your bike until it breaks down. I know more than a few cyclists who follow this "program." There's no denying that it's easier than taking the time to keep your bike rolling, but there are serious problems that result from such neglect. First, as a cyclist, independence is an important part of your life. You should make your own decisions on where and how far you want to ride, and not base them on the terrain or the condition of your bike. If your bike is always just a step away from breaking down, you're going to think twice before going for a long ride. An unexpected breakdown can ruin a ride or even an entire vacation.

Secondly, when something finally does go wrong, it will be much more serious and costly than if you had replaced the small parts as they wore out and kept the mechanism lubricated.

Of course, no preventive maintenance program is foolproof. You can spend more time inspecting your bike than riding it, but BLAM! one day you're going to run into a patch of glass, or SNAP! a shift or brake cable will break. It is as important to know how to cope with such common problems as it is to do your best to keep them from happening.

Without a doubt, the most common mishap is a flat tire. I consider myself an expert on them: to paraphrase Jimmy Durante, "I've had a million of them." It's not that flat tires are an everyday occurrence, but I've ridden thousands of miles testing the superlight wired-ons developed in the late 1970s. Many of those tires, unfortunately, were not so super, and there were days when I'd puncture four or five times.

Fortunately, most tires on the market are far sturdier. Even superlight models have given me 1,000 miles or more between flats.

I've learned two lessons from the flats I've had: careful riding and proper inflation will prevent most flats; and a puncture can virtually always be patched in less than five minutes.

You can avoid most tire problems just by keeping your tires at the recommended pressure, usually indicated on the sidewall of the tire. Buy an accurate air-pressure gauge and check your tires before every ride. Too much air can cause a blowout, while too little can pinch the tubes, crack the tire casings and make your tires more vulnerable to flats.

From time to time, "miracle" puncture-proofing solutions appear on the market. Some fill the tube with foam rubber, making your bike sluggish. Liquid fillers, which are supposed to pour into puncture holes and fill them, often pour right through and make patching impossible. Avoid these products; heavier tubes are a far saner and less expensive cure for frequent flats.

Likewise, avoid the solid tires that frequently are offered. Aside from making your ride harder (which is why they disappeared when pneumatic tires were developed), many have quirks such as working their way off the rims as you ride.

Do, however, use metal tire savers (also called nail pullers) that ride on top of the tires to remove debris before it can work its way into the tires. Adjust them so that the curved edge just touches the tires.

The most obvious invitation to a puncture is a bald tire. Check your tires at least once a month, and when you notice the casing showing where the tread used to be, replace the tire. You may be able to prolong the life of your tires by rotating them from front to back after each 1,000 miles of riding.

Even with proper care, you will inevitably have flats from time to time, even though they may be years between.

Wired-On Tire Repair

The first thing to do when you suspect you have a flat (a loud BANG! is grounds for suspicion, as is thumping up and down) is to get off the road and out of the way of cars and other cyclists. Look for a grassy spot to flip your bike upside down.

Remove the wheel from the bike. You may have to release the quick-release on the brake calipers so that the tire can clear the brake pads. If you don't have quick-release brakes, you may have to disconnect the brake cable from the brakes (see Chapter Twenty-Three). If it is the front tire that has punctured, flip the quick-release or remove the nuts and slip the wheel out of the fork blades.

Removing the rear wheel is trickier. Shift the chain onto the smallest rear freewheel cog. Loosen the quick-release or wheel nuts, and slide the wheel forward. Grab the derailleur body and pull it back so that the wheel can slide past it. When you put the wheel back in place, remember to line up the chain on the smallest cog.

Inflate the tire. Most bicycle tubes use Schrader valves, the same as those used on automobiles. To inflate, simply remove the valve cover and press the pump against the valve stem. Some pumps, however, require you to thread the air hose onto the end of the valve, or flick a locking lever to hold the pump on the valve.

If your bike tires have Presta valves, you should also start by removing the valve cap. Then grasp the end of the valve and unscrew counterclockwise. When the valve nut is all of the way out, press the pump onto the valve and inflate. When you think there is enough air in the tire, knock the pump away

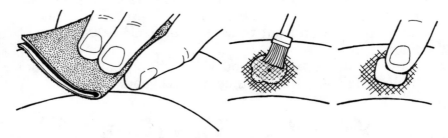

Patching a tube. Left to right, the steps are: sanding the tube, applying glue and applying the patch.

from the valve with a strong blow. If you try to twist the pump off, you'll probably pull the valve out of the tube. Screw in the valve nut in a clockwise direction to the closed position.

After the tire is partially inflated, listen for a leak. If you do not hear a leak, look for a puncture. A hole or piece of glass in the tire is a good indication of where the tube punctured. Deflate the tire.

Squeeze both sides of the tire toward the middle of the rim, working all the way around the rim. Insert a tire iron, not a screwdriver, under the tire bead directly opposite the valve and pry the bead over the rim. Hook the iron onto a nearby spoke. Insert another iron under the bead a few inches away and pop the bead over the rim at that point. Move on another few inches and repeat until the entire bead is free. If there is a locknut on the valve stem, remove it.

If you know where the puncture is, pull the tube out only in that area. If the puncture is near the valve, push up on the valve stem to remove it from the rim.

Inflate the tube slightly to pinpoint the puncture. If the tire has a Schrader valve, you may hear air rushing out of the valve stem. This means you have a loose valve core, which can be tightened inside the stem with a bobby pin or pronged valve cap. If the valve stem has a hole in it or near its base, replace the tube.

If you cannot find the puncture, remove the entire tube, noting how it was positioned. Inflate it until firm and, if possible, immerse it in water. Watch for bubbles. Hold your finger over the puncture, deflate and dry the tube. If you've had the foresight to carry a piece of chalk, mark the point of puncture.

Using sandpaper—and not the metal graters that come with many tire patch kits—rough an area around the puncture slightly larger than the patch you intend to use. Wipe off all sanding dust.

Apply a thin, even coat of glue (make sure you puncture the tube's spout before leaving home) to the roughed-up area and let dry until it looks dull and feels tacky to the back of your finger. You can speed up the process by blowing on the glue, but don't wet it.

Peel the backing off a patch, being careful not to touch the adhesive side, and press it firmly onto the tube. Hold the edges of the patch tightly in place for a minute.

If you have talcum, dust the tube with it to keep the tube from pinching inside the rim. Make sure the rim strip covers all the spoke heads.

Replace the tube as it was originally positioned inside the tire. If the puncture was on the inside of the tube, it was probably caused by a protruding spoke. Make sure all spokes are covered by the rim strip, and file the protruding spoke or spokes as soon as you can.

If the puncture was on the outside of the tube, check the tire directly above it and locate the puncture. If the tire has been badly cut or ruptured, repair it as soon as possible by gluing a piece of polyester ribbon or a piece of casing from an old tubular to the inside. Weldwood contact cement is good for doing this.

Inflate the tube slightly and listen for a leak. Make sure the patch is holding; there's nothing more frustrating than to have to stop and repair it again a mile down the road. Deflate the tube until it just holds its shape and push the valve stem partially out of its hole on the rim. Start slipping the bead back onto the rim there, working out from the valve in both directions at once. After the bead is in place, pull down on the valve stem to seat it.

When you reach the spot opposite the valve, you will be left with a small area of the tire that doesn't easily slip back onto the rim. Work at the section with your thumbs until it slips over the rim. An obstinate tire may call for delicate use of a tire lever, but be extremely careful. This is not the time to puncture the tire again.

Inflate the tire slowly to 10 to 15 psi, just so it has shape. Check the rim line on the tire to make sure it is the same distance from the rim all the way around. Deflate the tire to allow the tube to seat without binding, then reinflate to 10 to 15 psi and check for proper seating again. If everything looks good, inflate to full pressure and replace the wheel on your bike. If the tire has not seated properly, though, tug it into position before reinflating.

Make sure you set the brake quick-release correctly and tighten the axle nuts or quick-release, too.

Tubular Tire Repair

Tubular tires are much more complicated to repair. To repair a tubular, you must remove the tire from the rim, using only your hands. Then inflate the tire until firm, and slowly run it through water. A stream of bubbles will mark the puncture. Do not be fooled by bubbles coming out near the stem, though: this is merely the point of least resistance for them to escape. Hold your finger over the puncture, deflate and dry the tire, then mark the puncture with chalk.

Pry away three or four inches of rim tape from the bottom of the tire on each side of the puncture. With chalk, make a line on each end of the casing where you will cut the threads

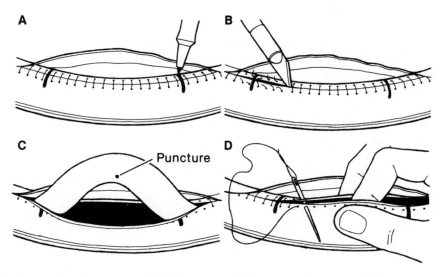

Repairing a tubular tire. Steps include: marking lines on casing (A), cutting stitching (B), pulling tube from casing (C), sanding tube, applying glue and patch (shown in preceding illustration), and pinching sides of casing (D) while restitching.

to expose the tube. You can match these lines during reassembly to ensure that the tire will return to its proper shape. Cut the stitching about two inches from each side of the puncture, with your blade pointing away from the tube. Pull out the tube and locate the leak by inflating and immersing in water if necessary. Use the same repair procedure as for wired-on tubes.

After you have patched the puncture and dusted the tube with talcum, check to see what object caused the puncture and remove it from the casing if it is still imbedded. Repair casing breaks as described above. Insert the tube into the casing, inflate until firm and check for leaks.

If there are no leaks, deflate the tube and stitch the casing closed. Make sure the marks you made earlier line up exactly opposite each other and the tube is out of the way when stitching. Using the old holes, begin stitching, overlapping the existing stitches by about ½ inch. Pull the stitches firmly but not tightly. Stitch until about ½ inch beyond the cut, then knot the thread. Put a layer of glue on the casing and one on the rim tape and let dry. Then carefully press them together.

If you plan to take it easy on the ride back home or to camp, you can mount the tubular using the old glue or double-faced rim tape. If the possibility of rolling a tire off the rim does not appeal to you, apply glue to both the tire and the rim and allow it to dry until tacky.

After the surfaces become tacky, insert the valve into the rim and place the opposite side of the rim on a clean, solid surface. Starting at the valve, slowly work the tubular down onto the rim, carefully making sure that it is evenly distributed. Grab the final section with both hands and pull onto the rim. After again checking to make sure the tire is centered on the rim, inflate to full pressure. Allow enough time for the glue to set before riding or the tire may creep on the rim and bulge. Weldwood cement sets up in about 15 minutes, but waiting overnight is better. Weldwood is also reportedly more heat-resistant than other rim cements, not losing strength under hot weather or hard downhill braking. Unfortunately, Weldwood is so strong that you may have trouble when you have to take the tire off the rim again.

By the time you have repaired a tubular, you will have wasted a good deal of riding time. For this reason, cyclists who use tubulars always carry a spare or two and simply replace a tire that has punctured. After they arrive home, they take out the knife, needle and thread and do the tedious repair work.

Even though having a flat is never enjoyable, knowing these simple techniques will make your next flat only a minor inconvenience.

CHAPTER TWENTY-TWO
THE DRIVE TRAIN

Next to flat tires, the most frequent mechanical nuisances are the chain falling off the front chainrings or the gears jamming. Again, half the battle can be won by performing minor preventive maintenance and the other half by learning simple repair techniques.

If you have a single- or 3-speed bike, you don't have to worry about the chain falling off unless you replace the rear wheel incorrectly after repairing a flat or changing a tire. There should never be more than ½ inch of up or down play in the chain.

On a single-speed bike, there are no multiple gears to jam, either. Three-speed bikes have their gears packed into their rear hubs, often along with the braking mechanism. To keep them running smoothly, squirt a few drops of oil into the hub each month, adding it through the small hole in the hub. Do the same to rear single-speed hubs.

The shift cable on a 3-speed will stretch in time, making it impossible to use all three gears. If you have problems shifting, or if the cable is slack, you should adjust it.

Shift into high gear (third). Near the rear hub, find the barrel sleeve adjuster, held in place by a locknut. Loosen the locknut, and screw down the barrel adjuster until the cable has just a slight amount of slack. If there is still too much slack, even when the barrel adjuster is screwed all the way to its limit, screw it fully home and move the fulcrum clip that holds the cable housing on the bike frame until the slack disappears.

To make sure the gears will work, shift into neutral (second). Inside the right hub nut, an indicator rod should line up with the end of the axle. On some bikes, there will be a little "N" or "2" to line up in the nut. If the rod or figure does not line up, turn the screw on the barrel adjuster until it does.

Derailleur Adjustment

On derailleur bikes, the gear-changing and the braking mechanisms are separate from the hubs. They may look more complicated, especially the gear mechanisms, but they're simple enough that most children are able to adjust them.

Only when your derailleurs work their way out of adjustment will the chain fall off the chainrings or refuse to shift onto certain rear cogs. If you keep the derailleurs properly adjusted, this need never happen.

Anytime your bike does not shift properly or you have to pull the shift levers all the way back to shift into your largest or smallest sprockets, you should adjust your derailleurs. If you don't, your chain may rub on the derailleur cages, causing costly damage.

Front and rear derailleurs each have a set of screws that limit their travel. One screw on each limits how far out the cage can push the chain; the other, how far in. Many derailleur problems can be remedied simply by tightening or loosening the appropriate screw(s) to allow the chain to travel farther or to limit its travel.

If doing this alone does not eliminate your problems, or if you have ridden for more than a year without adjusting your derailleur cables, you should give your derailleurs an overhaul.

With your bike upside down, or hanging with the wheels off the ground, shift so that your shift levers are all the way forward.

Find the cable binder bolt on your front derailleur and then the one on your rear derailleur. Loosen them so that the cables come free.

Check your cables. Remove them from the housings and inspect them for fraying. If they are frayed or if the housings are kinked or broken, replace the cables and housings. If the cables are good, lubricate them with WD-40 or white grease and thread them back into the housings in the opposite direction of which the cables are wound, to keep them from fraying at the ends.

If you are installing new cables and housings, you will have to cut them to the proper size. Make sure each housing is long enough to curve gracefully into position. Using cable cutters, if possible (about ten dollars a pair, but worth it), cut the housing between the wire coils. File the sharp edges off the cut ends of the housings.

Do not cut the cables until you thread them through the housings and derailleur binder bolts, or they may fray while

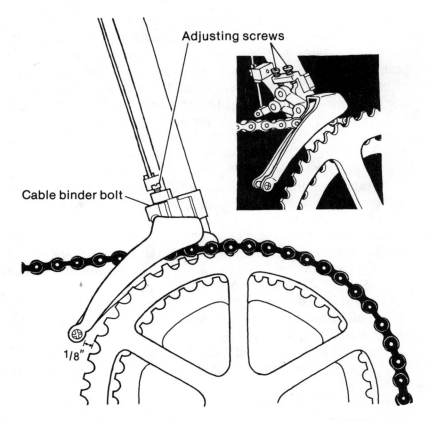

View of front derailleur. When properly adjusted, front derailleur cage should be approximately ⅛ inch above teeth of large sprocket. Note the adjusting screws and the cable binder bolt.

doing so. If you want to be professional, solder the ends of the cables after you cut them with the cable cutters. Crimping on an aluminum cap will do the same job, but will make it harder to remove the cables on the road.

Check the front derailleur cage. It should be parallel to the bicycle frame, and the bottom of the cage should sit about ⅛ inch above the teeth of the large sprocket (when the cage is positioned over that sprocket—you may have to push it into position to check). If not, loosen the derailleur mounting bolt and adjust it.

Next, back off the two adjusting screws on the front derailleur. Then run the cable through the cable binder bolt. Pushing the derailleur cage in line over the proper sprocket (some front derailleurs line the cage up over the outer sprocket when the shift lever is all the way forward; others work just the opposite), tighten the bolt. If the cage is not lined up with the large chainring, shift so that it is.

Now move to the rear derailleur. If there is a barrel adjuster on it where the cable enters, make sure the adjuster is screwed on tight.

If your derailleur has a horizontal adjusting screw (many Japanese derailleurs have them), adjust the screw so the body of the derailleur is parallel to the seatstay.

Back off the high- and low-gear adjusting screws. Insert the cable into the derailleur and push the chain roller cage in line with the smallest rear cog. Pull the cable tight, and tighten the cable binder bolt.

Now let go of the derailleur cage and adjust the high-gear (small sprocket) adjusting screw until the rollers line up exactly with the outer sprocket.

Move back to the front derailleur and tighten the high-gear (large sprocket) adjusting screw until the cage lines up with the outer sprocket.

Shift the chain onto the inner front and rear sprockets and adjust the low-gear adjusting screws until the cages line up with the inner sprockets.

As your cables stretch with use, you will periodically have to back off the barrel adjuster on your rear derailleur or screw in the derailleur adjusting screws to take up slack.

If you align your derailleurs properly, and keep the slack out of the cables, the chain should not jump off the sprockets, rub against the derailleur cages or refuse to shift onto any sprockets. If any of these things happen, the adjusting screws have not been properly adjusted.

To keep your derailleurs shifting smoothly, spray the springs, pivot points and your shift levers with LPS-1 or WD-40 every two weeks.

If the chain refuses to stay on the sprocket you shift it onto, you may have to adjust the tension of your shift levers.

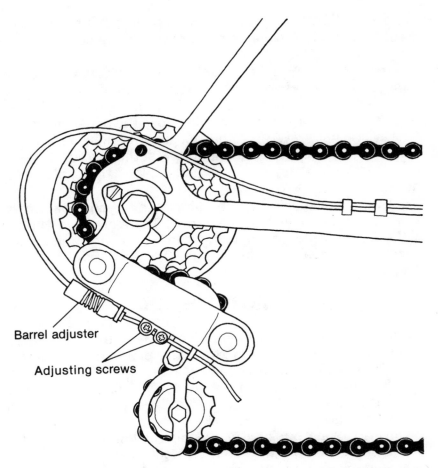

Barrel adjuster

Adjusting screws

View of rear derailleur. Note adjusting screws and barrel adjuster.

Down-tube and stem-mounted levers usually have tension screws or wing nuts on the sides. Make sure these are tight, but not so tight that they make it hard to shift. If you have handlebar-end shifters, check the bolts running through the levers.

It is normal for your chain to rattle after you shift if it falls between sprockets. Jiggling the shift lever will usually stop the noise. If it doesn't, however, your derailleur cages may be bent, preventing the chain from lining up with the cogs.

Either snug a crescent wrench around the bent cage and carefully bend it into alignment, or replace the bent parts or the entire derailleur.

If shifts are delayed or difficult and you have not yet removed the cables to clean the derailleurs, do so. Delayed shifts are usually the result of kinks in the cable housings, frayed cables or the cables hanging up in the housings. If the cables are not frayed, or the housings broken or kinked, spray the cables with lubricant and twist them around inside the housings. If they still hang up, replace the cables and housings.

Even after making these adjustments, your chain may still fall off the inner front chainring. There are several possible causes, and you should have a qualified mechanic check for the cause of the problem.

Chain Repair

Poor shifting and chain hopping may also be caused by a worn or dirty chain. Remedying the problem may call for cleaning or replacing the chain.

To remove the chain on a single- or 3-speed bike, just find the master link and pop it free.

If you have a derailleur bike, you have to separate the chain by driving out one of the pins holding the links together. You do this with a chain tool (also called a rivet remover). Shift into the smallest front and rear sprockets. Back off the tool so that the chain fits into the slot, then turn the tool's handle clockwise. Make sure that the pin is exactly in line with the chain rivet. Turn the handle gently until the pin is nearly all the way out, then remove the chain from the tool. If you cannot pry the links apart, put the chain back in the tool and turn the handle another time or two. Be careful not to drive the pin all the way out.

Before removing your chain, check it for wear. Shift onto the large front sprocket. Grab the chain from the front edge of the sprocket and pull it forward. If you can pull it far enough so that you can see more than half of the sprocket tooth, replace the chain.

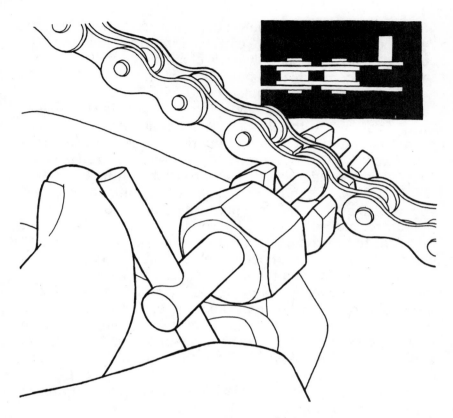

Removing a rivet from a derailleur chain with a chain tool. The tool's pin drives rivet out the opposite side of the chain. Be careful not to drive the rivet completely out of the outer chain plate.

If the chain is still good, wipe the links of the separated chain clean and paint the bottom outside edge of the outer link plate. This allows you to replace the chain exactly as it was, which has two benefits: you'll be able to shift smoothly, and your chain will last longer, since you won't weaken it at a different spot every time you remove it for cleaning. A better alternative is to remove the pins on both sides of the outer plate and replace it with a special master link that comes apart with a screwdriver or a flick of the chain. These links cost about five dollars.

Drop the chain into a can of kerosene and shake the can. When the kerosene becomes filthy, remove the chain and dump the kerosene. Shake the can to remove excess kerosene and grit. Wipe the can clean, put the chain back in, and add clean kerosene. Swirl the chain inside the can. If the kerosene becomes black again, replace it.

Remove the chain, shake it and hang to dry.

After the chain dries, you must lubricate it. The easiest way is to spray it with LPS-3, Bullshot chain lube, Tri-Flon or a similar product. You can alternatively soak the chain in a can of warm oil or drop a drop of oil into each pivot pin. In any case, wipe the side plates clean after lubricating them.

This is work, and some experts recommend that you should do it after every eight hours of riding. If you don't have the time or motivation to do so, you can get by with a shot of lubricant to the chain every week. It won't look as good, and won't last as long, but chains are not that expensive.

When you replace the chain, make sure it goes through the derailleur cages properly. Place the chain on the ridge of the chain tool farthest from the handle, and positioned so that the pin you drove out faces the tool's driving pin. Make sure the pins line up and work the chain pin back into place. Stop when the pin barely sticks out on the side you're working from.

Back off the tool and flex the chain at the pin to make sure the link is not stiff. If it is, place the chain on the ridge of the chain tool nearest the handle and give the handle some quarter-turns, working on alternating sides of the chain, until the link is no longer stiff. If other links tighten at any time, free them the same way.

Stiff links will make your chain skip every few seconds. You can find the stiff ones by slowly pedaling the chain backward, watching each link as it comes off the bottom chain roller of the rear derailleur or goes onto the rear cog. Remedy the stiff links as described above, or by flexing the chain at the links.

If you're installing a new chain, you may have to cut it to the proper length. For single- and 3-speed bikes, line the old chain up with the new one and use the chain tool to remove the excess links.

For derailleur bikes, you can do the same, but some

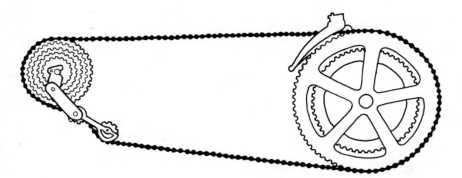

To determine proper chain length, shift the chain onto the large front and rear sprockets. Remove or add links until the cage of the rear derailleur is at a 45-degree angle to the ground.

derailleur bikes do not come with the correct-size chain. If you've changed freewheels or front chainwheels, you may also need to change the length of the chain.

Put the chain on the bike, with the derailleurs set so that the chain runs over the largest front and rear sprockets. Overlap the ends of the chain until the rear derailleur cage is at a 45-degree angle to the ground. Remove the extra links, but make sure you end up with an inner link meeting an outer link.

Following these simple maintenance procedures will take a little of your time, but you will be repaid with hours of carefree riding. And if something does go wrong on the road, you'll be ready.

CHAPTER TWENTY-THREE BRAKES

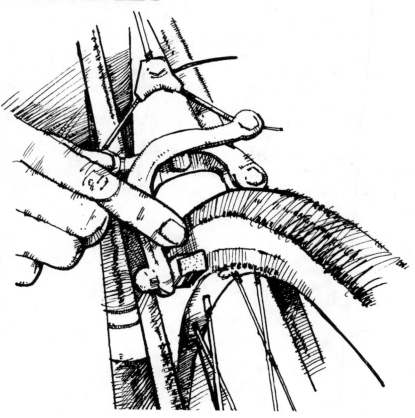

Your life could depend on your brakes working well. Keeping them properly adjusted is essential to ensure safe riding.

All single-speed bikes and many inexpensive 3-speeds have coaster brakes. The brake mechanisms are tucked inside the rear hub, and you merely add a few drops of oil each month. If the brakes lock or lose their stopping power, you have to take the wheel to a shop for repair.

More expensive 3-speeds and all derailleur bikes use caliper brakes, either centerpull or sidepull. With either type, it is important that the brakes are securely mounted to the frame. Loose brakes will twist to the side and pull forward when you try to stop, greatly reducing your braking power. Make sure the nuts on the brake mounting bolts are as tight as possible.

The brakes must also be centered over the rims. With some inexpensive brakes, you have to hold the calipers in position as you tighten the mounting nuts. Better brakes have flats on the mounting bolts that you can grip with a cone wrench, allowing you to position the calipers after the brake bolt is tightened. This doesn't always work, though: some inexpensive sidepulls will not line up properly no matter how long you attack them with a cone wrench. And sidepulls without adjusting flats are notoriously hard to center.

The only thing you can do if your brakes refuse to cooperate is to place the blade of a large, flat screwdriver on the side of the spring that is farther from center, then hit it delicately until the brake moves to center. Usually you will overshoot on the first try and will have to attack from the other side to align the brakes properly.

Next, check the brake pads. If they are worn beyond the pattern that was stamped into them, replace them. You don't have to buy the same brand, but do get good ones, not the four-for-a-dollar variety.* If your present pads are only slightly worn, wipe them clean with acetone or wash and file off the outer layer of glaze and road grime.

---

* If you replace the pads and holders, make sure the open ends of the holders face the rear, so the pads won't slide out as you brake.

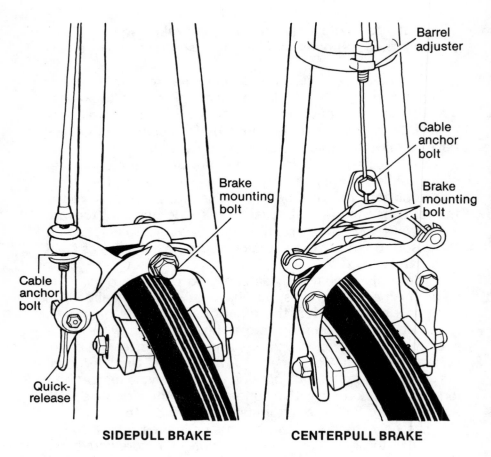

SIDEPULL BRAKE   **CENTERPULL BRAKE**

Views of sidepull (left) and centerpull (right) brakes with brake-mounting bolt, cable anchor bolt, quick-release and barrel adjuster identified. (Note that on centerpulls, the quick-release is not actually on the brake but on the lever or cable holder.)

Make sure the brake pads are aligned with the rims. The pad holders are held in place with nuts or allen bolts that must be loosened in order to change the vertical position of the pads.

Line up the brake pads so that they hit squarely on the rims and not against the tires. Since brake holders usually turn when you tighten the nuts, set them slightly counter-clockwise before a final tightening. As you tighten the nuts, the pads should move into position.

When you apply your brakes and the pads hit the rims, the momentum of the rims will twist the caliper arms so that only the rear of the brake blocks will hit the rims. To counteract this, toe in the brake pads so that the fronts of the pads are closer to the rims than the rear parts are. When the caliper arms twist, the entire pads will hit the rims.

The exact amount of toe-in will depend upon the brakes and pads you are using. Thin caliper arms and sticky brake pads cause the most twisting, and so require a toe-in of up to ⅛ inch. Stronger caliper arms and softer pads keep deflection to a minimum, and call for little toe-in. The best setups have strong arms and sticky pads, calling for medium toe-in.

Unless you are using brake blocks that include adjustable washers, the only way you can toe in your pads and keep

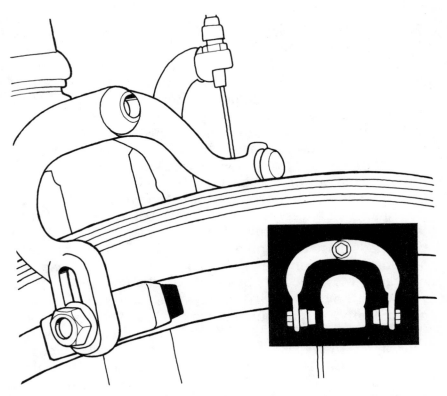

When properly aligned with rim, brake pads should cover it, but not ride too high or too low. The brake holder bolt allows the pad to be moved up, down and out of level.

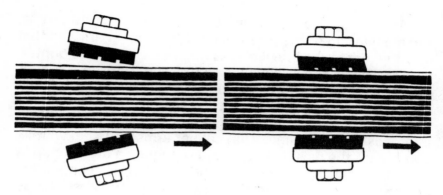

On the left, toed-in brake pads at rest (exaggerated). On the right, toed-in pads in action. The forward motion of the rim yanks pads inward, giving even contact.

them toed-in is by twisting the caliper arms. You can do this by grabbing the arms with a crescent wrench or sticking a large screwdriver blade through the slots in the caliper arms and twisting. You may have to remove the pads to do this. Experiment until you find the best toe-in position.

Incorrect toe-in can make your brakes squeal, as can new brake pads. There are two reasons new pads squeal: they are coated with a glaze that takes time to wear off, and most pads are designed to work with both flat and angled rims, and initially do not line up with either. To quickly cure both problems, you may want to file the pads before using.

Almost all brakes today come with barrel adjusters that let you take up slack in the cables as they stretch, to keep the brake pads close to the rims. For best performance, the pads should sit $\frac{1}{16}$ to $\frac{1}{8}$ inch away from the rims. You can keep this clearance within bounds by using barrel adjusters.

When the barrel adjusters have been screwed all the way out, though, you must run more of the brake cables through the brake cable binder bolts. Screw the barrel adjusters all the way in, then loosen the brake binder bolts. On sidepull brakes, the binder bolts are on the brake arms. On center-pulls, the binder bolt is on the saddle that carries the small transverse cable above each brake.

Now pull the cables from the housings and check them as you did with the derailleur cables. Be even more critical: a brake cable splitting as you try to stop in the middle of a 40-mph descent is much more dangerous than a missed shift.

After you remove the cables, you can also check to make sure your brake levers are securely mounted. If you can jiggle them, they should be tightened. To do this, you must hold the levers open and turn the internal bolts or nuts clockwise. Most levers require a special T-tool or deft maneuvering with a pair of small, flat-nosed pliers. Some new designs make adjustments easier by using allen bolts.

Reinsert the cables, lubricating and threading them as you did the derailleur cables. Pass the end of the front cable through the cable binder bolt on the front brake (sidepulls) or though the cable anchor bolt on the front cable anchor (centerpulls). Then squeeze the brake pads against the rim, either with your hand, a friend's hand or a third hand tool.

With sidepull brakes, the next step is to pull the brake cable tight through the cable binder bolt. Tighten the bolt and release the pads. Squeeze the front brake lever three or four times. If the pads end up more than ¼ inch from the rim, squeeze the pads against the rim again, loosen the bolt and take up more slack. Test again, making sure the lever does not bottom out against the handlebars before locking the front wheel. Then adjust the rear brake the same way.

With centerpull brakes, you will also have to squeeze the front pads against the rim, but you will not be able to use your hand: you will need it to slide the cable anchor bolt as far as possible on the cable. If you work alone, you should use a fourth hand tool that will do this for you, freeing your hands to keep the anchor bolt straight as you tighten it.

After you have pulled the cable tight and tightened the anchor bolt, release the calipers and squeeze the front lever three or four times. If the pads end up more than ¼ inch from the rim, squeeze the pads against the rim again, and take up more slack. Adjust until the brake locks the front wheel before the lever bottoms on the handlebars, then repeat for the rear brake.

Screw the barrel adjusters back to take up excess slack. After every 100 miles or so of riding, screw back the adjusters to take up the increasing slack. When the adjusters are wound all of the way out, it is time to repeat the operation.

After your brakes are adjusted, take a look at your rims. Your rims play an important part in your braking performance. Keep them clean and free of brake streaks and oil by using solvents such as benzene, MEK or toluene. Make sure that your rims are trued, also, or your brakes could easily lock.

Every few weeks spray a light lubricant or drop a few drops of oil or a dab of grease on the cable anchor points on the brake caliper arms (sidepull brakes) or on the cable anchors (centerpulls). Lubricate the brake pivot points, where the caliper arms pivot against the springs, too. And spray the pivots inside the brake levers with a light lubricant. Regular lubrication and maintenance will keep your brakes working like new, and may save your life.

CHAPTER
TWENTY-FOUR
MISCELLANEOUS
MAINTENANCE

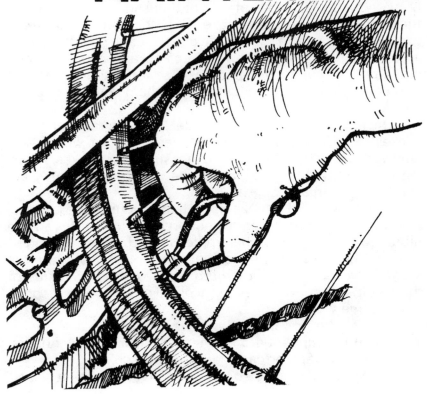

These maintenance procedures are by no means the only ones that your bike may require. But virtually all other maintenance procedures require expensive tools, a good deal of time and a precise feel for proper adjustment that a novice can only guess at. With bike shop rates climbing past the ten-dollar-an-hour mark, there is increasingly more reason for cyclists to do all their own maintenance work. But until you find a skilled mechanic willing to sit down with you and give you lessons, you're probably better off taking your bike to the shop for an overhaul once or twice a year. As long as you keep the gears, brakes, tires and chain in good shape, the bill shouldn't be high.

Replacing a Broken Spoke

Still, there are a few procedures you may need to know. One is how to replace a spoke. If your wheels have been built properly, you should be able to get thousands of miles under them without breaking a spoke. But when one does break, you could be stuck in the middle of nowhere if you don't have a spare or don't know how to replace a spoke. Just one broken spoke can throw your wheel so far out of line that it won't clear your brakes, or can start a chain reaction of other spokes breaking.

On long rides, it's a good idea to carry two or three spokes exactly the same size as the ones your wheels are built with. You should be able to measure your spokes, allowing for the threaded end inside the rim, to get a fairly accurate approximate length.

You'll also need a spoke wrench to fit your spoke nipples.

If a spoke on the front wheel breaks, first unthread the nipple from the spoke. The nipple is the tip that is inserted through the rim and threaded onto the spoke. Note how the spoke is woven through the other spokes and which side of the hub it enters. Remove it and install a replacement spoke in the same way.

Deflate the tire, in case you overtighten the new spoke. Then spin the nipple onto the new spoke with your fingers. Put a piece of tape or paper on the new spoke.

Turn your bike upside down and spin the wheel. It will hit

against one brake pad. With your spoke wrench, tighten the new spoke three or four turns. When the nipple is on the side of the wheel near the ground, you tighten by turning counter-clockwise.

Spin the wheel again. If it still hits the same pad, tighten a few more turns. If it hits the opposite pad, loosen a turn or two. Repeat the procedure, making smaller and smaller adjustments, until the rim passes between the pads without hitting either.

If a spoke breaks on the left side of the rear wheel, the procedure for replacing it is the same. But if it breaks on the right side of a derailleur bike, where the freewheel is, or even on the left side if the freewheel is large, you must remove the freewheel to replace the spoke.

To do this, you'll need a 10- or 12-inch adjustable crescent wrench, and a freewheel-removing tool that matches the notches or splines in your freewheel body.

Remove the nut and washer (or, on quick-release hubs, conical nut and spring) from the rear wheel hub. Engage the freewheel-removing tool in the slots in freewheel body, then screw the axle nut on finger-tight to hold the tool in position.

Use the wrench to break the freewheel loose, working counterclockwise. This will take effort. You may have to stand the wheel on end and kick the wrench with your heel to get the leverage you'll need. If you don't like the possibility of freewheel teeth sinking into your calf because of a misplaced kick, you can buy a freewheel holder that slips into a workbench vise and work on it there. After the freewheel breaks free, loosen the retaining nut and spin the freewheel off the axle.

Replacing the spoke is exactly the same as for the front wheel. When the spoke is replaced and tightened, spin the freewheel back onto the hub by hand as tight as possible. It will tighten as you ride.

Taping the Handlebars

From time to time, your handlebar tape will grow ragged and filthy. You can make your bike look new again by replacing the tape.

To make taping easy, it's good to release your brake cables and move them out of the way. Unscrew or pry out the plugs in the ends of the handlebars.

If your bike has handlebar-end shift levers, release your derailleur cables, too. Then loosen the bolts holding the levers in place and pull each lever from its housing. Inside will be a 6-mm hexagonal hole. Insert a 6-mm allen wrench and turn clockwise. The housing will loosen; remove it from the end of the handlebars.

Starting at the ends of the bars, unwrap the tape. Throw it away. If your brake levers have rubber hoods, roll them up away from the handlebars.

You will need two rolls of cloth tape. Don't use plastic tape: it becomes slippery when you sweat and looks terrible. Cloth tape is more comfortable, absorbing your sweat and cushioning your hands, and more attractive.

Cut two 2½-inch pieces of tape from the end of one roll. Wrap one around the bottom of your right brake-lever mounting bracket, then overlap the other piece.

Stand on the right side of the bike. Unroll about three inches of tape, and stick it on the right side of the handlebars, about two inches from the stem. Some handlebars have a raised center section; start the tape against the edge of this section if your bars have one.

Wrap the tape counterclockwise around the bars, overlapping each new turn over about a third of the previous turn.

When you reach the brake lever, work carefully. The tape will come from behind the top of the lever. Swing it around and under the lever, bringing it out parallel to the bottom of the lever. This may take several attempts. When it's done right, there should not be a gap around the brake lever: the entire area should be covered with tape.

If you have handlebar-end shifters, tape the cable housings in place on the lower portion of the handlebars using electrical tape, checking to make sure the cable is positioned so that it does not dig into your hand. I find that there is only one position where the cable doesn't bother me. Make sure the end of the cable housing protrudes just slightly beyond the end of the handlebars.

Finish taping the bottom half of the handlebars, covering the cable housing if you have bar-end shifters.

There's a good chance that you will run out of tape before you reach the end of the bars. You may be able to pick up the amount of tape you need by carefully unwrapping and retaping the bottom of the bars. If you are more than two turns short, you will have to completely unwrap the bars and start over.

When you finally reach the end of the bars, wrap the tape around the opening and cut it off, leaving about an inch extending. Tuck this inside the bar end and replace the plug. With handlebar shifters, do the same but replace the lever housing. Tighten the housing by turning the allen wrench counterclockwise, insert the shift lever, and tighten the mounting screw and bolt. Reinsert the cable, threading it through the cable housing. Tighten the derailleur and brake cables.

The procedure is exactly the same for the left side of the bars, except that you must tape in a CLOCKWISE direction from the top.

Sometimes just retaping your handlebars isn't enough to make your bike look like new when it's covered with mud, sweat and grit. That's when it's time to give your bike a bath.

Bathing your bike may sound crazy, but it's not. A good cleaning washes away rust-causing sweat, Gatorade and road dirt that's accumulated over the months. Top racers wash their mounts after each race, dumping them into the nearest creek or river if nothing better is available.

Take both wheels off your bike. Fill a bucket with warm, soapy water. Any soap will do, but an auto wash with built-in wax is best.

Set your bike in the tub or laundry basin, grab a rag and scrub it. Use a soft brush to get the hard-to-reach spots. When the bike's clean, cover the saddle with a plastic bag (do the same with lights or generator) and rinse with two or three buckets of water.

Letting your bike air-dry is best, but you can speed the process and reduce water spotting by wiping it dry with a soft towel. After the bike dries, lubricate the chain, as well as the brake and derailleur pivot points.

While your bike is free of grit, check for nicks and chips in the paint. Small nicks can be spotted with matching paint (Schwinn makes a wide range of touch-up colors), but bigger spots should be sanded and primed before painting. If you do any touch-up work, allow the paint to dry for a day before you ride.

To protect your frame and keep it looking its best, wax it after you wash it. DuPont Rain Dance wax is recommended by some bicycle manufacturers and gives good results.

One other way to keep your frame in good shape is to remove the front derailleur, pump clip, bottle-cage clamp, shift-lever clamp and any other frame clamps, then wrap a piece of handlebar tape around the frame where each item mounts. This will protect the frame from scratches.

If your bike has a leather saddle, there are a few tricks you should use to keep it looking good and to help break it in to your contours. The most important step is to regularly condition your saddle with saddle soap. The saddle soap will help preserve and soften the leather. If you ride in or get caught in the rain, let your saddle dry naturally, away from heat. After it dries, use saddle soap on it and saturate it from underneath with neat's-foot oil (available in hardware stores).

These steps will help the saddle break in, but the only truly effective way to break in a leather saddle is to ride many miles on it. Other methods of softening the leather weaken it, and can shorten your saddle's life. Saddle soap is good for the saddle and has only one minor drawback: it will cause the saddle to stain your riding pants, so be sure to wear black ones or use a saddle cover.

With these simple procedures, you can keep your bike looking as good as it works for years to come.

CHAPTER
TWENTY-FIVE
THE END
OF THE ROAD

Now you know all you need to know about keeping yourself and your bike going mile after mile, year after year. You are free to enjoy the rewards of cycling whenever the spirit moves you, and there is nothing that can spoil your enjoyment.

That is one of the biggest joys of cycling: it is an independent endeavor, and helps you become more independent. Anytime you are ready, the world is yours for the taking. And as a cyclist, you are among the few who take from nature without raping it.

Cycling offers such independence because it is a simple sport. As such, it is perfect for the times. In many ways, life has gotten out of hand and we have become slaves to our inventions. Our attempts to simplify life through technology continually complicate it and remove us from the essence of living. It's no coincidence that cycling has been reborn amidst a growing awareness that the simplest things in life are often the best, that the best way to enjoy life is by eliminating the gadgets that shield us from it. In every area of life, people are returning to the simpler ways and values of generations past, to the most sensible ways of doing things.

Cycling is bound to play a continuing role in this return to functionalism. It is not merely a practical way to save our lives, environment and resources, but makes doing so fun.

More than anything else, it is that fun, that spine-tingling joy of cycling that will keep people riding. No matter why you ride, don't ever lose track of this truest joy of cycling: the wind and sun in your hair, the sights, scents, moods and undulations of nature filling your senses. Be adventurous—don't let yourself be tied down. Explore the back roads, climb the forbidding hills, change your course when the spirit moves you. You'll be amazed at the surprises waiting for you there.

APPENDIX A
MAJOR ANNUAL RECREATIONAL RIDES

These tours are scheduled from March through August and appear in roughly chronological order. Consult particular ride organizers for details. All rides are one day unless otherwise noted.

Annual Wheelmen's Winter Rendezvous. Five days. Harold Ditzler, 678 NW Ninth Street, Homestead, FL 33030.

Annual Spring Sonoita–Bisbee Tour. Two days, 129 miles. Jack Laird, Bisbee Rotary Club, PO Box 21, Bisbee, AZ 85603. 602/432-2226.

Annual Wildflower Century. Send a SASE to San Luis Obispo Bike Club, Inc., PO Box 1585, San Luis Obispo, CA 93406.

Annual Tour of the Rio Grande Valley. Send a SASE to New Mexico Wheelmen, 9713 Morrow Road NE, Albuquerque, NM 87112.

Mid-Ohio Century. 50 or 100 miles. Tom Dillman, Delaware Bicycle Club, PO Box 566, Delaware, OH 43015. 614/369-4244.

Davis Double Century. Davis Bicycle Club, c/o B & L Bike Shop, 610 Third Street, Davis, CA 95616.

Across Florida Ride. 150 miles. Spacecoast Freewheelers, c/o Mike Schular, 390 Saint Charles Avenue, Merritt Island, FL 32952.

Five Borough Bike Tour. 35 miles. Elliot Winick, Metropolitan New York Council AYH, 132 Spring Street, New York, NY 10012.

Hemet Double Century. Hemet Wheelmen, PO Box 2621, Hemet, CA 92343. 714/925-0288.

Tour of the Scioto River Valley (TOSRV). Two days, 210 miles. TOSRV Communications, PO Box 23111, Columbus, OH 43223.

Great Western Bike Rally. Three days. Ralph D. Doething, Chairman, Great Western Bike Rally, PO Box 7000-618, Redondo Beach, CA 90277.

Tour of the Swan River Valley (TOSRV WEST). Two days, 231 miles. Missoula Bicycle Club, PO Box 8903C, Missoula, MT 59807.

Huffman 100. 100/50/25. Send a SASE to Dayton Cycling Club, c/o Jerry Hopfengardner, 272 Napoleon Drive, Kettering, OH 45429. 513/294-7724.

Biking across Kansas. Larry Christie, 809 North Parkwood, Wichita, KS 67208. 316/682-4006.

Amish Tour. 25 or 50 miles. Send a SASE to Cleveland Touring Club, Harold Albus, 22721 Shore Center Drive, Euclid, OH 44123. 216/289-5133 or 932-5485.

Freewheel. Seven days. Tulsa Wheelmen, Rick Mattioni, 820 East Third, Tulsa, OK 74120. 918/584-6008 or 583-2511.

WAG. Two days, 15 to 100 miles each. Slippery Rock, Pennsylvania. Western Pennsylvania Wheelmen, PO Box 6952, Pittsburgh, PA 15212. 412/367-0398.

Annual Bicycle Jamboree. 25, 50, or 100 miles. Shasta Wheelmen, c/o Jack Ennis, 196 Oleander Circle, Redding, CA 96001. 916/241-0962.

Seattle to Portland. One to three days, 200 miles. Cascade Bicycle Club/Puget Sound Cycling Club. Paul Boyer, PO Box 12774, Seattle, WA 98111. 206/783-8145.

Great Canadian Bicycle Rally. Three days, 15 to 100 miles each. Jean Ross, Ingersoll Avenue, Woodstock, ON N4S 2J7 Canada. 519/539-3681.

Great Eastern Rally (GEAR). Four days, 15 to 90 miles each. Send a SASE to GEAR, PO Box 4097, Virginia Beach, VA 23454.

Mid-West Double Century. Two days, 100 to 200 miles. Lima Council AYH, Elton Hammond, PO Box 173, Lima, OH 45802. 419/222-7301.

Tour of the Mississippi River Valley (TOMRV). Send a SASE to Linda Powers, 1807 Forty-Second Street, Rock Island, IL 61201.

Register's Annual Great Bike Ride across Iowa (RAGBRAI). Eight days, 425 miles. Don Larson, PO Box 24163, Dayton, OH 45424. 513/325-2101.

GO LAW Rally. Send a SASE to GO LAW Rally, Bob Larson, PO Box 24163, Dayton, OH 45424. 513/325-2101.

Amishland and Lakes Weekend. Michiana Bicycling Association, Marvin Scher, 50657 Blackhawk Court, Granger, IN 46530. 219/272-8700.

Tandem Rally. Four days. Tandem Club of America. Send a SASE to Scott and Nan Steketee, 4639 Spruce Street, Philadelphia, PA 19139.

Sentinel's Active Americans Great Bicycle Ride across Wisconsin (SAAGBRAW). Seven days, 300 miles. Wisconsin Wheelmen, PO Box 650, Milwaukee, WI 53201.

Hokaton Classic. 25, 50, or 100 miles. Valley Spokesmen Touring Club, PO Box 2630, Dublin, CA 94566.

Hancock Horizontal 100. Hancock 100, c/o Corey T. Foust, PO Box 232, Findlay, OH 45840. 419/422-7473.

Northwest Century and Half-Century Runs. Send a SASE to Fred Strong, 3411 Seventy-Seventh Place SE, Mercer Island, WA 98040. 206/232-7311.

Rosarito to Ensenada Fun Bicycle Ride. Bicycling West, PO Box 15128, San Diego, CA 92115.

North East Ohio Century (NEOC). NEOC Communications, c/o Robert C. Green, 25 Scott Lane, Girard, OH 44420. 216/539-4853.

APPENDIX B
MOUNTING CLEATS

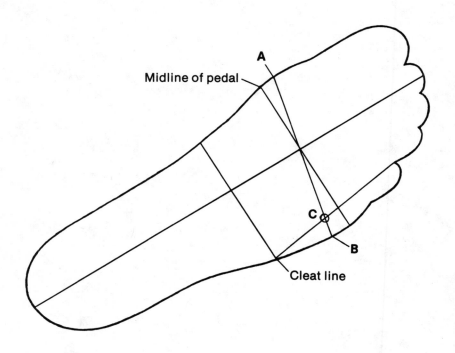

A

Midline of pedal

C

B

Cleat line

Cycling with cleats can make a big difference in your performance and comfort. But unless those cleats are mounted correctly, you can do more harm than good.

The following method of mounting cleats is based on the findings of Harlan Meyer of Hi-E Engineering:

The leg acts as a column when pushing on the pedal, so thought should be given to keeping the force near the center when viewing the leg from the front or rear. The force should pass through the center of the knee and ankle joints. Any deviation introduces a movement that strains the muscles and joints.

Fore and aft, the foot is a lever that pivots at the ankle. The lever is used by pressing mainly on the pad of the foot. To find your center of pressure, take a sheet of paper and make an outline of your foot.

Next, raise your toes and heel, leaving the pad of your foot on the floor. Make a mark (A and B) on each side about the center of where your foot is resting on the paper. From this, you can draw the center line of the pressure pad.

For the fore-and-aft line, mark a point (C) in from the outside edge about the width of your little toe. The little toe and outside edge of the foot are used for balancing and maneuvering. This area should not be used for pressure during direct, maximum effort.

Now make a mark on the pressure-pad center line, halfway between the inside of the foot (A) and point C, and another halfway at the heel. Connect these points with the fore-and-aft line, and then draw a perpendicular where it intersects the pressure line. This should be the center line of the pedal. Transfer the center line of the pedal to the bottom of your shoe and check it against the pedal marks made on your shoe while riding without cleats.

Repeat the process for your other foot.

Mount your cleats to correspond with the center line and the fore-aft line on each shoe. You may feel strain at first, but it should soon disappear. If it doesn't, adjust your cleats until the pain diminishes.

FURTHER
READING

Astrand, Per-Olaf, and Rodahl, Kaare. *Textbook of Work Physiology.* New York: McGraw-Hill, 1977. "The bible of exercise physiology." Explains physiological and bio-mechanical changes that take place during exercise. Assumes reader has elementary background in chemistry, anatomy and physiology.

Ballantine, Richard. *Richard's Bicycle Book.* 2d ed. New York: Ballantine, 1978. Limited but helpful information on buying and riding a bike. This book's maintenance section, which takes up nearly half of the pages, is the best of its kind around.

Beinhorn, George. "Getting Centered on a Bike." *Bike World,* January 1976. A look at the psychic aspects of cycling.

Berto, Frank. "Build Your Own Super-Tourer": Parts I, II, III. May, June and July 1976.

———. "The Custom-Built Superbike: What Makes It So Special?" *Bicycling,* October 1976. These four articles are must reading for anyone who is considering building his own bike. Even if the thought never crossed your mind, it may convince you to try building your own.

———. "All about Gear Shifting." *Bicycling,* October 1978.

———. "Gearing for Loaded Touring." *Bicycling,* June 1979.

Bicycling magazine editors. *Basic Bicycle Repair.* Emmaus, Pennsylvania: Rodale Press, 1980. Explains all major repair problems and gives easy-to-understand advice for correcting them.

———. *Basic Riding Techniques.* Emmaus, Pennsylvania: Rodale Press, 1979. Provides information on basic cycling techniques designed to help the reader derive maximum benefit and pleasure.

————. *Best Bicycle Tours.* Emmaus, Pennsylvania: Rodale Press, 1980. A review of 18 bicycle tours with information on special attractions along each route.

————. *Bicycle Commuting.* Emmaus, Pennsylvania: Rodale Press, 1980. A handbook for cyclists who want to use a bike for commuting. Also contains a consumer's guide to commuting bikes, accessories and equipment.

————. *Get Fit with Bicycling.* Emmaus, Pennsylvania: Rodale Press, 1979. Written by two doctors who give precise medical advice about general health, training schedules, nutrition and more—specifically for cyclists.

————. *The Most Frequently Asked Questions about Bicycling.* Emmaus, Pennsylvania: Rodale Press, 1980. This book answers all of the questions cyclists have been asking about bicycles and bicycling.

————. *Reconditioning the Bicycle.* Emmaus, Pennsylvania: Rodale Press, 1979. This is a step-by-step guide to overhauling the bicycle.

Bikecentennial. *The Cyclists' Yellow Pages.* Missoula, Montana: Bikecentennial, 1979. A slim but excellent guide to maps, accommodations and many other resources for cycle touring; includes information on Bikecentennial's routing service and other publications.

Bike World magazine editors. *Bicycle Track Racing.* Mountain View, California: World Publications, 1977. The only book of its kind, offering a thorough look at the subject.

————. *International Bicycle Touring.* Mountain View, California: World Publications, 1976.

Bond, Robert E. "About Hypoglycemia." *American Wheelmen,* June 1979. A look at how even healthy people can develop this potentially serious condition, and how to avoid it.

Brand, Mary Walsh. "The Special Needs of Women Cyclists." *Bicycling,* November 1978.

Bridge, Raymond. *Bike Touring: The Sierra Club Guide to Outings on Wheels.* San Francisco: Sierra Club, 1979. An excellent and comprehensive guide to cycle touring.

British Cycling Bureau. *Cycling: The Healthy Alternative—A Digest of Ten Reports to the British Cycling Bureau.* London: The British Cycling Bureau, 1978. A fascinating collection of ten papers examining the social role of cycling and its role in better health.

Brown, Jim and Crystal. "The Medium Is the Massage." *Bike World,* October 1977. The art of massage for your aching muscles.

Brown, Lester R.; Flavin, Christopher; and Norman, Colin. *Running on Empty: The Future of the Automobile in an Oil-Short World.* New York: W. W. Norton, 1979. A concise analysis of the auto's role in today's and tomorrow's society, and options to auto use.

Brown, Robert S.; Ramirez, Donald; and Taub, John M. "The Prescription of Exercise for Depression." *Physician and Sportsmedicine,* December 1978.

Brubaker, Clifford E. et al. "Cross-Country Bicycling: Physiological Effects." *Physician and Sportsmedicine,* July 1978. Study of weight loss and other effects on cyclists who ride cross-country.

Burden, Dan, and Burgess, Bruce. *Bicycle Safety Highway User's Information Report.* Washington, D.C.: U.S. Department of Transportation, National Highway Traffic Safety Administration, 1978. A study of accidents on the Bikecentennial trail.

Burke, Ed. *Inside the Cyclist: Physiology for the Two-Wheeled Athlete.* Brattleboro, Vermont: *Velo-News,* 1979. A collection of *Velo-News* articles by Burke and others on cycling physiology, particularly useful to cycle racers.

Business Week magazine editors. "A Guide to Bicycle Shopping." *Business Week,* 9 July 1979.

————. "The Oil Crisis Is Real This Time." *Business Week,* 30 July 1979.

Caldwell, John. *Cross-Country Skiing Today.* Brattleboro, Vermont: The Stephen Greene Press, 1977. An excellent guide to the winter sport that's most compatible with cycling.

Chisel, Dewey. "Bicycle for Transportation." *Bicycling,* March 1977.

Cooper, Jo. "Biking with Babies." *Bicycling,* October 1974. An interview with racer/tourist Darryl LeVesque, who has been carrying the kids along since they were born.

Cooper, Kenneth H. *The New Aerobics.* New York: M. Evans, 1970. The revised guide to aerobic conditioning by "the father of aerobic exercise."

de la Rosa, Denise M., and Kolin, Michael J. *Understanding, Maintaining, and Riding the Ten-Speed Bicycle.* Emmaus, Pennsylvania: Rodale Press, 1979. Thorough guide to bicycle adjustment and maintenance.

Durham, Roger. "Fighting the Battle of Inertia." *Bike World,* November 1976. A look at the effects of rolling weight, specifically of wired-on vs. tubular tires.

Faria, Irvin. *Cycling Physiology for the Serious Cyclist.* Springfield, Illinois: Charles C. Thomas, 1978. A look at scientific studies and their practical application for the serious cyclist, particularly the racer.

————. "Putting Foxy Grandpa to the Test." *Bike World,*
November 1977. What makes old-timer Ed Delano tick.

Fixx, James F. *The Complete Book of Running.* New York:
Random House, 1977. The perennial best-seller. An
excellent beginner's guide to the sport, with much useful information on training and exercise in general.

Forester, John. *Cycling Transportation Engineering.* Palo
Alto, California: Custom Cycle Fitments, 1977. "Must"
reading for bikeway advocates and planners.

————. *Effective Cycling.* Palo Alto, California: Custom Cycle
Fitments, 1978. The most thorough discussion of
cycling, particularly notable for its information on riding
with traffic.

————. "Is Cycling the Intelligent, Independent, Enjoyable
Choice?" *American Wheelmen,* October 1979. A look at
anticycling discrimination.

————. "More Miles, Faster, with Less Strain." *American
Wheelmen,* March 1980. A credible theory of why spinning works.

Gallwey, Timothy, and Kriegel, Bob. *Inner Skiing.* New York:
Random House, 1977. Excellent guide to mastering skiing by eliminating inner distractions. Applies just as well
to cycling and other sports.

Gaston, Eugene A. "Preventing Bikers' Knees." *Bicycling,*
July 1979.

————. "Bicycling, Cholesterol and Your Heart." *Bicycling,*
March 1980.

Hidgon, Hal, ed. *The Complete Diet Guide for Runners and
Other Athletes.* Mountain View, California: World Publications, 1978. Dispels diet myths and gives simple,
straightforward look at what's necessary for good health
and top performance. Best of its kind.

Hoyt, Creig et al. *Food for Fitness.* Mountain View, California: World Publications, 1975. No-nonsense guide to nutrition; good companion to *The Complete Diet Guide for Runners and Other Athletes.*

————. *Traveling by Bike.* Mountain View, California: World Publications, 1974.

Ice, Randy. "The S.C.O.R. Cardiac Cyclists." *American Wheelmen,* February 1978. Cycling after coronaries.

Jackson, Shaun. "Packing for a Tour." *Bicycling,* June 1978. Highly recommended how-to guide.

Kolin, Michael J., and de la Rosa, Denise M. *The Custom Bicycle: Buying, Setting Up, and Riding the Quality Bicycle.* Emmaus, Pennsylvania: Rodale Press, 1979. A guide to frames, master frame builders, and bicycle design and setup. Reliable information on what to look for when buying a quality bike or custom components.

Krygowski, Frank. "Geological Survey Maps for Cycling." *Bicycling,* April 1979. Excellent guide to using topographical maps for cycle commuting and touring.

Kulund, Daniel N., and Brubaker, Clifford E. "Injuries in the Bikecentennial Tour." *Physician and Sportsmedicine,* June 1978. A study of cyclists who traveled the 4,500-mile transcontinental cycling trail.

LaFetra, Jan. "The Art of Drafting for Moderate Riders." *American Wheelmen,* June 1977. Beginner's guide to drafting.

Lehman, Josh. "A Primer for City Cycle Commuters." *Bicycling,* March 1978.

————. "A Million Words and More—Maps for Bicycle Touring." *Bicycling,* April 1978. A helpful guide to selecting maps for your tour.

Lieb, Thom. "From Dawn to Dusk and Back Again." *Bike World*, May/June 1978. An inside look at one of the most demanding types of cycling: the 24-hour time trial.

————. "Custom Bicycle Frames" and "Basic Frame Geometry." *Bicycling*, July 1979. An in-depth discussion of choosing a frame to match your style of cycling.

McCullagh, James C. *American Bicycle Racing*. Emmaus, Pennsylvania: Rodale Press, 1976. Well-written look at the different types of racing and, most importantly, the people that make cycle racing a fascinating sport.

Marino, John J. *Wheels of Life*. This slim, self-published volume details Marino's journey from sickness to becoming a transcontinental cycling record holder. Some good information on nutrition and an interesting account of his cross-country ride.

Matheny, Fred. "Throwing Caution into Your Training Schedule." *Bike World*, November 1977. Avoiding overtraining and its detrimental effects.

————. "Mental Guidelines for a Beginning Racer." *Bike World*, December 1977. Conditioning the mind, as well as the body.

Mirkin, Gabe, and Hoffman, Marshall. *The Sportsmedicine Book*. Boston: Little, Brown, 1978. Concise guide to training, injuries and a wealth of other topics. Also includes running program for the beginner.

Monkerud, Don. "The Effects of Air Pollution." *Bike World*, September 1978.

————. "A Cyclist Who Pedals Politics." *Bike World*, September/October 1979. Interview with bicycle activist Ellen Fletcher.

Mullholland, Owen. "Bike Handling: The Art of Staying Alive in the Peleton." *Bicycling,* August 1974.

Murphy, Michael, and White, Rhea A. *The Psychic Side of Sports.* Reading, Massachusetts: Addison Wesley, 1978. Fascinating look at what happens during those "weird" moments in sports.

Nass, Alice. "Cheating the Blues." *Bicycling,* February 1979. An interview with John Griest on cycling as a cure for depression.

————. "One Bicycle on Rye to Go—Hold the Mayo." *Bicycling,* February 1979. Cycling the road to recovery from a coronary.

Novak, Michael. *The Joy of Sports.* New York: Basic Books, 1976.

Parade magazine editors. "Running from Depression," "Coronary-Prone Kids" and "Weekend Warning." *Parade,* 21 October 1979.

Quinn, William. "Transcontinental Meditations." *American Wheelmen,* November 1979. Inspiring thoughts of a cross-country cyclist.

Reynolds, Bill. *Complete Weight Training Book.* Mountain View, California: World Publications, 1976. Guide to weight training, an important facet of training for the racing cyclist and others looking to improve overall fitness. Includes specific programs for cycling and many other sports.

Rowe, Nina Dougherty. "Tips for Beginning Bicycle Commuters." *Bicycling,* September 1978.

Runner's World magazine editors. "Interview with Dr. Kenneth Cooper." *Runner's World,* December 1979. Informative talk with "the father of aerobics."

Sanders, William. *The Bicycle Racing Book*. Chicago: Domus, 1979. In a sea of dull, thick books, this one stands out as refreshing and to the point. The best guide available for the novice racer.

———. "Surviving Car–Bike Crashes." *Bike World*, October 1973.

———. "Taking the Tots Along." *Bike World*, February 1974.

———. "The First Time." *Bike World*, March 1974. Hilarious account of Sanders' very belated first bike ride.

———. "Advanced Dogmanship." *Bike World*, July 1974. Most thorough advice available for dealing with canines.

———. "Teaching Children to Ride." *Bike World*, July 1974. Two essential articles for parents.

———. "Rip-Off Artists and Thugs." *Bike World*, October 1974. Dealing with thieves and psychopaths on the cycle paths.

———. "In Search of a Path: Parts I, II, III. *Bike World*, March, April and May 1975.

———. "Taking the Mystery Out of Sew-Ups." *Bike World*, November 1977. The clearest, most comprehensive advice ever written on choosing and using tubular tires.

———. "How to Survive a Bicycle Crash." *Bike World*, May/June 1979. "Must" reading for any cyclist. Good common sense advice that could save your life, and will make you a much more confident cyclist.

Sanders, William et al. "A Hard Look at Helmets." *Bike World*, August 1977. Rationale for wearing a helmet and an evaluation of several models.

Schubert, John. "Why Cyclists Should Ride with Traffic." *Bicycling,* June 1979. If you need more evidence that riding against traffic is insane, here it is.

Schubert, John, and Seman, Stewart. "Expert Tips on Buying a Used Bike." *Bicycling,* September/October 1979.

Sheehan, George A. *Dr. Sheehan on Running.* Mountain View, California: World Publications, 1975. Not to be confused with his pretentious books of philosophy, this lean volume takes a good look at fitness, sport and fun.

Simes, Jack, and George, Barbara. *Winning Bicycle Racing.* Chicago: Contemporary Books (formerly named Henry Regnery), 1976.

Simpson, Jerry. "The European Charm." *Bike World,* March 1978. Advice on touring Europe.

————. "Proper Crankarm Lengths: Resolution of the Revolutions." *Bike World,* September 1979. Good look at an obscure but potentially important topic.

Smith, David L. "Female Cycling Performance." *Bicycling,* November 1978. How women measure up to men in cycling—and vice versa.

————. "Training for a Century Ride." *Bicycling,* April 1979. A bit too structured, but helpful in setting up a training schedule for that first 100-miler.

————. "Training for Longevity." *Bicycling,* May 1979. An eloquent rationale for cycling.

————. "The Cyclist's Foot." *Bicycling,* January/February 1980.

————. "The Cyclist's Foot Revisited." *Bicycling,* April 1980. This pair of articles looks at how the foot operates, and how to keep it functioning properly.

Teague, Jack and Chris. "Touring with Your Pre-Teens." *Bicycling,* August 1974.

U.S. *News and World Reports* magazine editors. "Your Summer Sports: Just How Dangerous?" *U.S. News and World Reports,* 31 July 1978.

van Aaken, Ernst. *Van Aaken Method.* Mountain View, California: World Publications, 1976.

Van Der Plas, Rob. "Staying Alive at Night": Parts I, II. *Bicycling,* December 1978, January 1979. An enlightening look at bicycle lights.

Weaver, Susan. "Family Touring." *Bicycling,* June 1978. Taking the kids along on tours and recreational rides.

————. "A Buyer's Guide to Sleeping Bags." *Bicycling,* July 1978.

————. "A Buyer's Guide to Stoves and Bivouac Sacks." *Bicycling,* August 1978.

————. "A Buyer's Guide to Tents": Parts I, II. *Bicycling,* September and October 1978. These four articles provide a detailed discussion of essential touring gear. "Must" reading for the first-time tourist.

————. "Successful Mountain Touring." *Bicycling,* August 1979.

————. "What? Exercise and Lift Weights for Cycling?" *Bicycling,* January/February 1980. Weight training for the cyclist.

Weaver, Susan, and Lehman, Josh. "Bikepacking Technique." *Bicycling,* June 1979. Mastering the loaded touring bike.

Weaver, Susan, and Smith, John. "A Buyer's Guide to Seat Bags." *Bicycling,* August 1979.

Whitt, Frank R., and Wilson, David G. *Bicycling Science: Ergonomics and Mechanics.* Cambridge, Massachusetts: The MIT Press, 1975. A well-researched and fairly easy-to-read look at human power and bicycle physics.

Wilcockson, John et al. *Complete Bicycle Time Trialing Book.* Mountain View, California: World Publications, 1977.

Wilhelm, Tim and Glenda. *The Bicycle Touring Book.* Emmaus, Pennsylvania: Rodale Press, 1980. An excellent book exclusively devoted to planning, undertaking and enjoying bicycle touring.

————. "The Desert," "A Change in the Wind," "Rocky Mountain High," "Catch a Falling Leaf." *Bicycling,* April, July, August, and October 1977. This four-part series captures the joys and heartbreaks of the Wilhelms' cycle crossing of the United States with their nine-year-old daughter and two-year-old son.

Williams, John E., and Vogt, Charlotte. "The Woman Seat." *Bicycling,* November 1978. Customizing a bicycle seat to fit a woman's anatomy.

Wolfe, Frederick L. *The Bicycle: A Commuting Alternative.* Edmonds, Washington: Signpost Books, 1979.

Wood, Peter D. "Smoking and Running." *Runner's World,* September 1979.

————. "Does Running Help Prevent Heart Attacks?" *Runner's World,* December 1979.

INDEX